Book B

Vocabulary for the High School Student

Book B

Vocabulary for the High School Student

Harold Levine

Norman Levine

Robert T. Levine

When ordering this book, you may specify:
either **R 509 W** or
Vocabulary for the High School Student,
Book B

Amsco School Publications, Inc.

315 Hudson Street/New York, N.Y. 10013

Authors of Vocabulary for the High School Student, Book B

Harold Levine
Chairman Emeritus of English,
Benjamin Cardozo High School, New York

Norman Levine
Associate Professor of English,
City College of the City University of New York

Robert T. Levine
Professor of English,
North Carolina A & T State University

Vocabulary Books by the Authors

Vocabulary and Composition Through Pleasurable Reading, Books I–VI
Vocabulary for Enjoyment, Books 1, 2, and 3
Vocabulary for the High School Student, Books A and B
Vocabulary for the High School Student
Vocabulary for the College-Bound Student
The Joy of Vocabulary
A Scholarship Vocabulary Program, Courses I–III

Please visit our Web site at:

www.amscopub.com

ISBN 0-87720-793-3

Copyright © 1991 by Amsco School Publications, Inc.
No part of this book may be reproduced in any form without written permission from the publisher.

Printed in the United States of America

To the Student:

If you are in the first year of high school or the final year of junior high school, this may be a valuable book for you. It will help you do the following things enjoyably:

1. Add 1000 important words to your vocabulary.
2. Read closely for meaning, especially implied meaning.
3. Write concisely—that is, using as few words as necessary. If you use more, you will probably be less effective.
4. Unravel the meanings of unfamiliar words whenever possible from their context, or by separating those words into their component parts.
5. Build new words with prefixes, suffixes, and roots—with due attention to spelling.
6. Think analytically.

For a sample of the rewarding experiences you are likely to have as you use this book, turn now to Lesson 1.

Harold Levine
Norman Levine
Robert T. Levine

CONTENTS

Lesson

1. People Words *1*
2. Fighting Words *6*
3. Wordbuilding With Latin Roots *11*
4. -*ATE* Words *16*
5. Review and Enrichment *20*

6. "One Who" Words *26*
7. Wordbuilding: -*ILE* Words *30*
8. Words of Honesty and Dishonesty *35*
9. Burning Words *40*
10. Review and Enrichment *44*

11. Words for Human Strengths and Weaknesses *51*
12. More Wordbuilding With Latin Roots *56*
13. Words of Abundance *62*
14. "Taking" Words *66*
15. Review and Enrichment *71*

16. Wordbuilding With Five Latin Roots *78*
17. Power Words *83*
18. -*ICS* Words *88*
19. "All" Words *93*
20. Review and Enrichment *98*

21. New Words From Synonyms in the Context *105*
22. New Words From Antonyms in the Context *110*
23. Words of Chance and Fortune *116*
24. Wordbuilding With Five Latin Roots *121*
25. Review and Enrichment *126*

26. New Words From Commonsense Context Clues   *133*
27. Monosyllabic Words for Persons   *139*
28. Disyllabic Words for Persons   *144*
29. Uncomplimentary Words   *149*
30. Review and Enrichment   *153*

31. Polysyllabic Words for Persons   *159*
32. Complimentary Words   *164*
33. Wordbuilding With Four Latin Roots   *169*
34. "Little" Words   *174*
35. Review and Enrichment   *179*

36. Loanwords Ending in US   *186*
37. Loanwords Ending in IUM   *191*
38. Loanwords Ending in OR   *196*
39. Loanwords Ending in UM   *201*
40. Review and Enrichment   *206*

Dictionary of the Words Taught in This Book   *213*
Pronunciation Key   *inside back cover*

Lesson 1. People Words

There was a famine in China. No one in Wang Lung's family had eaten for several days. The best he could do for his children was to feed them a mixture of earth and water to ease the pain in their stomachs.

At this time, three well-fed strangers from the city came to Wang Lung's farm to buy his land, knowing that he desperately needed money for food. They deliberately offered him only a few pennies per acre. Wang Lung was furious. At that price, he screamed, they would be stealing his land from him. The strangers, however, stood by their offer, saying that they never paid more when buying land from the starving.

Wang Lung is the main character in *The Good Earth* by Pearl S. Buck.

QUESTION: What does the above incident tell us about the strangers?

ANSWER: They didn't care about **what is morally right or proper.** They had no conscience.

QUESTION: Is there a shorter way to describe the strangers?

ANSWER: Yes. You can do it in one word: They were **unscrupulous.**

Unscrupulous does the work of many words. It means "without a conscience," or "having no concern for what is morally right or proper."

The words you are about to learn, like **unscrupulous,** are words that describe people. For this reason, let us call them "people" words.

affluent (*adj.*)
af′ lōō wənt
: wealthy; rich; prosperous; in possession of an abundance of money or property
  ant. **destitute; indigent**

astute (*adj.*)
ə stōōt′
: shrewd; clever; crafty
  ant. **gullible**

biased (*adj.*)
bī′ əst
: favoring one side too much; partial; prejudiced
  ant. **impartial**

conscientious (*adj.*)
kän′ shē en′ shəs
: 1. always trying to do what is right; controlled by **conscience** (a sense of right and wrong that governs behavior); honest; scrupulous
  ant. **unscrupulous**

  2. careful; painstaking; meticulous

destitute (*adj.*)
des′ tə toot′
lacking necessary things, such as food, shelter, or clothing; extremely poor; impoverished; indigent
    ant. **affluent**

frugal (*adj.*)
froo′ g'l
sparing; thrifty; not wasteful
    ant. **lavish**

gullible (*adj.*)
gul′ ə b'l
easily deceived or cheated; credulous
    ant. **astute**

impartial (*adj.*)
im pär′ shəl
not favoring one side more than the other; free of **bias** (prejudice); not partial
    ant. **biased**

lavish (*adj.*)
lav′ ish
too free in giving or spending; extravagant; prodigal
    ant. **frugal**

unscrupulous (*adj.*)
un skroo′ pyə ləs
having no concern for what is morally right or proper; unconscionable
    ant. **conscientious**

EXERCISE 1.1: LESSON WORDS. In each blank space, write the most appropriate boldfaced word from the left column of the preceding list. **Do not use any of these words more than once.** The first answer has been entered as a sample.

1. Janet is frequently short of cash because she is a(n) __lavish__ spender.

2. The refugees lost everything they had in the flood. It left them _____.

3. Dorothy suspected that the umpire was favoring the visiting team, but I did not think he was _____.

4. You don't believe that the vacant house is haunted, do you? Surely, you are not so _____.

5. Millions of people regularly purchase lottery tickets, hoping in this way to become _____.

6. Our neighbors were victimized by a(n) _____ dealer who sold them a used car without telling them about its defects.

7. Before the trial, I favored neither the plaintiff nor the defendant. I was completely _____.

8. The town's reservoirs are low, so we will have to be _____ in our use of water.

9. I made a move that I thought would win the game for me, but my opponent was too _____ to fall into the trap.

10. The guards who were asleep when they should have been on patrol will have a hard time convincing anyone that they are _____ employees.

RELATED WORDS. The lesson words you have just learned have close relatives that we may call **related words**. Learn the boldfaced **related words** in the middle column below, together with their meanings.

Lesson Words	Related Words	Meanings of Related Words
affluent (*adj.*)	**affluence** (*n.*)	wealth
astute (*adj.*)	**astuteness** (*n.*)	cleverness
biased (*adj.*)	**bias** (*n.*)	prejudice
conscientious (*adj.*)	**conscience** (*n.*)	sense of right and wrong
destitute (*adj.*)	**destitution** (*n.*)	extreme poverty; indigence
frugal (*adj.*)	**frugality** (*n.*)	thrifty management; thrift
gullible (*adj.*)	**gullibility** (*n.*)	capability of being easily fooled
impartial (*adj.*)	**impartiality** (*n.*)	freedom from bias
lavish (*adj.*)	**lavishness** (*n.*)	extravagance
unscrupulous (*adj.*)	**unscrupulously** (*adv.*)	unconscionably

EXERCISE 1.2: RELATED WORDS. Fill each blank below with the most appropriate **related word** from the middle column of the preceding list. **Do not use any of the related words more than once.**

1. That was a clever suggestion you made. I congratulate you on your _____.

2. Joe spends too freely. If he doesn't curb his _____, he will soon be heavily in debt.

3. When Dee found $10 in the locker room, she took it to the Lost-and-Found Office. Her _____ would not allow her to keep the money.

4. The judge has a reputation for _____. No one has ever accused him of showing favoritism.

5. Our club did not have much money, but it was able to meet its expenses because of the treasurer's _____.

6. A classmate borrowed my notes but did not return them. When I asked for them, she said I never gave them to her. How can anyone act so _____?

7. Our grandparents suffered in the Great Depression of the 1930's. It was a time of widespread _____.

8. At first, I thought the librarian had treated me unfairly, but I realized afterward that she had no _____ against me.

9. P.T. Barnum was convinced of the _____ of human beings. He once said, "A sucker is born every minute."

10. A part of the American dream is the belief that a person who works hard can rise to _____ from poverty.

EXERCISE 1.3: BRAINTEASERS. Each line below ends in a partially spelled word. Fill in the missing letters. The first partially spelled word has been completed as a sample.

1. Mary never wastes anything, but her brother is not so **f** r u g **a** **l**.

2. Have you no sense of right and wrong? Have you no __ __ __ s c i e n c e?

3. To own a yacht, you must be a person of __ __ f l u __ __ __ __.

4. When we root for a team, we make no attempt to conceal our __ __ a s.

5. People are fooled sometimes, but they are not always g u l l __ __ __ __.

6. The refugees had no resources at all. They were totally __ __ d i g __ __ __.

7. We did not take sides. We tried to be __ __ p a r t __ __ __.

8. She does her work carefully. She is __ __ t i c __ __ __ __ __.

9. They spend too freely. Why are they so e x t r a __ __ __ __ __ __?

10. Peter is very clever. I wish I had his __ __ __ __ t e n __ __ __.

EXERCISE 1.4: ANALOGIES. Which lettered pair of words—**a, b, c,** or **d**—most nearly has the same relationship as the numbered pair? Circle the letter of your answer.

1. POVERTY : AFFLUENCE
    - *a.* anxiety : pain
    - *b.* depression : prosperity
    - *c.* ecstasy : joy
    - *d.* craving : desire

2. IMPARTIAL : BIAS
    - *a.* innocent : guilt
    - *b.* furious : rage
    - *c.* envious : jealousy
    - *d.* remiss : neglectful

3. FRUGAL : EXTRAVAGANCE
    - *a.* blunt : outspokenness
    - *b.* humble : arrogance
    - *c.* enthusiastic : zeal
    - *d.* remorseful : regret

4. GULLIBLE : DECEIVE
    - *a.* persistent : discourage
    - *b.* obstinate : persuade
    - *c.* unintelligible : comprehend
    - *d.* timid : frighten

5. CONSCIENCE : BEHAVIOR
    - *a.* food : nourishment
    - *b.* fuel : warmth
    - *c.* pollutant : contamination
    - *d.* thermostat : temperature

Lesson 2. Fighting Words

Mr. Jarvis Lorry, 60, has the difficult task of breaking the news to Lucie Manette, 17, that her father—missing for 18 years and presumed dead—has been rescued from a French prison. Hearing this news, Lucie faints, and Lorry calls for help. A wild-looking red-haired woman enters, grasps Lorry with her brawny hand, and sends him flying across the room. As he is about to hit the wall, he thinks, "This must really be a man!" The **assailant** is Miss Pross, Lucie's devoted servant. "Couldn't you tell her what you had to tell her," she shouts at him, indignantly, "without frightening her to death?"

Let us call **assailant,** in the above paragraph, a "fighting" word. An **assailant** is "someone who attacks with blows or words." Miss Pross, as you have seen, does both. The incident in which she assails Lorry occurs in the early pages of *A Tale of Two Cities* by Charles Dickens.

Learn the following "fighting words" and their meanings:

aggression (*n.*) ə gresh′ ən	unprovoked attack; warlike act; encroachment by one nation on the territory of another
assailant (*n.*) ə sāl′ ənt	person who **assails** (violently attacks with blows or words); attacker
belligerent (*adj.*) bə lij′ ər ənt	fond of fighting; warlike; quarrelsome; pugnacious *ant.* **friendly**
belligerent (*n.*) bə lij′ ər ənt	nation engaged in a war; person involved in a fight; warrior
implacable (*adj.*) im plā′ kə bəl	unable to be **placated** (made peaceful); unappeasable; unrelenting; unforgiving *ant.* **placable; forgiving**
intimidate (*v.*) in tim′ ə dāt′	make **timid** (fearful); frighten; scare; discourage from acting by threats or violence *ant.* **calm**
invincible (*adj.*) in vin′ sə bəl	incapable of being **vanquished** (conquered, defeated, or subdued); insuperable; insurmountable *ant.* **conquerable**
mercenary (*n.*) mur′ sə ner′ ē	soldier serving for pay in a foreign army

mercenary (*adj.*) serving merely for pay or gain; greedy
mur′ sə ner′ ē

pugilist (*n.*) prizefighter; boxer; person who fights with fists
py$\overline{oo}$′ ji list

strife (*n.*) bitter conflict; fighting; discord; antagonism
strīf *ant.* **accord; peace**

vanquish (*v.*) subdue by superior force; conquer; defeat; overcome
vaŋ′ kwish

EXERCISE 2.1: LESSON WORDS. In each blank space, write the most appropriate boldfaced word from the left column of the preceding list. **Do not use any of these words more than once.**

1. My cousin is going into nursing not just for the pay, but because she wants to help the sick. She is certainly not _____.

2. Many a(n) _____ has to give up boxing because of injuries suffered in the ring.

3. One look at the huge, ferocious watchdog is enough to _____ most burglars and keep them from trying to enter the premises.

4. Japan's seizure of Manchuria from China, in 1931, was condemned by the League of Nations as an act of _____.

5. His first impulse when he differs with someone is to quarrel and fight. Why must he be so _____?

6. After losing the first two sets, the champion rallied and went on to _____ his opponent.

7. The victim injured in the attempted robbery gave the police a good description of her _____.

8. Both sides are so _____ that an early settlement of the strike seems unlikely.

9. General Braddock, believing that his troops were _____, paid little attention to Washington's warnings of a possible Indian ambush.

10. The Hundred Years War (1337-1453) between England and France went on for more than a century. It seemed the _____ would never end.

Fighting Words

RELATED WORDS. Learn the boldfaced **related words** in the middle column below, together with their meanings.

Lesson Words	Related Words	Meanings of Related Words
aggression (*n.*)	**aggressor** (*n.*)	person or nation that attacks first
assailant (*n.*)	**assail** (*v.*)	attack with blows or words
	unassailable (*adj.*)	not open to attack or doubt
belligerent (*adj.*)	**belligerence** (*n.*)	fondness for fighting; pugnacity
implacable (*adj.*)	**implacably** (*adv.*)	unrelentingly
	placate (*v.*)	make peaceful; appease
intimidate (*v.*)	**timid** (*adj.*)	fearful
	timidity (*n.*)	fear
invincible (*adj.*)	**invincibility** (*n.*)	unconquerability
pugilist (*n.*)	**pugilism** (*n.*)	boxing

EXERCISE 2.2: RELATED WORDS. Fill each blank below with the most appropriate **related word** from the middle column of the preceding list. **Do not use any of the related words more than once.**

1. Beginning swimmers are usually afraid of the water, but they gradually overcome their _____.

2. Until her recent defeat, Barbara had a reputation for _____. She had never lost an election.

3. A boxer who intentionally fouls an opponent is no credit to the sport of _____.

4. One of the warring nations is now ready to make peace, but the other is _____ opposed to the idea.

5. I didn't start this fight. You were the _____.

6. We have no reason to doubt the information we have received since it comes from a(n) _____ source.

7. Andrea initially rejected the part that was offered to her because she was too _____ to appear on stage, but she later joined the cast.

8. I now realize that I hurt Bill's feelings when I voted against him. He isn't talking to me, and I have been unable to _____ him.

9. The police have found two witnesses who saw the suspect _____ the victim.

10. When the bill comes up for discussion, its opponents will refuse to compromise. They are known for their _____.

EXERCISE 2.3: BRAINTEASERS. Each line below ends in a partially spelled word. Fill in the missing letters.

1. Switzerland stayed out of the war. She was not a(n) _ _ _ _ _ _ r e n t.

2. Her uncle knows how to box. He once was a(n) _ _ _ _ l i s t.

3. The fighting has gone on long enough. It is time to end the _ _ r i f e.

4. Two guards fought off an attack by an armed _ _ s a i l _ _ _.

5. An undefeated champion is hard to v a n _ _ _ _ _.

6. Don't be afraid. All is well. There is no reason for t i m i d _ _ _.

7. Our foes refuse to discuss peace. They are _ _ _ _ _ c a b l e.

8. Everyone was friendly to us. We encountered no _ _ t a g _ _ _ _.

9. Troublemakers seek to create _ _ _ c o r d.

10. Our neighbors still fight. They have not reduced their _ _ _ _ _ c i t y.

EXERCISE 2.4: ANALOGIES. Which lettered pair of words—**a, b, c,** or **d**—most nearly has the same relationship as the numbered pair? Circle the letter of your answer.

1. PUGILIST : RING
   - *a.* dramatist : play
   - *b.* actor : stage
   - *c.* carpenter : wood
   - *d.* conductor : band

2. INVADER : AGGRESSION
   - *a.* liar : credibility
   - *b.* novice : experience
   - *c.* braggart : humility
   - *d.* counterfeiter : forgery

3. UNASSAILABLE : ATTACK
   - *a.* mortal : death
   - *b.* invincible : defeat
   - *c.* irresponsible : blame
   - *d.* despicable : contempt

4. PUGNACIOUS : FIGHT
    - *a.* indolent : work
    - *b.* selfish : share
    - *c.* impatient : wait
    - *d.* curious : learn

5. IMPLACABLE : FORGIVE
    - *a.* unaccommodating : oblige
    - *b.* grateful : appreciate
    - *c.* extravagant : squander
    - *d.* gregarious : socialize

Lesson 3. Wordbuilding With Latin Roots

In this lesson, we will be building words with the following Latin roots:

ROOT	MEANING
combusti	burn
dispensa	do without; dispense with
exhausti	use up
intelligi	understand
percepti	notice; perceive
perturba	disturb; excite
practica	put into practice; accomplish
reprehensi	blame
satia	satisfy
tena	hold; defend

EXERCISE 3.1: WORDBUILDING. On each line below, first insert the necessary root. Then write the complete word. Choose all your roots from the above list. The first two words have been built as samples.

		ROOT				WORD
1. im	+	practica	+	ble	=	impracticable
						(not able to be put into practice)
2.		tena	+	ble	=	tenable
						(capable of being defended)
3.		_____	+	ble	=	_____
						(able to be noticed)
4. in	+	_____	+	ble	=	_____
						(not able to be dispensed with)
5. un	+	_____	+	ble	=	_____
						(not able to be understood)
6. im	+	_____	+	ble	=	_____
						(not able to be excited)
7.		_____	+	ble	=	_____
						(capable of being used up)

8. _____ + ble = _____
   (capable of burning easily)

9. in + _____ + ble = _____
   (incapable of being satisfied)

10. _____ + ble = _____
    (deserving to be blamed)

Here are the words that you were asked to build, listed alphabetically and accompanied by fuller definitions. Learn those definitions.

combustible (*adj.*)
kəm bus′ tə bəl
: able to catch or be set on fire and burn easily; inflammable; ignitable
  ant. **incombustible; noncombustible**

exhaustible (*adj.*)
eg zôst′ ə bəl
: capable of being **exhausted** (used up completely)
  ant. **inexhaustible**

imperturbable (*adj.*)
im′ pər tur′ bə bəl
: incapable of being **perturbed** (agitated or disturbed); not easily excited; calm; cool
  ant. **touchy**

impracticable (*adj.*)
im prak′ ti kə bəl
: incapable of being put into practice; unworkable; impractical; impossible
  ant. **feasible; practicable**

indispensable (*adj.*)
in′ di spen′ sə bəl
: incapable of being done without; necessary; imperative; essential
  ant. **dispensable; unessential**

insatiable (*adj.*)
in sā′ shə bəl
: incapable of being **satiated** (satisfied); always wanting more; unsatisfiable
  ant. **satiable**

perceptible (*adj.*)
pər sep′ tə bəl
: able to be **perceived** (noticed through one or more of the senses); detectable; discernible
  ant. **imperceptible**

reprehensible (*adj.*)
rep′ ri hen′ sə bəl
: deserving to be **reprehended** (blamed or scolded); blameworthy; censurable

tenable (*adj.*)
ten′ ə bəl
: capable of being held, maintained, or defended; defendable; justifiable
  ant. **untenable**

unintelligible (*adj.*)
un′ in tel′ i jə bəl
: incapable of being understood; difficult to comprehend; incomprehensible
  ant. **intelligible; understandable**

EXERCISE 3.2: LESSON WORDS. In each blank space below, write the most appropriate boldfaced word from the left column, above.

1. Your idea is _____. It will not work.

2. Certain odors that humans cannot detect are _____ to dogs.

3. Drinking water is _____. We cannot do without it.

4. His reply was _____. None of us could understand it.

5. Is your opinion _____? Can you justify it?

6. She is calm and _____. Nothing seems to upset her.

7. Our oil supply is _____. Some day it will all be gone.

8. A(n) _____ cleaning fluid must not be used near a flame.

9. Hikers have _____ appetites, so take along some extra food.

10. Why should any of us be blamed? We definitely have not done anything _____.

RELATED WORDS. Learn the boldfaced **related words** in the middle column below, together with their meanings.

Lesson Words	Related Words	Meanings of Related Words
combustible (*adj.*)	**combustion** (*n.*)	act or process of burning
exhaustible (*adj.*)	**exhaustive** (*adj.*)	thorough; leaving nothing out
	exhaustion (*n.*)	extreme weariness; fatigue
	exhaust (*n.*)	spent gas escaping from an engine
imperturbable (*adj.*)	**perturb** (*v.*)	trouble greatly; disturb
insatiable (*adj.*)	**satiate** (*v.*)	satisfy to the full; sate
perceptible (*adj.*)	**perception** (*n.*)	knowledge; understanding
	perceptive (*adj.*)	having keen insight; observant
tenable (*adj.*)	**tenacious** (*adj.*)	holding firmly; stubborn
	tenacity (*n.*)	stubbornness; courage

Wordbuilding With Latin Roots

EXERCISE 3.3: RELATED WORDS. Fill each blank below with the most appropriate **related word** from the middle column of the preceding list. **Do not use any of the related words more than once.**

1. Al was tackled but held the ball securely in his _____ grip.

2. With wet firewood, proper _____ is impossible.

3. The noise was almost imperceptible. It did not _____ me.

4. A(n) _____ search led to the recapture of the escapees.

5. Some have a craving for sweets that is impossible to _____.

6. The _____ from automobile engines pollutes our air.

7. Our museum visits have given us a better _____ of the past.

8. The fort did not fall, thanks to the _____ of its defenders.

9. I was so weary that I nearly collapsed from _____.

10. Dee saw the danger first. She is more _____ than most of us.

EXERCISE 3.4: BRAINTEASERS. Each line below ends in a partially spelled word. Fill in the missing letters.

1. Did you understand his reply? I found it _ _ _ _ t e l l _ _ _ _ _ _.

2. They wanted to know everything. Their curiosity was _ _ s a t _ _ _ _ _.

3. There must be no delay. Immediate action is _ _ _ e r a _ _ _ _ _.

4. A smoky campfire is the result of poor _ _ _ b u s _ _ _ _.

5. You are very perceptive. I am not so _ _ _ _ _ _ a n t.

6. The defect is so slight as to be almost i m p _ _ _ _ _ _ _ _ _.

7. We must have clean air. It is _ _ _ _ _ p e n s _ _ _ _ _.

8. The invaders were hard to dislodge. They were t e n _ _ _ _ _ _.

9. A miser's greed is impossible to _ _ _ _ a t e.

10. We don't approve of what you are doing. It is _ _ _ _ _ h e n s _ _ _ _.

14 Vocabulary for the High School Student, Book B

EXERCISE 3.5: ANALOGIES. Which lettered pair of words—**a, b, c,** or **d**—most nearly has the same relationship as the numbered pair? Circle the letter of your answer.

1. PERTURB : DISTURB
   - *a.* intimidate : encourage
   - *b.* vanquish : conquer
   - *c.* squander : save
   - *d.* gratify : displease

2. DISPENSABLE : ESSENTIAL
   - *a.* feasible : practicable
   - *b.* intelligible : incomprehensible
   - *c.* perceptible : detectable
   - *d.* insuperable : invincible

3. COMBUSTION : HEAT
   - *a.* monopoly : competition
   - *b.* friction : harmony
   - *c.* indolence : promotion
   - *d.* ambiguity : doubt

4. REPREHENSIBLE : COMMENDATION
   - *a.* credible : trust
   - *b.* imperfect : criticism
   - *c.* despicable : respect
   - *d.* pure : contamination

5. TENACIOUS : YIELD
   - *a.* kind : sympathize
   - *b.* frugal : conserve
   - *c.* vindictive : forgive
   - *d.* gullible : believe

Wordbuilding With Latin Roots

Lesson 4. *-ATE Words*

At four o'clock one summer morning, Aram, 9, heard a tapping on his window. Looking out, he saw someone on a beautiful white horse. It was his cousin Mourad, 13, who had come to invite him for a ride. Now, Aram knew that Mourad did not own that horse because Mourad's family, like Aram's, was very poor. He also knew that Mourad sometimes behaved strangely, so it did not entirely surprise him that Mourad should **appropriate** a horse that didn't belong to him.

Aram is the main character in *My Name Is Aram,* a collection of short stories by William Saroyan.

You have probably guessed the meaning of **appropriate** from its context. Note that **appropriate** and the other new words in this lesson all end with the suffix *-ate,* meaning "make." For this reason, let us call them "*-ate*" words.

ameliorate (*v.*)
ə mēl′ yə rāt′
 make better; improve; become more tolerable
  ant. **worsen; deteriorate**

appropriate (*v.*)
ə prō′ prē āt′
 make oneself the owner of something without permission or right; take possession of; annex; steal

facilitate (*v.*)
fə sil′ ə tāt′
 make easier; make less difficult

frustrate (*v.*)
frus′ trāt′
 make ineffectual; cause to have no effect; block; thwart
  ant. **fulfill**

humiliate (*v.*)
hyoo mil′ ē āt′
 make someone feel ashamed; lower someone's pride or dignity; degrade; embarrass

incapacitate (*v.*)
in′ kə pas′ ə tāt′
 make unable or unfit; deprive of **capacity** (ability to do something); disable

invigorate (*v.*)
in vig′ ər āt′
 make strong; give **vigor** (strength) to; fill with life and energy; enliven; strengthen
  ant. **debilitate**

necessitate (*v.*)
nə ses′ ə tāt′
 make necessary; require; demand

obliterate (v.)   make nonexistent; erase; efface; blot out; delete; remove all
ə blit′ ər āt′   traces of; destroy completely

perpetuate (v.)   make **perpetual** (lasting forever or for a long time); cause to
pər pech′ ōō āt′   continue or be remembered; immortalize
                ant. **obliterate**

EXERCISE 4.1: LESSON WORDS. In each blank space, write the most appropriate boldfaced word from the left column of the preceding list. Do not use any of these words more than once.

1. The cleaning fluid did not _____ the stains. I can still see traces of them.

2. Our opponents tried to thwart us, and we did our best to _____ them.

3. The city's bus and train services need to be improved. Is anything being done to _____ them?

4. I am opposed to your motion. The slight increase we have had in the club's expenses does not _____ a doubling of the dues.

5. Wouldn't it _____ him if he were the only one who was not invited? I am sure it would be a blow to his pride.

6. The electric dishwasher was supposed to _____ our work, but we had to work harder because it did not dry the dishes properly.

7. Sheila's injury did not _____ her for a long time, and she was soon able to rejoin the team.

8. Please forgive me. I took your pen without realizing what I was doing. Of course, I did not mean to _____ it.

9. The many cities and towns named after Columbus are a sign that Americans want to _____ the memory of that great explorer.

10. You are exhausted. Get some rest. It will _____ you.

RELATED WORDS. Learn the boldfaced **related words** in the middle column below, together with their meanings.

Lesson Words	Related Words	Meanings of Related Words
ameliorate (v.)	**amelioration** (n.)	improvement
appropriate (v.)	**proprietor** (n.)	owner of a store or business
facilitate (v.)	**facility** (n.)	ease; skill
frustrate (v.)	**frustration** (n.)	disappointment; defeat
humiliate (v.)	**humiliating** (adj.)	degrading
incapacitate (v.)	**incapacity** (n.)	lack of ability; unfitness
invigorate (v.)	**vigorous** (adj.)	strong; powerful; energetic
	vigorously (adv.)	forcefully; energetically
perpetuate (v.)	**perpetual** (adj.)	everlasting
	perpetually (adv.)	forever

EXERCISE 4.2: RELATED WORDS. Fill each blank below with the most appropriate **related word** from the middle column of the preceding list. **Do not use any of the related words more than once.**

1. For us, the season ended in _____. We lost every game.

2. Under no circumstance will we beg Jim to get his cooperation. Such behavior on our part would be _____.

3. Things are getting better. We see many signs of _____.

4. If I were to practice on my drums late at night, I am sure the neighbors would object _____.

5. Some complain that writing is hard. Others write with _____.

6. A candidate who shows _____ for leadership will not get my vote.

7. Mrs. Drew does not own this shop. Her aunt is the _____.

8. The waves are _____ in motion. The sea is never at rest.

9. I feel much better, but I am still not nearly as _____ as I was before coming down with the flu.

10. Marie Curie's discovery of radium won her _____ fame.

EXERCISE 4.3: BRAINTEASERS. Each line below ends in a partially spelled word. Fill in the missing letters.

1. A stubborn stain is hard to _ _ _ _ _ e r a _ _.
2. It seemed like a difficult task, but they did it with _ _ _ _ l i t _.
3. Who owns this shop? Is she the p r o p _ _ _ _ _ _ ?
4. Things are getting better. There are signs of _ _ _ _ _ _ r a t i o n.
5. The defeat was a blow to our pride. It was h u m _ _ _ _ _ _ _.
6. Expenses keep rising. It seems they will go up _ _ _ p e t _ _ _ _ _.
7. He humiliates people. He keeps looking for someone to _ _ b a r _ _ _ _ _.
8. How many are disabled? What is the nature of their _ _ c a p _ _ _ _ _ ?
9. I know you are disappointed. I understand your _ r u s t _ _ _ _ _ _ _.
10. Slow down a bit. You don't have to exercise so _ _ _ _ _ _ _ c a l l _.

EXERCISE 4.4: ANALOGIES. Which lettered pair of words—*a*, *b*, *c*, or *d*—most nearly has the same relationship as the numbered pair? Circle the letter of your answer.

1. FACILITATE : EASY
    a. amplify : inaudible
    b. immobilize : movable
    c. complicate : difficult
    d. rectify : incorrect

2. PERPETUAL : TEMPORARY
    a. permanent : durable
    b. unnecessary : indispensable
    c. partial : biased
    d. crucial : important

3. RUST : DETERIORATION
    a. applause : disapproval
    b. vigor : health
    c. bickering : harmony
    d. aloofness : sociability

4. HUMILIATE : DIGNITY
    a. antagonize : hostility
    b. encourage : confidence
    c. demote : rank
    d. intimidate : fear

5. FAILURE : FRUSTRATION
    a. injury : pain
    b. defeat : exultation
    c. variety : boredom
    d. knowledge : ignorance

Lesson 5. Review and Enrichment

EXERCISE 5.1: SYNONYMS. For the boldfaced word in each sentence below, find two synonyms. Choose all your synonyms from the list at the end of this exercise. The first two synonyms have been entered as samples.

1. We shall **vanquish** our adversaries. _defeat   overcome_
2. Paper is highly **combustible**. _____
3. Are they **lavish** spenders? _____
4. I did not try to **frustrate** you. _____
5. This proposal is **impracticable**. _____
6. Our rivals are **astute**. _____
7. The enemy was **implacable**. _____
8. Try to **obliterate** the defeat from your memory. _____
9. Their threats did not **intimidate** us. _____
10. Your cooperation is **indispensable**. _____

LIST OF SYNONYMS

block	essential	impractical	shrewd
crafty	extravagant	inflammable	thwart
defeat	frighten	overcome	unappeasable
delete	ignitable	prodigal	unforgiving
erase	imperative	scare	unworkable

EXERCISE 5.2: ANTONYMS. Replace each boldfaced word with an **antonym** from the list at the end of this exercise. The first antonym has been entered as a sample.

1. His health is beginning to **ameliorate**.   1. _deteriorate_
2. We thought they were **conscientious**.   2. _____
3. You have a(n) **pugnacious** disposition. 3. _____
4. It was a time of **strife**.   4. _____
5. Their response was **unintelligible**.   5. _____

6. Did the climb **invigorate** you? 6. _____

7. Some of the residents are **affluent**. 7. _____

8. Why should we **perpetuate** this practice? 8. _____

9. Their appetites are **unsatisfiable**. 9. _____

10. It is clear that she is **impartial**. 10. _____

11. Some shoppers are **gullible**. 11. _____

12. I see you are **implacable** today. 12. _____

13. The change was **discernible**. 13. _____

14. Her claims are entirely **justifiable**. 14. _____

15. These decorations are **necessary**. 15. _____

LIST OF ANTONYMS

agreeable	deteriorate	peace
astute	dispensable	satiable
biased	forgiving	understandable
debilitate	imperceptible	unscrupulous
destitute	obliterate	untenable

EXERCISE 5.3: SENTENCE COMPLETION. Two words are missing in each sentence below. Select those words from the following list, and enter them where they belong. Do not use any of the words on the list more than once.

affluence	imperative
appropriate	invincibility
bias	placate
conscience	prodigal
humiliating	pugilist

1. Having never lost a bout, the _____ is confident of his _____ .

2. Despite their _____ , they are not _____ spenders.

3. The weaker nation found itself in the _____ position of having to _____ an aggressor.

4. It is _____ that a judge should be free of _____.

5. If she found someone's purse, her _____ would not allow her to _____ it.

Continue, as above, but select your words from the following list:

assail insuperable
discernible obliterate
facility perceptive
frustration perpetually
incapacitate reprehensible

6. A(n) _____ person may be still able to detect the damage because we could not _____ every trace of it.

7. How can anyone _____ his character if he has never done anything _____?

8. After an hour, I gave up on the problem in _____, but my sister solved it with surprising _____.

9. The fall did not _____ her for more than a moment, and she resumed play with no _____ loss of vigor.

10. Napoleon's defeat at Waterloo will _____ remind us that no one is _____.

EXERCISE 5.4: ROOTS. Fill each blank with the required root from the following list:

combusti perturba
dispensa practica
exhausti reprehensi
intelligi satia
percepti tena

The first entry has been made as a sample.

1. Nothing seems to disturb her. She is im__**perturba**__ble.

2. Your scar is hard to perceive. It is almost im_____ble.

3. Our patience is not in_____ble. Sooner or later, it will run out.

22   **Vocabulary for the HIGH SCHOOL Student, Book B**

4. Non_____ble materials are incapable of burning.

5. The idea is im_____ble. We couldn't put it into practice.

6. You are in_____ble to the team. It cannot do without you.

7. A miser's craving for wealth is in_____ble. It cannot be satisfied.

8. It is impossible to make sense out of an un_____ble remark.

9. He denies his conduct was _____ble. He refuses to accept any blame.

10. Her opinion seems un_____ble. How will she be able to defend it?

EXERCISE 5.5: SPELLING. Enter the two missing letters. The first word has been completed as a sample.

1. fa_c_il_i_tate
2. ne___ess___tate
3. inflam___ ___ble
4. dec___ ___ve
5. perpet___ ___l
6. unscr___p___lous
7. di___ ___ernible
8. deter___ ___rate
9. int___m___date
10. ex___aust___ble
11. con___cient___ous
12. i___pe___turbable
13. h___mil___ating
14. incapa___ ___tate
15. amel___ ___rate
16. insat___ ___ble
17. extrav___g___nt
18. pugna___ ___ous
19. approp___ ___ate
20. prej___di___e
21. uncon___ ___ionable

EXERCISE 5.6: CONCISE WRITING. Each of the following sentences uses ten or more words to express a thought. Express that same thought in *no more than four words*. The first sentence has been rewritten as a sample.

1. The position that I found myself in was one that I could not defend.
   My position was untenable.

2. The suggestion that you made is not capable of being put into practice.

3. We did nothing for which we deserve to be blamed.

4. Are these materials capable of catching on fire and burning easily?

5. She came into possession of a great deal of wealth.

6. Some people have no concern for what is morally right or proper.

7. Did anyone use threats or violence to discourage you from taking action?

8. She did not favor one side more than the other.

9. Encroachment by one nation on the territory of another is not to be tolerated.

10. The ease with which he can be fooled or cheated is hard to believe.

EXERCISE 5.7: CLOSE READING. Carefully read the following passages, and answer the questions below them.

PART ONE

When Kino and Juana, a Mexican-Indian couple, took their infant son Coyotito to a doctor, the doctor refused to treat him because they had no money. Kino and Juana are the main characters in *The Pearl,* by John Steinbeck.

Johnny Tremain, a young teenager, was apprenticed to Silas Lapham, a master silversmith. One day, John Hancock, the wealthiest person in New England, came to Silas Lapham's shop to order a silver sugar basin. While working on that sugar basin, Johnny burned his hand so badly that he had to enter another trade. Johnny is the main character in *Johnny Tremain,* by Esther Forbes.

QUESTIONS

1. Who was affluent? _____
2. Who was destitute? _____
3. Who was incapacitated? _____
4. Who was unconscionable? _____
5. Who was a proprietor? _____

PART TWO

In the war between the Greeks and the Trojans, Zeus, the king of the gods, tried to be neutral. However, the goddess Hera—his wife—favored the Greeks, and the goddess Aphrodite—his daughter—sided with the Trojans.

Achilles was the foremost of the Greek warriors. Without him, the Greeks could not win. As the result of a bitter quarrel with the Greek commander-in-chief Agamemnon, Achilles refused to fight. Agamemnon finally admitted he had been wrong, but even that did not satisfy Achilles because Agamemnon had insulted him so deeply. So, while the Greeks were being beaten on the battlefield, Achilles remained in his tent.

Hector, the bravest of the Trojans, prepared for battle by putting on his armor. When he extended his arms to embrace his son Astyanax, the infant shrieked in terror. He was frightened by his father's bronze helmet with its crest of waving horsehair. Hector laughed, removed his helmet, and took Astyanax in his arms.

The above incidents take place in *The Iliad* by Homer.

QUESTIONS

6. Who was implacable? _____

7. Who was intimidated? _____

8. Who tried to refrain from bias? _____

9. Who was partial to the Greeks? _____

10. Who was indispensable to the Greeks? _____

Lesson 6. "One Who" Words

Andy intended the pass for me, but he threw it right into the arms of an opposing player, and we lost the game. Later, Andy said that I should have caught the pass. Isn't that outrageous? Why didn't he admit that we lost because of his poor passing? Why should I be the **"one who bears the blame for another's mistakes"**?

What word can take the place of the last eight words in the above paragraph? You will find that word among the "one who" words, below.

QUESTION: What is a "one who" word?

ANSWER: A "one who" is a word whose meaning begins with "one who," or "a person who."

Here are some "one who" words to add to your vocabulary:

accomplice (*n.*) one who participates with another in wrongdoing or in a
ə käm′ plis crime; partner in crime; confederate

amateur (*n.*) one who engages in an activity for pleasure rather than for
am′ ə chər money; person who lacks professional skill; nonprofessional

drudge (*n.*) one who does hard, boring, or disagreeable work
druj

fugitive (*n.*) person who flees or tries to escape from danger, justice, etc.;
fyo͞o′ ji tiv runaway

peer (*n.*) person or thing that is of equal standing with another; equal
pir

prodigy (*n.*) one who has extraordinary talent or ability; marvel; wonder
präd′ ə jē

prophet (*n.*) one who foretells or predicts; predictor
präf′ ət

scapegoat (*n.*) one who bears or is made to bear the blame for the mistakes
skāp′ gōt′ or crimes of another or others

sponsor (*n.*) one who supports or assumes responsibility for another
spän′ sər person, or for a thing; supporter; backer

vandal (*n.*) one who willfully destroys or damages valuable private or
van′ dəl public property; defacer

EXERCISE 6.1: LESSON WORDS. In each blank space below, write the most appropriate "one who" word from the left column of the preceding list.

1. Mozart appeared in his first concert when he was six. He was a child _____.

2. How can I tell what the future will bring? I am not a(n) _____.

3. Betty is our best dancer. In our club she has no _____.

4. The perpetrator of this crime must have had at least one _____.

5. When the president asked who was recommending Sally for membership, I said that I was her _____.

6. While her stepsisters went to parties and dances, Cinderella stayed home and did all the chores. She was the _____ in the family.

7. A reward has been offered for information leading to the arrest of the _____ who defaced the entrance of the museum.

8. An athlete who accepts pay to appear in a sports event can no longer be considered a(n) _____.

9. Why don't you take responsibility for your blunders and stop looking for a(n) _____?

10. The suspect fled when he heard that a warrant had been issued for his arrest. He has been a(n) _____ for nine months.

RELATED WORDS. Learn the boldfaced **related words** in the middle column below, together with their meanings.

Lesson Words	Related Words	Meanings of Related Words
accomplice (*n.*)	**complicity** (*n.*)	partnership in wrongdoing or in a crime
amateur (*n.*)	**amateurish** (*adj.*)	inexpert; unskillful
drudge (*n.*)	**drudgery** (*n.*)	disagreeable, dull, or hard work
fugitive (*n.*)	**refuge** (*n.*)	shelter; place of safety
peer (*n.*)	**peerless** (*adj.*)	unrivaled; without equal
prodigy (*n.*)	**prodigious** (*adj.*)	amazing; wonderful; marvelous
prophet (*n.*)	**prophecy** (*n.*)	prediction
	prophesy (*v.*)	predict; foretell
sponsor (*n.*)	**sponsorship** (*n.*)	financial support; backing
vandal (*n.*)	**vandalism** (*n.*)	mischievous defacement or destruction of property

EXERCISE 6.2: RELATED WORDS. Fill each blank below with the most appropriate **related word** from the middle column, above. Do not use any of them more than once.

1. Some people like housework. Others consider it _____.

2. Peggy never forgets anything. She has a(n) _____ memory.

3. Your _____ that our team would win did not come true.

4. The driver of the getaway car was charged with _____ in the crime.

5. Symphony orchestras depend on the _____ of affluent music lovers.

6. Don't be gullible. No fortune-teller can _____ your fate.

7. The play was enjoyable, but the acting was somewhat _____.

8. Guards have been stationed in the museum to prevent _____.

9. The fugitive found temporary _____ in an abandoned barn.

10. William Tell was a(n) _____ archer. No one could match his skill with the bow and arrow.

EXERCISE 6.3: BRAINTEASERS. Each line contains a partially spelled word. Enter the missing letters.

1. Almost every professional was once a(n) __ m a t e __ __.

2. A few windshields were smashed. The police later caught two __ __ __ d a l s.

3. Some tire easily. Others have a p r o d __ __ __ __ __ __ amount of energy.

4. He wanted me to take the blame, but I refused to be the __ c a p e __ __ __ __.

5. Did the spy act alone, or did he have a(n) __ __ __ __ __ __ __ r a t e?

6. To avoid trial, the suspect became a(n) __ __ __ i t __ __ __.

7. To her parents, the child is not merely bright; she is a(n) __ __ __ d i g __.

8. Terry predicts we will win. What is your __ __ __ __ h e __ __?

9. I could not have become a member without your __ __ __ __ __ __ __ s h i p.

10. Since he had a part in the theft, he was convicted of __ __ __ __ __ __ c i t y.

EXERCISE 6.4: ANALOGIES. Which lettered pair of words—**a, b, c,** or **d**—most nearly has the same relationship as the numbered pair? Circle the letter of your answer.

1. SCAPEGOAT : VICTIM
    a. child : adolescent
    b. accomplice : wrongdoing
    c. heir : beneficiary
    d. student : sophomore

2. INN : REFUGE
    a. ship : harbor
    b. beverage : thirst
    c. thorn : comfort
    d. sun : warmth

3. PRODIGIOUS : AMAZEMENT
    a. loathsome : disgust
    b. humiliating : dignity
    c. diverting : boredom
    d. unintelligible : comprehension

4. VANDALISM : PROPERTY
    a. burglary : crime
    b. alcoholism : addiction
    c. vilification : reputation
    d. altruism : unselfishness

5. PEERLESS : EQUAL
    a. tireless : energy
    b. unscrupulous : conscience
    c. destitute : fear
    d. imperfect : flaw

Lesson 7. Wordbuilding: -ILE Words

The Latin suffix *-ile* has two principal meanings: "capable of" and "having to do with."

In this lesson, we will be adding the following roots to the suffix *-ile*. Learn their meanings:

ag	act; move	**mercant**	trade; merchants
doc	teach; instruct	**tact**	touch
fac	do	**text**	weave
frag	break	**versat**	turn; change
juven	young	**volat**	fly

EXERCISE 7.1: WORDBUILDING. Build the words defined in parentheses. Just enter the appropriate root from the above list in the first blank. Then write the complete word in the second blank. The first word has been constructed as a sample.

ROOT + SUFFIX = WORD

1. **frag** + ile = **fragile** (capable of breaking)
2. _____ + ile = _____ (capable of being taught)
3. _____ + ile = _____ (having to do with trade)
4. _____ + ile = _____ (capable of flying)
5. _____ + ile = _____ (having to do with the young)
6. _____ + ile = _____ (capable of moving)
7. _____ + ile = _____ (capable of turning)
8. _____ + ile = _____ (capable of being woven)
9. _____ + ile = _____ (capable of being done)
10. _____ + ile = _____ (having to do with touch)

Here are the words you should have built, listed alphabetically and accompanied by fuller definitions. Learn those definitions.

agile (*adj.*)
aj′ əl
    capable of moving quickly and easily; nimble; spry
        ant. **torpid; sluggish**

docile (*adj.*)
däs′ əl
    1. capable of being easily instructed; teachable; obedient; tractable
        ant. **ungovernable; unruly**
    2. lacking in independence; submissive

facile (*adj.*)
fas′ il
    1. capable of being easily done; easy; effortless
        ant. **arduous**
    2. arrived at without due effort; superficial

fragile (*adj.*)
fraj′ əl
    capable of being easily broken or damaged; delicate; frail
        ant. **durable**

juvenile (*adj.*)
jo͞o′ və nəl
    having to do with young persons; suitable for the young; immature; childish
        ant. **adult**

mercantile (*adj.*)
mʉr′ kən tīl′
    having to do with trade or merchants; commercial

tactile (*adj.*)
tak′ təl
    1. having to do with the sense of touch
    2. perceivable by touch; tangible; palpable

textile (*adj.*)
teks′ tīl′
    capable of being woven; suitable for weaving

textile (*n.*)
teks′ tīl′
    cloth; fabric made by weaving

versatile (*adj.*)
vʉr′ sə təl
    1. capable of turning easily from one occupation to another; able to do many things well; many-sided
    2. having many uses or applications; adaptable

volatile (*adj.*)
väl′ ə təl
    capable of evaporating rapidly; likely to shift unpredictably; unstable; inconstant

EXERCISE 7.2: LESSON WORDS. Fill each blank below with the most appropriate boldfaced word from the left column, above.

1. Food prices used to be fairly stable. Now, they are up one day and down the next. What makes them so _____?

2. You see a smile—a visual sensation. You hear a greeting—an auditory sensation. You feel your hand clasped—a(n) _____ sensation.

3. Adult readers are generally not interested in _____ books.

4. We edged our rivals by a score of 3-2, after fourteen innings. It was not a(n) _____ victory.

5. The _____ gymnast outperformed her rivals in the finals.

6. To accommodate shoppers, many _____ establishments remain open until ten on some nights.

7. Cotton, nylon, and silk are common _____ fibers.

8. Joanne's unruliness interferes with her learning. Her sister is more _____ and does much better.

9. My uncle's only sport is golf. He is not a(n) _____ athlete.

10. Glassware requires careful handling because it is so _____.

RELATED WORDS. Learn the boldfaced **related words** in the middle column below, together with their meanings.

Lesson Words	Related Words	Meanings of Related Words
agile (*adj.*)	**agility** (*n.*)	nimbleness
docile (*adj.*)	**docility** (*n.*)	submissiveness
facile (*adj.*)	**facilitate** (*v.*)	make easy; simplify
fragile (*adj.*)	**fragment** (*n.*)	part broken off
juvenile (*adj.*)	**rejuvenate** (*v.*)	make young again
mercantile (*adj.*)	**merchandise** (*n.*)	goods bought and sold; wares
tactile (*adj.*)	**intact** (*adj.*)	untouched; with nothing missing or damaged
textile (*adj.*)	**texture** (*n.*)	surface of something woven
versatile (*adj.*)	**versatility** (*n.*)	adaptability
volatile (*adj.*)	**volatility** (*n.*)	instability

EXERCISE 7.3: RELATED WORDS. Fill each blank below with the most appropriate **related word** from the middle column of the preceding list. Do not use any of them more than once.

1. In a corner of the kitchen, I just noticed a(n) _____ of the jar you broke yesterday.

2. The stolen money was found _____. Not a cent had been taken.

3. Jeeps have many uses in the army, on the farm, and in industry. They are prized for their _____.

4. Ponce de Leon expected the Fountain of Youth to _____ him.

5. At first, the people submitted to the harsh rule of the dictator. Their _____ made it appear that they would never rebel.

6. Your brother can fly into a sudden rage. The _____ of his temper makes it hard for others to deal with him.

7. Needle threaders _____ the task of getting a thread through the eye of the needle.

8. The stores are amply stocked with _____ for the holiday season.

9. Garments made of silk or nylon have a very smooth _____.

10. Some had to walk around the puddle because they didn't have the _____ to leap over it.

EXERCISE 7.4: BRAINTEASERS. Each sentence below contains a partially spelled word. Enter the missing letters.

1. Our old set of dishes is still i n _ _ _ _. Nothing is broken or missing.

2. Rubbing alcohol evaporates so quickly on your skin that you don't need to dry yourself. It is much more _ _ _ a t _ _ _ than water.

3. A(n) _ _ _ c a n _ _ _ _ bank serves the needs of merchants and businesses.

4. Joel wanted to play tag, but we told him it was too _ _ _ _ n i l _.

5. The baby-sitter expected the children to be tractable. However, they were by no means d o _ _ _ _.

6. You are __ __ __ s a t __ __ __. That's why we call you a jack-of-all-trades.

7. You have asked me a very important question, so give me some time to think. Otherwise, I might give you a f a __ __ __ __ answer.

8. The string I am using breaks too easily. Yours is more __ __ __ a b l e.

9. Economical shoppers know where to find the best __ __ __ __ h a n d __ __ __ at the lowest prices.

10. Most young people are better climbers than their elders because they have greater __ __ __ l i t __.

EXERCISE 7.5: ANALOGIES. Which lettered pair of words—**a, b, c,** or **d**—most nearly has the same relationship as the numbered pair? Circle the letter of your answer.

1. FRAGILE : BREAK
    - a. stable : change
    - b. volatile : evaporate
    - c. inanimate : breathe
    - d. inarticulate : speak

2. AGILE : SLUGGISH
    - a. astute : gullible
    - b. extravagant : lavish
    - c. partial : biased
    - d. boisterous : obstreperous

3. REJUVENATE : YOUNG
    - a. invigorate : feeble
    - b. heal : sick
    - c. reconcile : unfriendly
    - d. revive : conscious

4. DOCILE : REBEL
    - a. arrogant : boast
    - b. invincible : conquer
    - c. frugal : squander
    - d. grateful : appreciate

5. CORDUROY : TEXTILE
    - a. wool : warmth
    - b. flower : seed
    - c. copper : metal
    - d. towel : moisture

Lesson 8. Words of Honesty and Dishonesty

The most famous of all beauty contests was judged dishonestly. The contestants were three Greek goddesses—Hera, Athena, and Aphrodite. The judge was a young Trojan shepherd, Paris.

Each goddess tried to influence Paris's judgment by making him a promise. Hera promised him power over all of Europe and Asia if he would choose her as the fairest. Athena offered to make him a military hero who would lead the Trojans to victory over the Greeks. Aphrodite guaranteed that the most beautiful woman on earth would be his wife. After considering their promises, Paris announced that the winner of the beauty contest was Aphrodite.

Which word accurately describes what the goddesses in the above passage offered? You will find it among the following words of honesty and dishonesty.

acknowledge (*v.*)
ak näl′ ij
    admit to be true; confess; avow
        ant. **deny**

bribe (*n.*)
brīb
    money or a favor given or promised to a person to persuade that person to do something dishonest or illegal

candor (*n.*)
kan′ dər
    honesty in saying what one really thinks; frankness; outspokenness
        ant. **evasion**

corrupt (*adj.*)
kə rupt′
    influenced by bribes; dishonest; evil; mercenary

disinterested (*adj.*)
dis in′ tris tid
    free from selfish motives; unbiased; impartial
        ant. **biased; partial**

equivocate (*v.*)
ē kwiv′ ə kāt′
    use language that has a double meaning in order to mislead; hedge

ethical (*adj.*)
eth′ i kəl
    morally right; conforming to **ethics** (recognized rules for right conduct); upright; honorable
        ant. **immoral; unethical**

hypocrite (*n.*)
hip′ ə krit′

one who only pretends to have—but really does not have—desirable beliefs, principles, or attitudes; pretender

perjury (*n.*)
pur′ jə rē

willful telling of a lie while under oath; false swearing

shirk (*v.*)
shurk

get out of doing one's work or duty; evade; avoid

EXERCISE 8.1: LESSON WORDS. In each blank space below, write the most appropriate boldfaced word from the left column, above.

1. One or two tried to get others to do their work, but the rest did not _____ their responsibilities.

2. At first, the suspect refused to _____ that he had anything to do with the theft.

3. If you don't intend to come to the game, don't say you "will try" to come. Be straightforward. Don't _____ .

4. If my bitterest rival told me she was "delighted" that I had been elected, I would think she was a(n) _____ .

5. When he broke the vase, Timmy didn't say that it fell. Instead, with complete _____ , he admitted that he had dropped it.

6. The officer was offered $500 not to issue a summons, but he turned down the _____ .

7. It is not _____ for a public official to use his or her influence to get government positions for relatives.

8. You cannot say you were a(n) _____ observer of the fight. Wasn't one of the belligerents a close friend of yours?

9. The witness who gave false testimony was convicted of _____ .

10. Anyone who pays an official to get preferred treatment is just as _____ as the official who accepts the money.

RELATED WORDS. Learn the boldfaced **related words** in the middle column below, together with their meanings.

Lesson Words	Related Words	Meanings of Related Words
acknowledge (*v.*)	**acknowledgment** (*n.*)	admission; avowal
bribe (*n.*)	**bribery** (*n.*)	giving or taking of a bribe
candor (*n.*)	**candid** (*adj.*)	frank; outspoken; sincere
corrupt (*adj.*)	**incorruptible** (*adj.*)	incapable of being bribed
equivocate (*v.*)	**equivocal** (*adj.*)	having two or more meanings; ambiguous
	unequivocal (*adj.*)	unambiguous; clear
hypocrite (*n.*)	**hypocrisy** (*n.*)	pretense of being what one is not
	hypocritical (*adj.*)	insincere
perjury (*n.*)	**perjurer** (*n.*)	one who swears falsely
shirk (*v.*)	**shirker** (*n.*)	one who evades work or duty

EXERCISE 8.2: RELATED WORDS. Fill each blank below with the most appropriate **related word** from the middle column, above. Do not use any of them more than once.

1. Betty is industrious. She is not a(n) _____.

2. Tell us the whole truth. Be _____ with us.

3. Admit you are not an expert. You have nothing to lose by making that _____.

4. Those who pretend to be what they are not are guilty of _____.

5. The public was shocked when an official whom it regarded as _____ was convicted of taking a bribe.

6. Your remarks were so _____ that we couldn't tell whether you were for or against the motion.

7. Anyone who gives false testimony is a(n) _____.

8. We were _____ when we told our neighbors we would miss them. The truth is they were so noisy that we were glad they were moving.

Words of Honesty and Dishonesty

9. To secure the lucrative contract, the executive made illegal payments to a public official. Both of them were later convicted of _____.

10. When asked if she would accept membership on my committee, Sally said she would consider it. I would have preferred a(n) _____ answer.

EXERCISE 8.3: BRAINTEASERS. Each line below contains a partially spelled word. Enter the missing letters.

1. Every effort is being made to select a(n) _ _ _ _ _ _ r e s t e d jury.

2. Conscientious workers do not _ _ i r k their duties.

3. A person who is not completely honest may try to _ _ _ _ _ _ a t e.

4. Culprits are usually in no hurry to _ _ k n o w _ _ _ _ _ their guilt.

5. Those we elect to represent us must be _ _ c o r r u p t _ _ _ _.

6. It is _ _ _ _ c r i t i c _ _ to show friendship to someone you despise.

7. You spoke your mind. We admired your _ _ _ _ o r.

8. The instructions are easy to understand. They are _ _ _ b i g _ _ _ _.

9. To give untrue testimony is to commit _ _ _ j u r y.

10. To sell one's vote is to participate in _ _ _ b e _ _.

EXERCISE 8.4: ANALOGIES. Which lettered pair of words—**a, b, c,** or **d**—most nearly has the same relationship as the numbered pair? Circle the letter of your answer.

1. HEDGE : EQUIVOCATE
    a. censure : commend   b. placate : appease
    c. invigorate : debilitate   d. complicate : simplify

2. SHIRKER : RESPONSIBILITY
    a. belligerent : victory   b. fugitive : refuge
    c. hermit : society   d. scapegoat : blame

3. HYPOCRISY : SINCERITY
    a. astuteness : gullibility b. acknowledgment : confession
    c. destitution : poverty   d. thrift : frugality

4. DISINTERESTED : BIAS
    - *a.* vindictive : hatred
    - *b.* healthy : sickness
    - *c.* haughty : pride
    - *d.* malicious : ill will

5. BRIBERY : CRIME
    - *a.* goodwill : asset
    - *b.* gratuity : service
    - *c.* chaos : order
    - *d.* coin : dime

Lesson 9. Burning Words

Ab Snopes had a cowardly way of getting back at a farmer he did not like. In the middle of the night, he would set the farmer's barn on fire. Snopes, a suspect in a number of barn burnings, is a character in the stories of William Faulkner.

Can you find a word in the list below that fitly describes Ab Snopes? Be sure to consider the whole list before making your choice. All of these words, as you will see, have something to do with burning.

ardent (*adj.*)
ärd′ 'nt
burning with enthusiasm; fervent; zealous; impassioned
ant. **cool**

arsonist (*n.*)
är′ sə nist
one who maliciously burns or tries to burn a building or other property; incendiary

caustic (*adj.*)
kôs′ tik
1. burning or destroying flesh; corrosive
2. severely critical; sarcastic; sharp; biting
ant. **genial**

conflagration (*n.*)
kän′ flə grā′ shən
huge destructive fire; holocaust; inferno

fervor (*n.*)
fur′ vər
great warmth of feeling or expression; enthusiasm; zeal; passion; ardor

flammable (*adj.*)
flam′ ə bəl
easily set on fire; inflammable; combustible
ant. **incombustible**

glaring (*adj.*)
gler′ iŋ
shining so brightly as to hurt the eyes; too obvious to escape notice; flagrant
ant. **unnoticeable**

ignite (*v.*)
ig nīt′
1. set on fire; cause to burn; kindle
2. catch on fire; start burning

kindling (*n.*)
kind′ liŋ
bits of dry wood or other easily lighted material for starting a fire

pyromaniac (*n.*)
pī′ rō mā′ nē ak′
one who has an uncontrollable, insane impulse to set things on fire

EXERCISE 9.1: LESSON WORDS. In each blank space below, write the most appropriate boldfaced word from the left column of the preceding list.

1. The great Chicago fire of 1871 raged for two days. A large part of the city was destroyed in that _____.

2. Anyone who has to pour concrete should wear rubber gloves because concrete, until it hardens, is very _____.

3. The fires were set by a(n) _____ who subsequently was committed to a mental institution.

4. Beverly became a(n) _____ tennis player, though at first she had only a lukewarm interest in the sport.

5. It is foolhardy for anyone to smoke in bed because bedding is extremely _____.

6. The _____ confessed that he had started the blaze to collect money from the insurance company.

7. It was such a(n) _____ error that almost everyone noticed it immediately.

8. Bruce volunteered to find some _____. We will need it to start our campfire.

9. The woods are so dry now that all it would take to _____ them is one lighted cigarette carelessly dropped by a thoughtless smoker.

10. Her supporters have been enthusiastic from the start of the campaign. They are working for her with undiminished _____.

RELATED WORDS. Learn the boldfaced **related words** in the middle column below, together with their meanings.

Lesson Words	Related Words	Meanings of Related Words
ardent (*adj.*)	**ardor** (*n.*)	great warmth of feeling; zeal
arsonist (*n.*)	**arson** (*n.*)	malicious burning of property

(*Related words are continued on next page.*)

Burning Words

caustic (*adj.*)	**caustically** (*adv.*)	very critically; sarcastically
....	**holocaust** (*n.*)	great destruction of life by fire
fervor (*n.*)	**fervent** (*adj.*)	intense; ardent; impassioned
flammable (*adj.*)	**nonflammable** (*adj.*)	not flammable; incombustible
glaring (*adj.*)	**glare** (*v.*)	stare angrily
ignite (*v.*)	**ignitable** (*adj.*)	burnable; combustible
kindling (*n.*)	**kindle** (*v.*)	set fire to; ignite
pyromaniac (*n.*)	**pyromania** (*n.*)	uncontrollable impulse to start destructive fires

EXERCISE 9.2: RELATED WORDS. Fill each blank below with the most appropriate **related word** from the middle column, above. Do not use any of them more than once.

1. It is very difficult to _____ damp logs.

2. Why did she _____ at him with such hostility?

3. The one who intentionally started the fire has been charged with _____ .

4. My fellow members were upset when I was an hour late for a committee meeting. "Aren't you a bit early?" one of them said, _____ .

5. The first trailer was hauling gasoline, which can catch fire easily. The second was transporting milk, a(n) _____ cargo.

6. The person accused of starting the blaze was said by his attorney to be suffering from _____, a form of insanity.

7. In spite of the insect bites and sore feet with which we returned from our last trip, our _____ for hiking has in no way diminished.

8. These napkins are _____ . Don't keep them too close to the stove.

9. The city's heroic firefighters quickly brought the tenement blaze under control and prevented it from becoming a(n) _____ .

10. I thanked my many friends for their encouraging cards and calls and their _____ wishes for my complete recovery.

EXERCISE 9.3: BRAINTEASERS. Each line below contains a partially spelled word. Enter the missing letters.

1. Store these materials away from heat. They are _ _ _ _ t a b l e.

2. The first step in building a campfire is to light the k i n d _ _ _ _.

3. That fire was no accident. It was the work of a(n) _ _ s o n _ _ _.

4. He has made several biting remarks. Why is he so _ _ _ _ t i c?

5. The welcome we got was polite but cool. It lacked _ _ _ _ o r.

6. A(n) _ _ _ _ m a n _ _ _ does not start fires merely to collect insurance money.

7. I did nothing to anger you. Why did you _ _ a r e at me?

8. A wind-driven fire can rapidly turn into a(n) _ _ _ f l a g _ _ _ _ _ _.

9. Wherever she goes, the star is worshiped by _ _ d e n _ fans.

10. Luckily, the smoke alarms in that hotel prevented a(n) _ _ _ _ _ _ u s _.

EXERCISE 9.4: ANALOGIES. Which lettered pair of words—**a, b, c,** or **d**—most nearly has the same relationship as the numbered pair? Circle the letter of your answer.

1. IGNITE : KINDLE
    - *a.* complicate : simplify
    - *b.* rectify : correct
    - *c.* antagonize : conciliate
    - *d.* purify : contaminate

2. ARSON : CRIME
    - *a.* perjury : justice
    - *b.* vandalism : property
    - *c.* clue : mystery
    - *d.* health : asset

3. GLARING : UNNOTICEABLE
    - *a.* peerless : unrivaled
    - *b.* belligerent : friendly
    - *c.* flammable : inflammable
    - *d.* amateurish : nonprofessional

4. CONFLAGRATION : FIRE
    - *a.* cloudburst : rain
    - *b.* pebble : rock
    - *c.* page : manuscript
    - *d.* seed : flower

5. ARDENT : ENTHUSIASM
    - *a.* mercenary : altruism
    - *b.* indigent : resources
    - *c.* uncertain : doubt
    - *d.* remorseless : pity

Burning Words 43

Lesson 10. Review and Enrichment

EXERCISE 10.1: SYNONYMS. For the boldfaced word in each sentence below, find two synonyms. Choose all your synonyms from the list at the end of this exercise. The first two synonyms have been entered as samples.

1. Don't try to **shirk** your responsibility. _____evade   avoid_____

2. Did they ever **acknowledge** that they were wrong? _____

3. I am not so **agile** as you. _____

4. My **fervor** for stamp collecting is cooling. _____

5. The parents think their infant is a(n) **prodigy**. _____

6. That was a(n) **caustic** remark. _____

7. He was not a(n) **disinterested** observer. _____

8. She has a(n) **prodigious** memory. _____

9. Lately, the weather has been **volatile**. _____

10. Who is their **sponsor**? _____

LIST OF SYNONYMS

amazing	inconstant
ardor	marvel
avoid	marvelous
avow	nimble
backer	sarcastic
biting	spry
confess	supporter
enthusiasm	unbiased
evade	unstable
impartial	wonder

EXERCISE 10.2: ANTONYMS. Replace each boldfaced word with an **antonym** from the list below. The first antonym has been entered as a sample.

1. These are **flammable** materials.
2. The testimony was remarkable for its **candor**.
3. Some of the toys are quite **fragile**.
4. I am not so **sluggish** as I was yesterday.
5. Her comments were more **caustic** than usual.
6. This is a(n) **glaring** imperfection.
7. It was a(n) **arduous** victory.
8. So far, we have had **ardent** support.
9. We mistakenly thought that you were **disinterested**.
10. The magician will have a(n) **adult** audience.
11. As a child, Ted was rather **docile**.
12. Did they **deny** their involvement?
13. She gave a(n) **equivocal** answer.
14. They answered us with **evasion**.
15. Do you think he was **sincere**?

1. incombustible
2. _____
3. _____
4. _____
5. _____
6. _____
7. _____
8. _____
9. _____
10. _____
11. _____
12. _____
13. _____
14. _____
15. _____

LIST OF ANTONYMS

acknowledge
agile
candor
cool
durable
evasion
facile
genial
hypocritical
incombustible
juvenile
partial
unambiguous
ungovernable
unnoticeable

Review and Enrichment

EXERCISE 10.3: SENTENCE COMPLETION. Two words are missing in each sentence below. Select those words from the following list, and enter them where they belong. Do not use any of the words on the list more than once.

> agile   ignite
> amateur   kindling
> bribe   peer
> confederate   shirker
> drudgery   unethical

1. It is _____ to offer or accept a(n) _____.

2. Even though the work was absolute _____, she refused to be a(n) _____.

3. _____s should compete with their _____s, rather than with professionals.

4. The _____ failed to _____ because it was too damp.

5. Before being arrested, the _____ pickpocket tried to slip the stolen wallet to a(n) _____ in the crowd.

Continue, as above, but select your words from the following list:

> ardent   fugitive
> arduous   hypocrite
> arsonist   intact
> docile   merchandise
> facilitate   scapegoat

6. The suspected _____ went into hiding soon after the conflagration and is still a(n) _____ from justice.

7. We were afraid the _____ might be damaged in transit, but all of it arrived _____.

8. What makes you think she is so _____ that she would permit anyone to use her as a(n) _____?

9. The work is _____, but we hope to find a way to _____ it.

10. If I pretended to be your _____ supporter but had no intention of voting for you, I would be a(n) _____.

EXERCISE 10.4: ROOTS. Fill each blank with the required root from the following list:

ag	mercant
doc	tact
fac	text
frag	versat
juven	volat

The first entry has been made as a sample.

1. Don't drop this carton. Its contents are __frag__ile.
2. Silk garments have a very smooth _____ure.
3. His temper is _____ile. He can very easily lose control of it.
4. It looked like a(n) _____ile trick, but it wasn't easy to do.
5. Was anything lost, or were the stolen records recovered in_____?
6. Monkeys are nimble. They move with remarkable _____ility.
7. This is not a(n) _____ile establishment. We do not sell anything here.
8. Darlene can play the guitar, the piano, and the recorder. She is a(n) _____ile musician.
9. Only in fairy tales can magicians re_____ate the elderly.
10. Her dog is hard to control. Yours is much more _____ile.

EXERCISE 10.5: SPELLING. Enter the two missing letters. The first word has been completed as a sample.

1. v__o__l__a__tility
2. equ__voc__l
3. inst__b__lity
4. m__rc__ntile
5. pr__d__gious
6. a__knowl__dge
7. p__r__maniac
8. h__pocr__sy
9. ag__l__ty
10. am__t__urish
11. acc__mpli__e
12. j__v__nile
13. m__rcen__ry
14. in__endi__ry
15. v__rs__tile
16. h__l__caust
17. p__rj__ry
18. ze__l__us
19. rej__v__nate
20. c__ust__cally
21. un__th__cal
22. inc__mb__stible
23. d__c__lity
24. h__pocrit__cal

Review and Enrichment 47

EXERCISE 10.6: CONCISE WRITING. Each of the following sentences uses ten or more words to express a thought. Express that same thought in *no more than four words*. The first sentence has been rewritten as a sample.

1. The giving or taking of bribes is not morally right.
   Bribery is unethical.

2. We admire your honesty in saying what you really think.

3. Ordinary glassware is capable of being easily broken or damaged.

4. One witness committed the crime of telling a lie while under oath.

5. The lights shone so brightly that they hurt our eyes.

6. Were you the one who was made to blame for the mistakes of the others?

7. Doesn't the willful destruction or damaging of valuable public or private property sicken you?

8. We despise those who pretend to have feelings and beliefs that they really do not have.

9. Harry has no one who can match him in ability or accomplishment.

10. People who have an uncontrollable insane impulse to start fires are extremely dangerous.

11. Was she the one who helped him commit the crime?

12. No one can predict whether prices will rise, fall, or remain stable.

13. Two employees who loafed and tried to get out of doing their work were dismissed.

14. They sometimes use language that has a double meaning in order to deceive others.

15. I am not a person of extraordinary talent or ability.

EXERCISE 10.7: CLOSE READING. Carefully read the following passages, and answer the questions below them.

All day long, day after day, Akaky sat at his desk, pen in hand, making copies of documents that were constantly being piled in front of him. Akaky is a government clerk in a story by Nikolay Gogol (1809-1852).

Silas Marner, a weaver by trade, is the main character in a novel by George Eliot (1819-1881).

Louis Braille (1809-1852) invented a system of printing and writing that makes use of the sense of touch. His system, known as Braille, uses patterns of raised dots, which are like little bumps, for letters and numbers. By running their fingers over these raised dots, sightless people can read.

Jim Thorpe (1888-1954), an American Indian, was the star of the 1912 Olympics, winning two gold medals in the track and field events. The following year, when the Olympic officials learned he had once received a small sum for playing baseball, they ruled that he was a professional, and he had to return the medals. Thorpe later became an outstanding professional football player, and he also played baseball with the New York Giants.

Christopher Columbus (1451-1506) was turned down when he asked John II (1455-1495) of Portugal to support the expedition that resulted in the discovery of America.

The following is from *A Tale of Two Cities,* a novel by Charles Dickens (1812-1870): "Monseigneur was about to take his chocolate. Monseigneur could swallow a great many things with ease, and was by some few sullen minds supposed to be rather rapidly swallowing France; but, his morning's chocolate could not so much as get into the throat of Monseigneur, without the aid of four strong men besides the cook."

QUESTIONS

1. Who was versatile? _____
2. Who was a drudge? _____
3. Who gave tactile clues? _____
4. Who was caustic? _____
5. Who was judged not to be an amateur? _____
6. Who dealt with textiles? _____
7. Who refused to be a sponsor? _____

Lesson 11. Words for Human Strengths and Weaknesses

A fox in a fable by La Fontaine is attracted by the smell of some fresh cheese that a crow, up in a tree, is holding in his beak.

"Master Crow, how handsome you are today," says the fox. The crow swells with pride at this delicious compliment. The fox continues, "If your voice is as pretty as your feathers, I would say that you are without question the most charming of all the creatures that inhabit these woods. Let me hear you sing."

Eagerly, the crow opens his beak to give the fox a sample of his voice and, as he does so, the cheese falls to the ground, where the crafty fox quickly devours it.

Like many human beings, the crow in the above fable suffers from a weakness that can be summed up in a single word. What is that word? You will find it among the words for human strengths and weaknesses, below.

apathy (*n.*)
ap′ ə thē

lack of emotion or feeling; lack of interest; unconcern; indifference
    ant. **zeal; enthusiasm**

avarice (*n.*)
av′ ə ris

excessive desire to gain and hoard wealth; greed for riches; cupidity
    ant. **prodigality**

benevolence (*n.*)
bə nev′ ələns

inclination to do good to others; good will; kindliness; generosity
    ant. **malevolence**

compassion (*n.*)
kəm pash′ ən

sympathy and sorrow for the sufferings and misfortunes of others, accompanied by a desire to help them; pity; commiseration; empathy
    ant. **mercilessness**

enterprise (*n.*)
ent′ ər prīz′

readiness to undertake new and daring projects; ambition; initiative

gluttony (*n.*)
glut′ 'n ē

habit of eating or drinking too much

malice (*n.*)
mal′ is
deep-seated meanness; desire to inflict injury on others or do mischief; spite
 ant. **benevolence; goodwill**

moderation (*n.*)
mäd′ ər ā′ shən
avoidance of excesses or extremes in behavior or expression; restraint; temperance

sagacity (*n.*)
sə gas′ ə tē
keen perception and sound judgment; intelligent application of knowledge; insight; shrewdness; wisdom

vanity (*n.*)
van′ ə tē
excessive pride in oneself or in one's appearance; self-admiration; vainness; conceit
 ant. **humility**

EXERCISE 11.1: LESSON WORDS. In each blank space below, write the most appropriate boldfaced word from the left column, above.

1. To have three or four desserts with a meal is senseless. What good can come from such _____?

2. Our _____ led us to take in and feed the hungry lost dog and to try to locate its owner.

3. A person who suffers from _____ is likely to spend an excessive amount of time in front of a mirror.

4. Some are totally unconcerned about what is happening to our environment. If everyone had such _____, our future would be very grim.

5. Surely, he doesn't think that tripping someone is a good joke. Only people with _____ in their hearts would do a thing like that.

6. When we feel that we are not wise enough to deal with a vexing problem, we should seek the advice of those who have greater _____.

7. *The Miser* by Molière is a play dealing with _____.

8. It is unwise and unsafe to go from overeating to eating almost nothing. Avoid both of these extremes. Use _____.

9. The Pilgrims must have had a great deal of _____ to embark in the tiny *Mayflower* on their risky voyage to America.

10. Our neighbors are kind people who do many favors for others. The whole community has been profiting from their _____.

RELATED WORDS. Learn the boldfaced **related words** in the middle column below, together with their meanings.

Lesson Words	Related Words	Meanings of Related Words
apathy (*n.*)	**apathetic** (*adj.*)	uninterested; unconcerned; indifferent
avarice (*n.*)	**avaricious** (*adj.*)	too eager for riches; greedy; covetous
benevolence (*n.*)	**benevolent** (*adj.*)	disposed to do good; kind; generous
compassion (*n.*)	**compassionate** (*adj.*)	deeply sympathetic; pitying; tender
enterprise (*n.*)	**enterprising** (*adj.*)	willing to undertake new projects; venturesome
gluttony (*n.*)	**glutton** (*n.*)	person who eats to excess
malice (*n.*)	**malicious** (*adj.*)	spiteful
moderation (*n.*)	**immoderate** (*adj.*)	more than is proper; excessive
sagacity (*n.*)	**sagacious** (*adj.*)	wise; discerning; shrewd
vanity (*n.*)	**vain** (*adj.*)	conceited

EXERCISE 11.2: RELATED WORDS. Fill each blank below with the most appropriate **related word** from the middle column, above. Do not use any of them more than once.

1. Andy takes too much pride in his clothes. He is quite _____.

2. Midas was _____. He wanted everything he touched to turn to gold.

3. If you need extra time to complete your report, ask for a few days or a week at most, but not a whole month. That would be _____.

4. The trouble is that I spoke too much. I am not yet _____ enough to know when to hold my tongue.

5. Sue turned down a third helping of that delicious apple pie because she didn't want to seem like a(n) _____.

Words for Human Strengths and Weaknesses

6. These people are _____. They wish everyone well.

7. At the age of seven, Darlene was _____ enough to set up her own lemonade stand.

8. Many did not bother to vote because they were not interested in the outcome of the election. I wonder what made them so _____.

9. A resident who noticed the stray dog was _____ enough to put out some food and water for the starved animal.

10. Some _____ person hid my belongings in one of the empty lockers, and I nearly went out of my mind trying to find them.

EXERCISE 11.3: BRAINTEASERS. Each sentence below contains a partially spelled word. Enter the missing letters.

1. Our antagonists are full of __ __ l i c e.

2. You have to be __ __ __ __ __ __ __ s i n g to be a pioneer.

3. Eat moderately. Don't be a(n) __ __ __ __ t o n.

4. Has she no sympathy for the needy? Where is her __ __ __ p a s s __ __ __?

5. The suspect was acquitted mainly because of his lawyer's __ __ __ __ c i t y.

6. Accumulating wealth is their principal goal. They are totally dominated by __ __ __ r i c e.

7. Our neighbors had said they were going to have a quiet party, but they made a(n) __ __ __ __ __ __ r a t e amount of noise.

8. Cora never misses an opportunity to remind us of her medals. She is obviously __ __ i n about her achievements.

9. The company has led in raising wages and improving working conditions. It is more __ __ __ __ __ l e n t to its employees than the average employer.

10. After we lost seven games in a row, our fans became __ p a t h __ __ __.

EXERCISE 11.4: ANALOGIES. Which lettered pair of words—**a, b, c,** or **d**—most nearly has the same relationship as the numbered pair? Circle the letter of your answer.

1. GLUTTON : FOOD
    - *a.* loafer : enterprise
    - *b.* snob : humility
    - *c.* drunkard : alcohol
    - *d.* opportunist : benevolence

2. ZEAL : APATHY
    - *a.* candor : evasion
    - *b.* tact : sagacity
    - *c.* belligerence : hostility
    - *d.* bias : partiality

3. EXTREMIST : MODERATION
    - *a.* spendthrift : extravagance
    - *b.* hermit : society
    - *c.* underdog : compassion
    - *d.* procrastinator : deferment

4. CONCEITED : VAIN
    - *a.* buoyant : depressed
    - *b.* gullible : shrewd
    - *c.* insincere : frank
    - *d.* covetous : avaricious

5. VANDALISM : MALICE
    - *a.* defection : disloyalty
    - *b.* alienation : harmony
    - *c.* impediment : progress
    - *d.* beverage : thirst

Words for Human Strengths and Weaknesses

Lesson 12. More Wordbuilding With Latin Roots

In this lesson, we will build some words with these Latin roots:

ROOT	MEANING
acri	sharp; bitter
fili	son or daughter
frater	brother
grav	serious; severe
mari	sea
mater	mother
omni	all
pater	father
rid	laugh
sed	sit

EXERCISE 12.1: WORDBUILDING. Complete each partially spelled word below by inserting the necessary root from the above list. The first insertion has been made as a sample.

1. Mother beams with ___mater___nal pride whenever anyone compliments one of her children.

2. After doing _____entary work, like reading or studying, I like to get up and move around.

3. The brothers have settled their quarrel. _____nal harmony has been restored.

4. A young child may think that adults know everything, but unfortunately they are not _____scient.

5. She laughed at him when he made a mistake, so he does not want to give her another opportunity to _____icule him.

6. Dad considers it his _____nal duty to teach his children to be safe drivers.

7. At the aquarium, we saw many fascinating _____ne plants and animals.

8. Why are they so bitter? Can't they speak to each other without _____mony?

9. Debbie and Andy showed their _____al devotion by making dinner and doing the dishes on their parents' anniversary.

10. The patient thought he was suffering from a cold, but he really had pneumonia. It shocked him to learn the _____ity of his condition.

Here are the words that you were asked to build, listed alphabetically and accompanied by fuller definitions for you to study.

acrimony (*n.*)   sharpness or bitterness of words, manner, or feeling; asperity
ak′ ri mō′ nē

filial (*adj.*)   befitting a son or daughter; expected from a son or daughter
fil′ ē əl
              ant. **unfilial**

fraternal (*adj.*)   of a brother; involving brothers; brotherly; like a brother; friendly
frə turn′ əl

gravity (*n.*)   seriousness; severity; danger; threat
grav′ i tē

marine (*adj.*)   1. of the sea; inhabiting, found in, or produced by the sea; oceanic
mə rēn′
            2. having to do with navigation or shipping; nautical

maternal (*adj.*)   characteristic of a mother; motherly
mə tur′ nəl

omniscient (*adj.*)   1. knowing all things; perceiving all things
äm nish′ ənt
            2. having extensive knowledge, awareness, or understanding

paternal (*adj.*)   characteristic of a father; fatherly
pə tur′ nəl

ridicule (*v.*)   make fun of; deride; mock; taunt
rid′ i kyool′

sedentary (*adj.*)   1. requiring much sitting
sed′ 'n ter′ ē
            2. accustomed to sit or rest much of the time or to do little exercise

More Wordbuilding With Latin Roots

EXERCISE 12.2: LESSON WORDS. In each blank space below, write the most appropriate boldfaced word from the left column of the preceding list.

1. There is an abundance of fish. The oceans are teeming with _____ life.

2. Bail for the murder suspect was set at a million dollars, in view of the _____ of the case.

3. The mother of the infants is on leave from her job because she feels they need her _____ care and affection.

4. I was afraid people would _____ me if I wore that T-shirt, but I got several compliments, and nobody laughed at me.

5. There was a great deal of _____ rivalry between Benjamin Franklin and his half-brother James.

6. Children who disregard their parents' requests or wishes are lacking in _____ obedience.

7. Since there is so much to know, how can any human being possibly be _____?

8. Coach Simpson took a(n) _____ interest in the youngsters he trained. He was like a father to them.

9. More and more office workers are spending part of their lunch hour jogging, as a counterbalance to their _____ work.

10. The debate between the candidates was marked by charges and countercharges. It was full of _____.

RELATED WORDS. Learn the boldfaced **related words** in the middle column below, together with their meanings.

Lesson Words	Related Words	Meanings of Related Words
acrimony (*n.*)	**acrimonious** (*adj.*)	bitter in speech or manner; caustic; biting
filial (*adj.*)	**affiliated** (*adj.*)	closely associated

(*Related words are continued on next page.*)

fraternal (*adj.*)	**fraternity** (*n.*)	1. brotherly feeling; brotherliness 2. men's or boys' social club
gravity (*n.*)	**grave** (*adj.*)	serious; likely to cause great harm or damage; threatening
marine (*adj.*)	**maritime** (*adj.*)	on, near, or bordering on the sea
maternal (*adj.*)	**matrimony** (*n.*)	marriage
omniscient (*adj.*)	**omnipotent** (*adj.*)	all-powerful; having unlimited power, authority, or influence
paternal (*adj.*)	**patrimony** (*n.*)	property inherited from one's father or ancestor; heritage
ridicule (*v.*)	**ridiculous** (*adj.*)	deserving to be laughed at; foolish; absurd; preposterous
sedentary (*adj.*)	**sediment** (*n.*)	matter that settles or sits at the bottom of a liquid; dregs

EXERCISE 12.3: RELATED WORDS. Fill each blank below with the most appropriate **related word** from the middle column, above. Do not use any of the related words more than once.

1. At some colleges, the female students may, if they wish, join a sorority, and the males may join a(n) _____ .

2. This apple juice is clear. I see no _____ at the bottom of the bottle.

3. Dad's union is now _____ with a national labor organization.

4. The wedding invitation from my cousin and her boyfriend surprised us. We did not know they were considering _____ .

5. At one point in their _____ dispute, the opponents nearly came to blows.

6. For centuries, the British Navy was _____ on the high seas.

7. The legislators looked worried, as if they had been discussing some _____ matters.

More Wordbuilding With Latin Roots

8. Martha's _____ consisted mainly of the farm on which her father had barely been able to make a living.

9. Florida, a(n) _____ state, has long coastlines both on the Atlantic Ocean and the Gulf of Mexico.

10. When a rumor spread that invaders had landed from Mars, some people believed it, but most thought it was _____.

EXERCISE 12.4: BRAINTEASERS. Each sentence below contains a partially spelled word. Fill in whatever letters are missing.

1. Never having lost a bout, the pugilist felt _ _ _ _ _ _ t e n t.

2. Because of the drought, the outlook for the new crops is _ r a v e.

3. The French were promised liberty, equality, and _ r a t e _ _ _ _ _.

4. June is the favored month for wedding bells and _ _ t r i m _ _ _.

5. When the discussion became _ _ r i m _ _ _ _ _ _, we decided to end it.

6. Supporting the family used to be considered a p a t _ _ _ _ _ obligation, until mothers, in increasing numbers, joined the work force.

7. Jones Beach, a(n) _ _ _ _ t i m e resort, is popular with ocean bathers.

8. This eating place is _ _ _ _ _ _ a t e _ with a nationwide chain of fast-food restaurants.

9. A postal carrier does not have a(n) _ _ _ _ _ t a r _ job.

10. Isn't it cruel to _ _ r i d e someone who makes a mistake?

EXERCISE 12.5: ANALOGIES. Which lettered pair of words—**a, b, c,** or **d**—most nearly has the same relationship as the numbered pair? Circle the letter of your answer.

1. OMNIPOTENT : POWER
   - *a.* hypocritical : sincerity
   - *b.* opportunistic : unselfishness
   - *c.* omniscient : knowledge
   - *d.* candid : evasiveness

2. HEIR : PATRIMONY
   - *a.* retiree : pension
   - *b.* culprit : punishment
   - *c.* creditor : bill
   - *d.* debtor : obligation

3. DERIDE : CONTEMPT
    a. vilify : respect
    b. accommodate : unkindness
    c. laud : disapproval
    d. antagonize : hostility

4. MARINE : NAVIGATION
    a. urban : farming
    b. mythological : history
    c. canine : cats
    d. mercantile : trade

5. ACRIMONY : PROGRESS
    a. drought : insolvency
    b. malnutrition : growth
    c. flexibility : change
    d. indigence : assets

Lesson 13. Words of Abundance

In 1985, Mel Fisher and his deep-sea divers found the Spanish treasure ship *Atocha,* which had sunk in a hurricane in 1622, in fifty-five feet of water, thirty-five miles off Key West, Florida. From the wreck, Fisher brought up forty-seven tons of gold and silver.

There is a word that aptly describes a discovery like Mel Fisher's. Do you know it? You will find it among the "words of abundance" below.

abound (*v.*)
ə bound′
1. be present in great quantities; be plentiful
2. be filled; teem

bonanza (*n.*)
bə nan′ zə
source of great and sudden wealth; place of great abundance; gold mine

cloying (*adj.*)
kloi′ iŋ
disgusting or distasteful because of excess; too sweet; too sentimental

congest (*v.*)
kən jest′
fill to excess; overcrowd; clog

copious (*adj.*)
kō′ pē əs
plentiful; abundant; ample
    ant. **meager**

glut (*n.*)
glut
excessive quantity; oversupply; plethora; surfeit

inordinate (*adj.*)
in ôr′ də nit
beyond reasonable limits; immoderate; excessive
    ant. **reasonable**

redundant (*adj.*)
ri dun′ dənt
using more words than necessary; wordy; verbose
    ant. **concise**

replete (*adj.*)
ri plēt′
well-filled; abundantly stocked; full

satiate (*v.*)
sā′ shē āt′
satisfy to excess; weary or disgust with too much; sate; gorge

EXERCISE 13.1: LESSON WORDS. In each blank space below, write the most appropriate word from the left column of the preceding list.

1. This cake is oversweet. It has a(n) _____ taste.

2. During the rush hours, endless streams of vehicles _____ our roads and highways.

3. The meager meal certainly did not _____ my appetite. It left me hungry.

4. Before these lakes and rivers became polluted, they used to _____ with fish.

5. Instead of "nothing was visible to the eye," just say "nothing was visible." Don't be _____ .

6. Because of its greater capacity, our new boiler is giving us a more _____ supply of hot water than we had in the past.

7. The taxi took a(n) _____ length of time to get us to the station. We could have gotten there faster if we had walked.

8. The lottery is generally a losing investment, but for the one who holds the winning ticket it can be a(n) _____ .

9. It was certainly no ordinary contest. Rarely has a final and deciding game been so _____ with tension and surprises.

10. Car dealers are unhappy. There is a(n) _____ of unsold new vehicles in their showrooms.

RELATED WORDS. Learn the boldfaced **related words** in the middle column below, together with their meanings.

Lesson Words	Related Words	Meanings of Related Words
cloying (*adj.*)	**cloy** (*v.*)	weary by too much of something pleasant; disgust
congest (*v.*)	**congested** (*adj.*)	filled too full; overcrowded
	congestion (*n.*)	overcrowding

(*Related words are continued on next page.*)

copious (*adj.*)	**copiously** (*adv.*)	abundantly; plentifully
glut (*n.*)	**glutton** (*n.*)	person who overeats; voracious eater
inordinate (*adj.*)	**inordinately** (*adv.*)	excessively; immoderately
redundant (*adj.*)	**redundancy** (*n.*)	needless repetition of words; verbosity
replete (*adj.*)	**deplete** (*v.*)	empty completely or partially; use up; exhaust
	.... **replenish** (*v.*)	refill; provide a new supply for
satiate (*v.*)	**insatiable** (*adj.*)	incapable of being satisfied

EXERCISE 13.2: RELATED WORDS. Fill each blank below with the most appropriate **related word** from the middle column, above. Do not use any of them more than once.

1. Our water shortage is easing. The recent heavy rains should _____ our reservoirs.

2. After the seven-course dinner, our guests asked, "What else is there to eat?" They were _____s.

3. The neighborhood is becoming _____ because so many new residents are moving into the area.

4. It took an hour for the ambulance to arrive. For the injured, that was a(n) _____ long wait.

5. The dessert is not too rich. It will not _____ your appetite.

6. At three in the morning, our busiest streets and roadways are practically deserted. There is no _____ at that hour.

7. Avoid _____ in your speaking and writing. Be concise.

8. Janet is a true scholar. She has a(n) _____ curiosity for knowledge.

9. If we do not begin conserving water, we may seriously _____ our supplies of this priceless natural resource.

10. Early shoppers can usually find what they want because every morning the shelves are _____ restocked with fresh merchandise.

EXERCISE 13.3: BRAINTEASERS. Each sentence below contains a partially spelled word. Enter the missing letters.

1. We have vindictive foes whose desire for revenge is __ __ s a t __ __ __ __ __ .

2. Avaricious people have a(n) __ __ __ __ d i n __ __ __ hunger for wealth.

3. A "rich millionaire" is obviously a(n) __ __ __ __ __ __ a n t expression.

4. Our grain reserves are depleted. When will they be __ __ __ __ __ __ __ s h e d?

5. The two brothers who came upon the rich ore deposit died before they could file their claim. For them, the discovery was not a(n) __ o n __ __ __ __ .

6. It tasted sweeter than honey. Some liked it, but I found it __ __ __ __ i n __ .

7. There is no dearth of materials. We have a(n) __ __ __ __ __ u s supply.

8. The heat wave is in its third week. We have had a s u r f __ __ __ of hot weather.

9. There have been times of scarcity and times of __ __ __ __ d a n c e.

10. The __ o r __ __ __ __ __ insects are devouring nearly everything in sight.

EXERCISE 13.4: ANALOGIES. Which lettered pair of words—**a, b, c,** or **d**—most nearly has the same relationship as the numbered pair? Circle the letter of your answer.

1. GLUTTONOUS : OVEREAT
    a. docile : rebel
    b. relentless : yield
    c. evasive : equivocate
    d. candid : falsehood

2. COPIOUS : MEAGER
    a. grave : serious
    b. vain : humble
    c. preposterous : ridiculous
    d. malicious : spiteful

3. TEEM : ABUNDANT
    a. thrive : unsuccessful
    b. loaf : industrious
    c. procrastinate : prompt
    d. bicker : quarrelsome

4. CLOYING : DISGUSTS
    a. vexing : irritates
    b. unequivocal : bewilders
    c. palatable : displeases
    d. fragile : endures

5. CONGESTION : MOBILITY
    a. extravagance : waste
    b. fatigue : efficiency
    c. acceleration : speed
    d. scarcity : price

Words of Abundance

Lesson 14. "Taking" Words

People do a great deal of taking in this world. For example, they take risks, they take pains, they take things apart, they take things for granted, and some take things that do not belong to them.

Each of the new words in this lesson has something to do with taking.

apprehend (*v.*)
ap′ rē hend′
1. take into custody; arrest; capture
2. grasp the meaning of; perceive
3. anticipate with anxiety or fear; dread

assume (*v.*)
ə sy$\overline{oo}$m′
1. take for granted; suppose to be a fact; postulate; presuppose
2. take upon oneself; undertake

comprehensive (*adj.*)
käm′ prē hen′ siv
taking in a great deal; dealing with all or many of the relevant details; inclusive; encompassing

dismantle (*v.*)
dis mant′ ′l
take apart; disassemble

entrepreneur (*n.*)
än′ trə prə nʉr′
person who organizes, manages, and takes the risks of a business undertaking

inalienable (*adj.*)
in āl′ yən ə bəl
incapable of being taken away; not transferable

meticulous (*adj.*)
mə tik′ y$\overline{oo}$ ləs
painstaking; extremely careful about small details; scrupulous; fussy

revoke (*v.*)
ri vōk′
annul by taking back or recalling; cancel; rescind
    ant. **confirm**

supersede (*v.*)
s$\overline{oo}$′ pər sēd′
take the place of; replace; force out of use; supplant; succeed

usurper (*n.*)
y$\overline{oo}$ zʉrp′ ər
one who wrongfully takes or assumes the office, rights, or powers of another

EXERCISE 14.1: LESSON WORDS. In each blank space below, write the most appropriate boldfaced word from the left column of the preceding list.

1. An adult encyclopedia deals with a vast number of topics. It is far more _____ than a juvenile encyclopedia.

2. Though the fugitive was armed, the police were able to _____ him without bloodshed.

3. A(n) _____ takes risks, hoping to make a profit.

4. Maybelle has not yet arrived, but we are expecting her. We have no reason to _____ that she is not coming.

5. The icebox is rare nowadays. It has been _____d by the electric refrigerator.

6. Since Cathy is the one who assembled the bookcase, she should know how to _____ it.

7. The dictator who overthrew the duly elected government is not popular with the inhabitants. They regard him as a(n) _____ .

8. No one can lawfully deprive an American of the right to a fair trial. It is a(n) _____ right guaranteed by the Constitution.

9. The speeder was fined $100, and his license was _____d.

10. A(n) _____ writer avoids redundant expressions.

RELATED WORDS. Learn the boldfaced **related words** in the middle column below, together with their meanings.

Lesson Words	Related Words	Meanings of Related Words
apprehend (v.)	**apprehension** (n.)	1. arrest 2. fear that something may go wrong; misgiving; foreboding
	...............**apprehensive** (adj.)	fearful; worried; anxious

(*Related words are continued on next page.*)

"Taking" Words

assume (v.)......................**assumption** (n.)		supposition; something that is taken for granted
......................**unassuming** (adj.)		not bold; not arrogant; unpretentious; humble
comprehensive (adj.).........**comprehend** (v.)		1. take into the mind; understand 2. take in; include; comprise
entrepreneur (n.) ....**enterprise** (n.)		1. initiative; ambition 2. risky undertaking; business venture
inalienable (adj.)...............**alienate** (v.)		make unfriendly; disunite; estrange
meticulous (adj.)...............**meticulously** (adv.)		very carefully; painstakingly; scrupulously
revoke (v.) ....**irrevocable** (adj.)		impossible to undo; unalterable
usurper (n.).....................**usurp** (v.)		seize and hold without right; commandeer; arrogate

EXERCISE 14.2: RELATED WORDS. Fill each blank below with the most appropriate **related word** from the middle column, above. Do not use any of them more than once.

1. The painters paid careful attention to every detail of their work. They did their job _____ .

2. Barry acts as if he is running the club. We have to remind him that Sally is our president. He should not try to _____ her authority.

3. I took it for granted that I would be able to buy my ticket just before the play. That, however, was a false _____ .

4. When the coach announced he was resigning, we tried to get him to change his mind, but he said his decision was _____ .

5. Please stop worrying. There is no need for _____ .

6. The two neighbors were once close friends, but now they don't talk to each other. What could have happened to _____ them?

7. A person who is humble and _____ is much better liked than one who is boastful and arrogant.

8. Some children are terrified on their first visit to the barber, but on subsequent visits they are less _____ .

9. The universe includes the earth, the sun, the moon, the stars, and all of space. It _____s everything there is.

10. Many employees have thought of quitting their jobs and going into business for themselves, but only a few have had the _____ to do it.

EXERCISE 14.3: BRAINTEASERS. Each line below contains a partially spelled word. Enter the missing letters.

1. When Dan proposed a climb to the top of the mountain, two of his friends said they would join him in the e n t e r _ _ _ _ _ .

2. For some pupils, the day before a final examination is always a time of _ _ _ _ _ h e n s _ _ _ .

3. The defeat of the Spanish Armada enabled England to s u p e r _ _ _ _ Spain as ruler of the seas.

4. Since my speech received only polite applause, I _ _ _ _ m e that it was not a great success.

5. You should be aware that the privilege of membership in the public library is not _ _ _ _ _ _ c a b l e. If you abuse it, it may be withdrawn.

6. Cheryl is not just careful. She is m e t _ _ _ _ _ _ _ .

7. The movers may have to _ _ _ m a n _ _ _ the grand piano to get it out of the studio.

8. Since the present ruler was never legally elected but seized power, he must be regarded as a(n) u s _ _ _ _ _ _ .

9. The Constitution clearly states the _ _ _ _ _ _ _ a b l e rights of which no person in this country may lawfully be deprived.

10. When you smell smoke, it is logical to make the _ _ s u m p _ _ _ _ that something is burning.

EXERCISE 14.4: ANALOGIES. Which lettered pair of words—**a, b, c,** or **d**—most nearly has the same relationship as the numbered pair? Circle the letter of your answer.

1. METICULOUS : CAREFUL
   - *a.* ecstatic : happy
   - *b.* eager : zealous
   - *c.* ordinary : outstanding
   - *d.* extravagant : frugal

2. IRREVOCABLE : UNDONE
   - *a.* inoffensive : tolerated
   - *b.* feasible : done
   - *c.* incombustible : ignited
   - *d.* edible : eaten

3. MANUFACTURER : ENTREPRENEUR
   - *a.* amateur : professional
   - *b.* senator : legislator
   - *c.* athlete : swimmer
   - *d.* ally : adversary

4. ASSEMBLE : DISMANTLE
   - *a.* postulate : assume
   - *b.* acknowledge : admit
   - *c.* revoke : cancel
   - *d.* accelerate : retard

5. APPREHENSIVE : ANXIETY
   - *a.* covetous : greed
   - *b.* benevolent : malice
   - *c.* disinterested : bias
   - *d.* merciless : compassion

Lesson 15. Review and Enrichment

EXERCISE 15.1: SYNONYMS. For the boldfaced word in each sentence below, find two synonyms. Choose all your synonyms from the list at the end of this exercise. The first two synonyms have been entered as samples.

1. The outlook is **grave**. _____serious   threatening_____

2. There was a(n) **glut** of potatoes on the market. _____

3. Many voters regard the coming election with **apathy**. _____

4. I came to the interview with some **apprehension**. _____

5. You just made a(n) **redundant** statement. _____

6. Don't be so **avaricious**. _____

7. We have respect for her **sagacity**. _____

8. New methods do not **supersede** old ones overnight. _____

9. The rivals greeted each other with **acrimony**. _____

10. Why do you **assume** that failure is inevitable? _____

LIST OF SYNONYMS

asperity
bitterness
covetous
foreboding
greedy
indifference
insight
misgiving
plethora
postulate

presuppose
serious
shrewdness
succeed
supplant
surfeit
threatening
unconcern
verbose
wordy

EXERCISE 15.2: ANTONYMS. Replace each boldfaced word with an **antonym** from the list below. The first antonym has been entered as a sample.

1. Your statement is **redundant**.   1. __concise__
2. We have had several examples of their **malice**.   2. _____
3. Their demands are **inordinate**.   3. _____
4. What impressed us most was his **vanity**.   4. _____
5. The team has a **copious** supply of new talent.   5. _____
6. There seemed to be no limit to his **avarice**.   6. _____
7. Some cravings are **insatiable**.   7. _____
8. At first, I was **apathetic** about bowling.   8. _____
9. Her parents say she is very **undaughterly**.   9. _____
10. The Supreme Court can **revoke** a decision of a lower court. 10. _____

LIST OF ANTONYMS

benevolence	humility
concise	meager
confirm	prodigality
enthusiastic	reasonable
filial	satisfiable

EXERCISE 15.3: SENTENCE COMPLETION. Two words are missing in each sentence below. Select those words from the following list, and enter them where they belong. Do not use any listed word more than once.

apprehensive	fraternal
assume	gorge
bonanza	marine
dismantle	meticulous
enterprising	voracious

1. The unfavorable _____ forecast made us _____ about going on the boat ride for which we had bought tickets.

2. If I had been more _____ when I first assembled the bench, I would not have had to _____ it and start all over again.

3. Those who have _____ appetites often _____ themselves.

72 Vocabulary for the High School Student, Book B

4. It is unsafe to _____ that brothers will always help one another, as some of them may have no _____ loyalty.

5. Each of the _____ Americans who joined in the California Gold Rush had high hopes of coming upon a(n) _____.

Continue, as above, but select your words from the following list:

alienate	inordinate
assumption	maternal
benevolence	replenish
comprehensive	sedentary
entrepreneur	usurp

6. Any _____ who takes _____ risks is inviting bankruptcy.

7. After doing _____ work indoors, try to get some outdoor exercise so that you may _____ your lungs with fresh air.

8. I took it for granted that the department store would sell sunglasses because it is supposed to have a(n) _____ variety of merchandise, and my _____ proved to be correct.

9. Dotty doesn't want to _____ the manager by making it seem that she is in charge and is trying to _____ his authority.

10. One neighbor took a(n) _____ interest in us—she was like a second mother—and we profited greatly from her _____.

EXERCISE 15.4: ROOTS. Fill each blank with the required root from the following list:

ROOT	MEANING
acri	sharp; bitter
fili	son or daughter
frater	brother
grav	serious; severe
mari	sea
mater	mother
omni	all
pater	father
rid	laugh
sed	sit

Review and Enrichment

The first entry has been made as a sample.

1. Switzerland is not a __mari__time nation. It has no seacoast.

2. There is no evidence of _____nal affection between the brothers. They fight all the time.

3. Is there any _____iment at the bottom of the bottle?

4. The rivals are full of bitterness. They cannot discuss anything without becoming _____monious.

5. Usually, Mother is the one who criticizes me for being late to dinner, but this time I got a(n) _____nal scolding, too.

6. I didn't wear that costume because I thought it would make me look _____iculous. Why should I be laughed at?

7. Some parents complain of _____al disobedience. They cannot get their children to obey them.

8. Zeus, the king of the Greek gods, was regarded as _____potent.

9. In some families, the father sometimes does the food shopping. It is not just a(n) _____nal responsibility.

10. There is really no cause for apprehension. The situation is not so _____e as we had thought.

EXERCISE 15.5: SPELLING. Enter the two missing letters. The first word has been completed as a sample.

1. insat__ia__ble
2. entrepren____r
3. conc____ted
4. frat____nal
5. s____plant
6. copi____s
7. init____tive
8. p____posterous
9. glut____nous
10. super____de
11. vora____ousness
12. ir____vocable
13. omnis____ent
14. assum____ion
15. fil____l
16. im____derate
17. repleni____
18. sc____pulous
19. malic____us
20. apath____ic
21. mat____mony
22. dismant____
23. us____per
24. surf____t

74 **Vocabulary for the High School Student, Book B**

EXERCISE 15.6: CONCISE WRITING. Each of the following sentences uses ten or more words to express a thought. Express that same thought in *no more than four words*. The first sentence has been rewritten as a sample.

1. Though I had already eaten enough to satisfy my hunger, I kept on eating and eating.
   I was a glutton.

2. Two individuals who were defacing and destroying public property were taken into custody.

3. The world needs people who are willing to organize, manage, and take the risks of business undertakings.

4. He has become accustomed to sit most of the time and does no exercise.

5. Their desire to acquire and hoard money is so great that it seems incapable of ever being satisfied.

6. The one who preceded her was extremely careful about small details.

7. They spoke without using bitter words or hurting each other's feelings.

8. This candy is too sweet to be appealing to the appetite.

9. Our friends sympathize with the unfortunate and want to help them.

10. Some people have a desire to hurt others or do mischief.

11. Does her report deal with all or most of the relevant details?

12. The sidewalks were filled to excess with throngs of pedestrians.

Review and Enrichment

13. Are they capable of seeing things clearly and making wise decisions?

    _____

14. There seemed to be no limit to the power and influence of our foes.

    _____

15. Good writers do not use more words than are necessary.

    _____

EXERCISE 15.7: CLOSE READING. Carefully read the following passages, and answer the questions below them.

PART ONE

After losing his position as caretaker in a fashionable London church where he had worked for sixteen years, Albert E. Foreman opened a tobacco shop. Foreman is the main character in *The Verger* by W. Somerset Maugham.

In 1500, when King Ferdinand and Queen Isabella of Spain heard that conditions in their colony of Hispaniola were very bad, they sent a new official to replace Christopher Columbus as governor. Columbus was sent back to Spain in chains.

The affluent Ebenezer Scrooge allowed himself only the smallest of fires, even in the coldest weather. Scrooge is the main character in *A Christmas Carol* by Charles Dickens.

Macbeth became King of Scotland by murdering King Duncan and taking over his throne. Macbeth and Duncan are characters in William Shakespeare's play *Macbeth*.

There used to be an inn in the notch of the White Mountains, where everyone was treated with homely kindness by the innkeeper—even those who came in only to warm themselves. This inn is the setting of *The Ambitious Guest*, a short story by Nathaniel Hawthorne.

QUESTIONS

1. Who was a usurper? _____

2. Who was benevolent? _____

3. Who became an entrepreneur? _____

4. Who was superseded? _____

5. Who was avaricious? _____

PART TWO

An elderly sailor, known as the Ancient Mariner, tells of a voyage that he went on in his younger days. His ship, caught in a storm, was driven toward the South Pole, but when an albatross landed on the deck, the weather changed for the better. The other members of the crew made a pet of the albatross, calling it a bird of good omen. One day, however, for no apparent reason, the mariner shot the albatross with his crossbow. The mariner's story is told in *The Rime of the Ancient Mariner* by Samuel T. Coleridge.

Morris Townsend asked Catherine Sloper to marry him, and she would gladly have accepted him, but her wealthy father Dr. Sloper opposed the match. An investigation into Morris Townsend's affairs convinced Dr. Sloper, who was very intelligent, that the marriage would be bad for his daughter. He told his daughter that the young man was probably a fortune-hunter who was interested in her only for her money, but she refused to believe this. So apprehensive was Dr. Sloper that the marriage would take place that he willed his entire estate to charity before he died. Dr. Sloper, his daughter, and Morris Townsend are characters in *Washington Square,* a novel by Henry James.

QUESTIONS

6. Who was suspected of seeking a bonanza? _____

7. Who was regarded as unfilial? _____

8. Who deprived someone of a patrimony? _____

9. Who proposed matrimony? _____

10. Who was malicious? _____

Lesson 16. Wordbuilding With Five Latin Roots

In this lesson, we will build some words with these Latin roots:

ROOT	MEANING
luc	light
nov	new
termin	end
trepid	fear
val	strong

EXERCISE 16.1: WORDBUILDING. Complete each partially spelled word below by inserting the necessary root from the above list. The first insertion has been made as a sample.

1. More light needs to be shed on this problem. Can anyone e __luc__ idate it for us?

2. They are full of _____ation. I wonder what they are afraid of.

3. The children had been to the circus many times, so to them it was not a _____elty.

4. The movie seemed in_____able. I thought it would never end.

5. Most of the excuses we heard were weak, but yours seemed _____id.

6. Inventors are daring and original. They have in_____ative ideas.

7. Your drapes are trans_____ent, but ours do not permit light to come through.

8. Most patients take about two weeks to get their strength back, but Dad was back at work in a week. He had a short con_____escence.

9. Unlike their in_____ captain, the crew was fearful that they might never see land again.

10. The drought has already lasted for a month. We cannot tell when it will _____ate.

Here are the words that you were asked to build, listed alphabetically and accompanied by fuller definitions. Learn those definitions.

convalescence (*n.*)
kän′ və ləs′ əns

gradual recovery of strength and health after an illness; period of recuperation

elucidate (*v.*)
ə lōō′ sə dāt′

throw light upon; explain; make clear; clarify

innovative (*adj.*)
in′ ə vā′ tiv

tending to introduce new methods or ideas; original; creative; inventive

interminable (*adj.*)
in tʉr′ mi nə bəl

having or seeming to have no end or limit; ceaseless; continual; perpetual

intrepid (*adj.*)
in trep′ id

brave; not afraid; fearless; bold; dauntless
  ant. **cowardly; craven**

novelty (*n.*)
näv′ əl tē

1. something new or unusual; innovation
2. newness

terminate (*v.*)
tʉr′ mə nāt′

1. bring to an end; put a stop to; end
   ant. **initiate**
2. come to an end; close; stop

translucent (*adj.*)
trans lōō′ sənt

letting light through, but not able to be seen through clearly

trepidation (*n.*)
trep′ ə dā′ shən

fear; fright; trembling; apprehension
  ant. **unapprehensiveness**

valid (*adj.*)
val′ id

having force; well-founded; sound; legally binding
  ant. **invalid**

EXERCISE 16.2: LESSON WORDS. In each blank space below, write the most appropriate boldfaced word from the left column, above.

1. Humans have been fighting each other since the beginning of time. There is _____ strife in the world.

2. When you make a report, try to include some examples and illustrations. They will help to _____ what you are talking about.

3. Instead of imitating others, make an effort to be _____.

4. Since I had never appeared on stage before, the thought of acting in a play filled me with _____.

5. Ellie's learner's permit is no longer _____. It expired two weeks ago.

6. Because the flu is so much more serious than a common cold, it may require a longer _____.

7. Frosted glass is _____. It admits light but does not permit a clear view of objects on the other side.

8. Most of the passengers had never been to the tropics, so to them palm trees were a(n) _____.

9. Test pilots are _____. Few of us have their courage.

10. The strike has been going on for some time. Both labor and management hope it will soon _____.

RELATED WORDS. Learn the boldfaced **related words** in the middle column below, together with their meanings.

Lesson Words	Related Words	Meanings of Related Words
convalescence (*n.*)	**convalesce** (*v.*)	gradually recover strength and health after sickness; improve; recuperate
elucidate (*v.*)	**lucid** (*adj.*)	clear; easy to understand; intelligible
innovative (*adj.*)	**innovator** (*n.*)	one who introduces something new; inventor; originator
	renovate (*v.*)	make new again; renew; modernize
intrepid (*adj.*)	**intrepidity** (*n.*)	bravery; fearlessness; valor
novelty (*n.*)	**novel** (*adj.*)	new; unusual; strange
terminate (*v.*)	**termination** (*n.*)	end; conclusion; cessation
valid (*adj.*)	**invalidate** (*v.*)	deprive of legal force; abolish; nullify
	validate (*v.*)	make valid; give legal force to; confirm; authenticate
	validity (*n.*)	force; effectiveness; legal soundness

EXERCISE 16.3: RELATED WORDS. Fill each blank below with the most appropriate **related word** from the middle column of the preceding list. Do not use any of the related words more than once.

1. The firefighters received high praise for their _____ in the face of danger.

2. A check has no _____ unless it is dated and signed.

3. Our kitchen will have a modernized look after we _____ it.

4. The instructions are so _____ that no one is likely to misunderstand them.

5. If found guilty, the defendant will probably appeal to a higher court in the hope that it may _____ the verdict.

6. This is not a(n) _____ idea. I have heard it many times before.

7. How long did it take you to _____ after your appendix was removed?

8. Prisoners on good behavior are usually given their freedom before the _____ of their sentences.

9. Charges with no evidence to _____ them are sure to be dismissed in court.

10. Fashion designers are _____s. They create new styles.

EXERCISE 16.4: BRAINTEASERS. Each sentence below contains a partially spelled word. Fill in whatever letters are missing.

1. Have you ever sat on the beach and watched the __ __ t e r m __ __ __ __ __ __ coming and going of the waves?

2. He is not a(n) __ __ __ __ __ __ __ o r, so we doubt that he will offer any original ideas or suggestions.

3. Lamp shades are made of __ __ __ __ __ __ __ c e n t material.

4. After a brief __ __ __ __ a l e __ __ __ __ __ __, the injured athlete should be back in competition.

5. To urbanites, traffic jams are not a n o __ __ __ __ __.

Wordbuilding With Five Latin Roots

6. At the __ __ __ __ n a t i o n of the war, the belligerents will face the huge task of rebuilding their ruined cities.

7. Since the insurance policy expired last year and was not renewed, it no longer has any __ __ l i d __ __ __.

8. The circus acrobats did their daring stunts on the high wires with incredible agility and __ __ __ __ __ __ __ __ i t __.

9. When I encounter something in my textbook that is not clear, I keep on reading, hoping that the next sentence or two will __ __ __ __ __ d a t e the matter.

10. There was a house down the road that was supposed to be haunted, and we never passed it on a dark night without some __ __ __ __ __ __ a t __ __ __.

EXERCISE 16.5: ANALOGIES. Which lettered pair of words—**a, b, c,** or **d**—most nearly has the same relationship as the numbered pair? Circle the letter of your answer.

1. INNOVATIVE : ORIGINALITY
   - *a.* conceited : humility
   - *b.* enthusiastic : apathy
   - *c.* docile : disobedience
   - *d.* compassionate : sympathy

2. INITIATE : TERMINATE
   - *a.* elucidate : explain
   - *b.* perpetuate : obliterate
   - *c.* cancel : revoke
   - *d.* arrest : apprehend

3. CONVALESCENCE : ILLNESS
   - *a.* dawn : sunrise
   - *b.* introduction : index
   - *c.* adolescence : childhood
   - *d.* dinner : dessert

4. LUCID : CLARITY
   - *a.* ambiguous : confusion
   - *b.* diverting : boredom
   - *c.* equitable : resentment
   - *d.* redundant : conciseness

5. INTREPID : FEAR
   - *a.* enterprising : ambition
   - *b.* unscrupulous : conscience
   - *c.* avaricious : greed
   - *d.* biased : prejudice

Lesson 17. Power Words

On August 6, 1926, the American swimmer Gertrude Ederle became the first woman to swim the icy, choppy English Channel from England to France. What is especially remarkable is that she completed the nineteen-mile crossing faster than any of the men who had swum the Channel before her.

Which of the lesson words below best describes a person like Gertrude Ederle? Note that each of these lesson words has something to do with power.

authorize (*v.*)
ô′ thər īz′

1. give someone **authority** (power or influence to do something); empower
2. give permission for; approve; sanction

dominate (*v.*)
däm′ ə nāt′

1. rule by superior power; control; govern
2. rise high above; tower over; overlook from a superior elevation

dynamo (*n.*)
dī nə mō′

1. machine for generating electricity; generator
2. forceful, energetic, hardworking person; go-getter; powerhouse

the Establishment (*n.*)
e stab′ lish mənt

controlling group; group of powerful leaders who represent the established order of society; ruling inner circle of a nation or institution

faculty (*n.*)
fak′ əl tē

1. power or ability to do a particular thing; special aptitude; skill; knack
2. one of the powers of the mind—for example, the **faculty** of memory, the **faculty** of reason, etc.
3. teaching staff of a school, college, or university

intellect (*n.*)
in′ tə lekt′

1. great mental power; high intelligence; brainpower
2. person of high intelligence

potent (*adj.*)
pōt′ ′nt

1. having or exercising great power; mighty
   ant. **weak; impotent**
2. achieving or bringing about a particular result; effective

potential (*n.*)
pō ten′ shəl

power or skill that may be developed; possibility; promise

sovereign (*adj.*)
säv′ rən

1. free; self-governing; independent; autonomous
2. supreme in power or authority

stamina (*n.*)
stam′ ə nə

power to endure or withstand fatigue, illness, hardship, etc.; endurance; vigor; strength

EXERCISE 17.1: LESSON WORDS. In each blank space below, write the most appropriate boldfaced power word from the left column, above.

1. You don't have to be a(n) _____ to understand this movie. It requires just ordinary intelligence.

2. Napoleon was not content to rule most of Europe. He wanted to _____ England and Russia, too.

3. Thomas Edison left school after three months. His teacher considered him uneducable. She failed to see that he had enormous _____.

4. Several fatigued runners dropped out of the marathon when they realized they did not have the _____ to reach the finish line.

5. Roger Williams was expelled from Massachusetts in 1635 because he believed in religious freedom, a view that displeased the _____.

6. Millions of lives have been saved by penicillin, a(n) _____ drug that fights bacterial infections.

7. Before July 4, 1776, the Thirteen Colonies were ruled by England. They were not a(n) _____ nation.

8. Our science teacher organizes field trips, conducts experiments, writes articles, and coaches tennis. He is a(n) _____.

9. Your cousin has a(n) _____ for making friends easily. That is why she is so popular.

10. A learner's permit allows a learner to drive if accompanied by a licensed driver. It does not _____ the learner to drive alone.

RELATED WORDS. Learn the boldfaced **related words** in the middle column below, together with their meanings.

Lesson Words	Related Words	Meanings of Related Words
authorize (*v.*)	**authority** (*n.*)	power to act, command, or judge
dominate (*v.*)	**dominant** (*adj.*)	most important; most powerful
	domineering (*adj.*)	tyrannical; dictatorial *ant.* **subservient**
	indomitable (*adj.*)	unconquerable; unyielding
dynamo (*n.*)	**dynamic** (*adj.*)	energetic; forceful; vigorous
intellect (*n.*)	**intellectual** (*adj.*)	requiring intelligence and clear thinking
potent (*adj.*)	**omnipotence** (*n.*)	power over all; unlimited authority
	potency (*n.*)	effectiveness; strength
	potentate (*n.*)	one who has great power; ruler; monarch
sovereign (*adj.*)	**sovereignty** (*n.*)	supreme and independent political authority; independence

EXERCISE 17.2: RELATED WORDS. Fill each blank below with the most appropriate **related word** from the middle column, above. Do not use any of the related words more than once.

1. A dictator may subdue a nation, but he cannot conquer its longing for freedom. That longing is _____ .

2. Prior to 1962, Algeria was a French colony and had no _____ .

3. Zeus was almighty because he controlled the thunder and lightning. That control gave him his _____ .

4. Ralph is forceful and energetic. He has a(n) _____ personality.

5. Taking part in a debate is a(n) _____ challenge. It requires a high degree of intelligence.

Power Words

6. Pip, an orphan, was raised very strictly by his _____ older sister, who often punished him unjustly.

7. When the first medicine was ineffective, the physician prescribed a drug with a higher _____, and that gave the patient some relief.

8. Police officials may make an arrest, but they do not have the _____ to administer punishment.

9. Scrooge was avaricious. Making and saving money were the _____ passions of his life.

10. The _____ whose fleet was destroyed by the Greeks at the Battle of Salamis was Xerxes I, King of the Persians.

EXERCISE 17.3: BRAINTEASERS. Each sentence below contains a partially spelled word. Fill in whatever letters are missing.

1. She will never give up. She has a(n) _ _ _ _ _ _ t a b l e will.

2. You must have _ _ a m _ _ _ if you hope to climb Mt. Washington.

3. Are you suffering from fatigue? You do not seem too _ _ _ _ g e t _ _.

4. A belligerent nation is a threat to the _ _ _ _ r e i g n _ _ of its neighbors.

5. The _ _ t a b _ _ _ _ _ _ _ is far more powerful than one ordinary individual.

6. The team showed great promise in spring training, but it failed to realize its p o t _ _ _ _ _ _.

7. Stop giving us commands. Don't be so _ _ _ _ _ _ r i n g.

8. Erica likes sports, but she is also interested in _ _ t e l l _ _ _ _ _ subjects, like science and foreign languages.

9. The huge twin towers of the World Trade Center d o _ _ _ _ _ _ downtown New York City.

10. A person under the influence of alcohol or drugs may not be in full possession of his or her _ _ _ _ _ t i e s.

EXERCISE 17.4: ANALOGIES. Which lettered pair of words—**a, b, c,** or **d**—most nearly has the same relationship as the numbered pair? Circle the letter of your answer.

1. BULLY : DOMINEERING
    a. tyrant : compassionate
    b. intellect : illiterate
    c. aggressor : belligerent
    d. altruist : selfish

2. MEMORY : FACULTY
    a. sewing : skill
    b. eating : nourishment
    c. speeding : accident
    d. convalescence : illness

3. SANCTION : AUTHORIZE
    a. squander : conserve
    b. supersede : supplant
    c. acknowledge : deny
    d. deplete : replenish

4. DYNAMIC : ENERGY
    a. intrepid : timidity
    b. indomitable : tenacity
    c. gullible : sagacity
    d. humble : vanity

5. BADGE : AUTHORITY
    a. hawk : peace
    b. oak : frailty
    c. flag : patriotism
    d. lion : cowardice

Power Words 87

Lesson 18. -ICS Words

You have probably done **calisthenics,** you have sometimes seen people go into **hysterics,** and you have occasionally been in places that have poor **acoustics.**

We are about to learn some useful and interesting words like **calisthenics, hysterics,** and **acoustics.** One thing they have in common is that they all end in *-ics*.

acoustics (*n. pl.*)
ə ko͞os′ tiks

1. science that deals with sound
2. qualities of a room, auditorium, or theater that determine how clearly sounds can be heard there; sound-producing qualities

ballistics (*n. pl.*)
bə lis′ tiks

science dealing with the firing of bullets, rockets, and missiles

calisthenics (*n. pl.*)
kal′ is then′ iks

systematic exercises for developing a healthy, strong, and trim body; light gymnastics

dynamics (*n. pl.*)
dī nam′ iks

1. science that makes it possible to determine or predict the motion of bodies acted on by forces
2. all the forces at work in any activity; driving forces

ethics (*n. pl.*)
eth′ iks

set of moral principles or values governing the behavior of an individual or group; recognized rules for right conduct

histrionics (*n. pl.*)
his′ trē än′ iks

1. art of acting; dramatics
2. artificial, showy display of emotion; theatricality

hysterics (*n. pl.*)
hi ster′ iks

fit of uncontrollable laughing or weeping

orthopedics (*n. pl.*)
ôr′ thō pē′ diks

branch of surgery that deals with problems of the spine, bones, and joints

pediatrics (*n. pl.*)
pē′ dē a′ triks

branch of medicine dealing with the development, care, and illnesses of children

tactics (*n. pl.*)
tak′ tiks

1. art of arranging and maneuvering military or naval forces to gain the advantage in combat
2. any methods used to gain an end

EXERCISE 18.1: LESSON WORDS. In each blank space below, write the most appropriate boldfaced "-ics" word from the left column of the preceding list.

1. After an hour or two of sedentary work, it feels good to get up and stretch, or do some _____.

2. Dr. Simmons was trained in _____. She specializes in the treatment of childhood diseases.

3. This auditorium is not the best place to listen to music. It has poor _____.

4. General Braddock's troops marched to battle in columns, but his foes used different _____. They fought from behind trees.

5. Everyone would agree that it is a violation of _____ for a mechanic to charge an automobile owner for unneeded repair work.

6. You are good in _____. Have you ever thought of going into acting?

7. The comedian had us in _____. We couldn't stop laughing.

8. A person who has suffered a fracture urgently needs the professional attention of a specialist in _____.

9. An expert in _____ testified that the bullet that wounded the police officer came from the weapon belonging to the suspect.

10. To be a success, an entrepreneur must become familiar with the _____ of business activity.

RELATED WORDS. Learn the boldfaced **related words** in the middle column below, together with their meanings.

Lesson Words	Related Words	Meanings of Related Words
acoustics (*n. pl.*) .... **acoustic** (*adj.*)		having to do with hearing or sound; designed for absorbing sound
dynamics (*n. pl.*) .... **dynamite** (*n.*)		powerful explosive
ethics (*n. pl.*) .... **ethical** (*adj.*)		conforming to moral standards; moral *ant.* **unethical; immoral**

(*Related words are continued on next page.*)

histrionics (*n. pl.*) ....**histrionic** (*adj.*)		having to do with actors or acting
hysterics (*n. pl.*) ....**hysteria** (*n.*)		uncontrollable outburst of emotion or fear
..............**hysterical** (*adj.*)		1. irrational because of emotional shock or fear 2. extremely comical; very funny
orthopedics (*n. pl.*) ....**orthopedist** (*n.*)		surgeon specializing in orthopedics
pediatrics (*n. pl.*) ....**pediatrician** (*n.*)		physician specializing in pediatrics
tactics (*n. pl.*) ....**tactical** (*adj.*)		having to do with tactics
.................**tactician** (*n.*)		expert in tactics

EXERCISE 18.2: RELATED WORDS. Fill each blank below with the most appropriate **related word** from the middle column, above. Do not use any of the related words more than once.

1. When a fire broke out in the crowded theater, there was panic and _____.

2. A quarterback directs the play of a football team when it goes on the offense. Therefore, he must be a good _____.

3. Engineers use _____ for blasting tunnels.

4. Practically all of a(n) _____'s patients are under twelve.

5. Our drama teacher thinks that Eunice has a great deal of _____ potential.

6. One of the patients came out of the _____'s office with her arm in a cast. Another emerged on crutches.

7. The first act was _____. It had the audience in stitches.

8. If not for the _____ tiles on the walls and the ceiling, the room would be much noisier.

9. As a beginner, I was poor in maneuvering my pieces on the chess board, but I gradually acquired that _____ skill.

10. Customers trust the proprietor. He has always been _____ in his dealings with them.

EXERCISE 18.3: BRAINTEASERS. Each sentence below contains a partially spelled word. Fill in whatever letters are missing.

1. A screen test can show whether a person has h i s _ _ _ _ _ _ talent.

2. You don't need gymnastic equipment to do _ _ _ _ _ t h e n _ _ _.

3. No one had an emotional outburst. There was no _ _ _ _ _ _ _ a.

4. _ _ _ _ _ _ _ _ _ _ a n s are experts in the prevention and treatment of childhood diseases.

5. A knowledge of _ _ _ l i s t _ _ _ enables engineers to plot the exact course of a missile.

6. Most speakers can be heard without the use of a microphone in this hall because it has excellent _ _ _ u s _ _ _ _.

7. A commander in chief has to be a good _ a c t _ _ _ _ _.

8. Exercises recommended by a(n) _ _ _ h o p _ _ _ _ _ may help patients who suffer from lower back pain.

9. Miners use _ _ _ _ m i t e to break up large masses of rock.

10. It is _ n e t _ _ _ _ _ for anyone to appropriate the belongings of another.

EXERCISE 18.4: ANALOGIES. Which lettered pair of words—**a, b, c,** or **d**—most nearly has the same relationship as the numbered pair? Circle the letter of your answer.

1. TACTICS : BATTLEFIELD
    - *a.* wages : income
    - *b.* histrionics : stage
    - *c.* laws : protection
    - *d.* manners : discourtesy

2. FUNNY : HYSTERICAL
    - *a.* good : excellent
    - *b.* docile : obedient
    - *c.* fair : average
    - *d.* potent : weak

3. PEDIATRICIAN : PHYSICIAN
    - *a.* protagonist : dramatist
    - *b.* playwright : author
    - *c.* parent : mother
    - *d.* legislator : senator

4. ACOUSTICS : SOUND
    - *a.* music : pleasure
    - *b.* mathematics : education
    - *c.* carpentry : tools
    - *d.* meteorology : weather

5. OPPORTUNISTIC : ETHICS
   - a. indolent : leisure
   - b. unbiased : fairness
   - c. rational : intelligence
   - d. foolhardy : caution

Lesson 19. "All" Words

Omnipotent (as in **omnipotent** ruler) may be called an "all" word because it means "*all*-powerful."

Comprehensive (as in **comprehensive** report) may also be considered an "all word" because it means "dealing with *all* or most of the relevant details."

Each of the following words for you to study is an "all word" because it has something to do with *all*.

absolute (*adj.*)
ab′ sə lo͞ot′
1. (as in **absolute** monarch) free from all restraint; not limited by a constitution, parliament, or congress
    ant. **limited**
2. (as in **absolute** honesty) complete; perfect

axiom (*n.*)
ak′ sē əm
statement accepted by all as true; self-evident truth; established rule or principle; maxim; truism

environment (*n.*)
en vī′ rən mənt
all the surrounding conditions that affect the development and behavior of a person, plant, or animal; surroundings

exclusive (*adj.*)
eks klo͞o′ siv
1. keeping all others from a part or share
2. disposed to deny admission to outsiders

general (*adj.*)
jen′ ər əl
1. having to do with all, nearly all, or most of a group; common; widespread
2. lacking in details; indefinite; not specific

pervade (*v.*)
pər vād′
spread through all parts of; extend throughout

society (*n.*)
sə sī′ ə tē
all people; humanity; humankind

totalitarian (*adj.*)
tō tal′ ə ter′ ē ən
having to do with a government in which one political party has complete control and excludes all others

uniform (*adj.*)
yo͞on′ ə fôrm′
1. all alike; not differing from one another
2. always the same; unvarying; identical
    ant. **irregular**

universally (*adv.*)
yo͞on′ ə vur′ səl ē
in all places; everywhere; in every case

EXERCISE 19.1: LESSON WORDS. In each blank space below, write the most appropriate boldfaced "all" word from the left column of the preceding list.

1. The smell of smoke lingers not only in the building where the fire occurred. It _____s the neighborhood.

2. We are sorry to hear that you are moving. We hope you will like your new _____.

3. The queen's authority is limited by a parliament and a constitution. She is not a(n) _____ monarch.

4. Since this is an urgent matter, I will stop doing everything else and give it my _____ attention.

5. _____ benefits from the work of those who fight disease and ignorance.

6. It is a(n) _____ that the shortest distance between two points on a flat surface is a straight line.

7. The people where we live believe that pollution is our number one problem. What is the _____ feeling about this matter in your area?

8. A knowledge of foreign languages can be useful to a world traveler because interpreters are not _____ available.

9. The general who seized power abolished the constitution, outlawed all opposition parties, and imposed _____ rule.

10. Potatoes differ from one another in shape and size, but peas tend to be _____.

RELATED WORDS. Learn the boldfaced **related words** in the middle column below, together with their meanings.

Lesson Words	Related Words	Meanings of Related Words
absolute (*adj.*)	**absolve** (*v.*)	free from guilt or blame; acquit; exonerate
axiom (*n.*)	**axiomatic** (*adj.*)	universally accepted as true
environment (*n.*)	**environs** (*n. pl.*)	district around a city; surroundings; vicinity

(*Related words are continued on next page.*)

exclusive (*adj.*) .... **exclude** (*v.*) — shut out; bar; expel
ant. **admit; include**

.... **exclusively** (*adv.*) — only; solely

general (*adj.*) .... **generalize** (*v.*)
1. make vague or indefinite statements
2. derive a broad conclusion from particular instances

pervade (*v.*) .... **pervasive** (*adj.*) — tending to spread throughout; thoroughly penetrating

society (*n.*) .... **socialize** (*v.*) — take part in social activities; mingle

uniform (*adj.*) .... **uniformly** (*adv.*) — steadily; evenly; smoothly

universally (*adv.*) .... **universal** (*adj.*) — present everywhere; omnipresent; ubiquitous

EXERCISE 19.2: RELATED WORDS. Fill each blank below with the most appropriate **related word** from the middle column, above. Do not use any of the related words more than once.

1. If Audrey persists in her refusal to pay her dues, the club may vote to _____ her from membership.

2. The dampness that arrived with yesterday's change in the weather is so _____ that it covers almost all of our region.

3. Lenore was a(n) _____ excellent student. She earned an A in every one of her high school courses.

4. It is _____ that a book cannot be judged by its cover.

5. The Nortons have kept pretty much to themselves. They do not _____ with any of their neighbors.

6. Some speakers _____ too much. They fail to give their listeners specific details or examples of what they are talking about.

7. XYZ products are sold _____ in XYZ stores. You cannot purchase them anywhere else.

8. Traffic congestion is increasing rapidly not only in the city, but in its _____, too.

"All" Words 95

9. People in all parts of the globe are tired of strife. Never has there been such a(n) _____ longing for peace.

10. The evidence against the suspect is strong. It is unlikely that the jury will _____ her.

EXERCISE 19.3: BRAINTEASERS. Each sentence below contains a partially spelled word. Fill in whatever letters are missing.

1. Some like the city. Others prefer a rural _ _ _ i r o n _ _ _ _.

2. You were too _ _ _ e r a _. Try to be more specific.

3. Jerry knows the accident was entirely his fault, but he has said nothing to _ _ s o l v e the other driver.

4. It is _ _ _ _ m a t _ _ that truth can be stranger than fiction.

5. Hermits live by themselves. They do not s o _ _ _ _ _ _ _.

6. Motorists do not maintain a(n) _ _ i f _ _ _ speed. Some drive faster than others.

7. The _ _ _ _ a s _ _ _ fog that completely immobilized traffic yesterday evening is beginning to lift.

8. Wherever we go, we find pollution. It seems to be _ _ _ q u i t _ _ _.

9. Our club is not a(n) _ _ _ _ u s _ _ _ organization. Anyone can become a member.

10. The rebels want to depose their _ _ _ _ l i t _ _ _ _ _ ruler and install a democratic government.

EXERCISE 19.4: ANALOGIES. Which lettered pair of words—*a*, *b*, *c*, or *d*—most nearly has the same relationship as the numbered pair? Circle the letter of your answer.

1. ENVIRONS : CITY
    a. waves : ocean
    b. stories : edifice
    c. shores : lake
    d. vehicles : bridge

2. EXCLUSIVE : BAR
    a. ethical : equivocate
    b. gregarious : socialize
    c. intrepid : fear
    d. implacable : forgive

3. UNIVERSAL : UBIQUITOUS
   - a. cloying : palatable
   - b. volatile : stable
   - c. novel : familiar
   - d. uniform : identical

4. GENERALIZE : VAGUE
   - a. originate : innovative
   - b. abound : scarce
   - c. divert : boring
   - d. conserve : extravagant

5. ABSOLVE : BLAME
   - a. humiliate : embarrassment
   - b. penalize : disadvantage
   - c. liberate : bondage
   - d. accommodate : favor

Lesson 20. Review and Enrichment

EXERCISE 20.1: SYNONYMS. For the boldfaced word in each sentence below, find two synonyms. Choose all your synonyms from the list at the end of this exercise. The first two synonyms have been entered as samples.

1. Competition requires **stamina**. ___endurance   vigor___
2. We are a(n) **sovereign** people. _____
3. Food is a(n) **universal** human need. _____
4. The suspects were **absolved**. _____
5. We are not **excluding** anyone. _____
6. The need is more **general** than we had thought. _____
7. Who **authorized** these expenditures? _____
8. She is **convalescing**. _____
9. You have a(n) **faculty** for getting the right answer. _____
10. We can do without your **histrionics**. _____

LIST OF SYNONYMS

acquitted	common	improving	self-governing
approved	dramatics	knack	theatricality
aptitude	endurance	omnipresent	ubiquitous
autonomous	exonerated	recuperating	vigor
barring	expelling	sanctioned	widespread

EXERCISE 20.2: ANTONYMS. Replace each boldfaced word with an **antonym** from the list at the end of this exercise.

1. You presented a(n) **potent** argument for your opinion. 1. _____
2. He didn't have to be so **domineering**. 2. _____
3. Who **terminated** the discussion? 3. _____
4. Some face the future with **trepidation**. 4. _____

5. Nobody was **excluded**.   5. _____

6. The motorist had a(n) **valid** driving license.   6. _____

7. The results have been **uniform**.   7. _____

8. I thought the transaction was **ethical**.   8. _____

9. Their **intrepid** behavior surprised everyone.   9. _____

10. Some rulers exercise **absolute** power.   10. _____

LIST OF ANTONYMS

admitted	irregular
craven	limited
immoral	subservient
initiated	unapprehensiveness
invalid	weak

EXERCISE 20.3: SENTENCE COMPLETION. Two words are missing in each sentence below. Select those words from the following list, and enter them where they belong. Do not use any listed word more than once.

absolve	ethics
ballistics	hysterical
elucidate	innovative
environment	society
Establishment	trepidation

1. If they have lied, they have committed a serious violation of _____, and we should not rush to _____ them.

2. In one country after another, the _____ turned Columbus down when he presented his _____ plan for sailing to India.

3. Those who contaminate the _____ are doing themselves and the rest of _____ a great disservice.

4. The _____ expert was asked to _____ how he had traced the recovered bullet to the weapon from which it was fired.

5. Some young children respond to threats of punishment with _____ and fits of _____ crying.

Continue, as above, but select your words from the following list:

acoustics	pediatrician
environs	pervasive
exclusive	renovate
invalidate	tactics
orthopedist	unethical

6. _____ people do not care what _____ they use to get what they want.

7. Millions are being spent to _____ the old concert hall and to improve its _____ .

8. A(n) _____ smog hovered over the industrial city and its immediate _____ .

9. On seizing power, dictators dissolve legislatures, _____ constitutions, and assume _____ control of the government.

10. A(n) _____'s patients are more like the general population than a(n) _____'s clientele.

EXERCISE 20.4: ROOTS. Fill each blank with the required root from the following list:

ROOT	MEANING
luc	light
nov	new
termin	end
trepid	fear
val	strong

The first entry has been made as a sample.

1. Joe's library card was not renewed. It is no longer __val__id.

2. Dora and Pat have stopped speaking to each other. No one knows what led them to _____ate their friendship.

3. An umbrella made of trans_____ent material cannot provide much shade.

4. The toy Junior received from his cousins was no _____elty because he had one exactly like it in his collection.

5. Audrey is an in_____ diver. I am too scared even to approach the diving board.

6. Counterfeit money has no _____idity.

7. It is very easy to understand what he says. He has a(n) _____id way of expressing himself.

8. Our president always has some original ideas. He is an in_____ator.

9. It takes considerable intellect and in_____ity to be an astronaut.

10. Some people are forever finding fault with things. They are in_____able complainers.

EXERCISE 20.5: SPELLING. Enter the two missing letters. The first word has been completed as a sample.

1. contin__ua__l
2. tyra_____ical
3. envi_____nment
4. soc_____lize
5. p_____vasive
6. domin_____ring
7. uny_____lding
8. sover_____gn
9. intellect_____l
10. ax_____matic
11. perpet_____l
12. auton_____ous
13. d_____ntless
14. translu_____nt
15. ac_____stics
16. pediatri_____an
17. th_____tricality
18. potent_____l
19. convales_____nce
20. cal_____thenics
21. interm_____able
22. soc_____ty
23. subserv_____nt
24. _____thopedist

EXERCISE 20.6: CONCISE WRITING. Each of the following sentences uses ten or more words to express a thought. Express that same thought in *no more than four words*.

1. Boys and girls in their teens like to take part in social activities.

2. These are problems that call for intelligence and clear thinking.

3. She stated something that everyone in the world accepts and recognizes as true.

4. It appeared that our troubles were never going to come to an end.

5. The group of influential leaders who represent the established order of society seems to have unlimited power.

6. Critics who review films do not like an artificial, showy display of emotion.

7. We need the power to withstand fatigue, illness, and other hardships.

8. What was the cause of this uncontrollable outburst of emotion?

9. We found fault with the methods that they were using to achieve their ends.

10. He was not the sort of person who would introduce a new method or come up with an original idea.

11. The conditions around us that affect the way we develop and behave are changing.

12. Though they let electric light through, frosted bulbs do not allow us to see through them.

13. Merinda does her assignments with such extraordinary vigor and energy that none of us can keep up with her.

14. That club was inclined to resist the admission of outsiders.

15. Barbarians are not governed in their behavior by a set of moral principles or values.

EXERCISE 20.7: CLOSE READING. Carefully read the following passages, and answer the questions below them.

PART ONE

Eris, the goddess of Discord, caused so much dissension wherever she went that the other goddesses and gods stopped inviting her to their parties.

When he was only 18, Ernest Hemingway—who was to become one of the greatest American writers of the 20th century—was severely wounded while serving as a volunteer ambulance driver in Italy during World War I. The Italian government decorated him for valor. On his release from the hospital, Hemingway joined the Italian infantry.

When she was just a child, Marian Anderson so moved the Philadelphia churchgoers who heard her sing in the choir that they raised money to help her further her musical education.

The Metropolitan Opera Company dates from 1883. Since 1966, it has been housed at the Lincoln Center for the Performing Arts in New York City, where the conditions for producing and listening to music are even better than they were at the company's former location.

QUESTIONS

1. Who recognized someone's intrepidity? _____
2. Who was excluded? _____
3. Who was provided with superior acoustics? _____
4. Who recognized someone's potential? _____
5. Who convalesced? _____

PART TWO

The Dutch East India Company, founded in 1602, was granted a monopoly by the government of the Netherlands to trade with the Dutch colonies in Asia.

Pip, the main character in *Great Expectations* by Charles Dickens, was brought up by his sister—Mrs. Joe Gargery—who was twenty years older. Mrs. Joe enforced discipline with a heavy hand. She often thrashed Pip for the slightest disobedience. For certain offenses, she would make Pip, and her husband, too, swallow large doses of tar-water, a nasty-tasting remedy.

One day, a stranger came to Joe Gargery's blacksmith shop and introduced himself as Jaggers, a lawyer from London. He told Joe and Pip that he had unusual business to transact with them and that he was acting as the confidential agent of another person whom he did not name.

QUESTIONS

6. Who was not specific? _____

7. Who had no sovereignty? _____

8. Who obtained an exclusive privilege? _____

9. Who was domineering? _____

10. Who was authorized by someone to do something? _____

Lesson 21. New Words From Synonyms in the Context

QUESTION: What does **mandatory** mean in the following passage?

Smoke alarms were first required only in certain apartment buildings. Now, they are **mandatory** in almost all households.

ANSWER: A careful reading of the above passage shows that **mandatory** has the same meaning as **required**.

Sometimes we can learn the meaning of an unfamiliar word from its **context**—the other words with which it is used. In the above passage, the clue to the meaning of the unfamiliar word **mandatory** is a nearby synonym—**required**.

EXERCISE 21.1: CONTEXT CLUES. What is the meaning of the boldfaced word in each passage below? Try to find the meaning of that word from its context.

The meanings of the first two boldfaced words have been entered as samples.

1. To many, the odor of garlic is objectionable. However, some do not find it **repugnant**.

    ANSWER: __**repugnant** means **objectionable**.__

2. I **spurned** her ridiculous offer of ten dollars for my old camera, and when she raised it to twenty, I refused that, too.

    ANSWER: __**spurned** means **refused**.__

3. Isn't it outrageous that criminals who showed no mercy to their victims should ask a judge for **clemency**?

    ANSWER: **clemency** means _____

4. The sun shone brightly, but for the fans emerging from the stadium it was a gloomy day. Their **somber** faces showed that the home team had lost.

    ANSWER: **somber** means _____

5. That willow tree has up to now been able to withstand the hurricane winds, but how much more punishment can it **sustain**?

    ANSWER: **sustain** means _____

6. Our instructor may forgive an occasional lateness, but she does not **condone** cheating.

   ANSWER: **condone** means _____

7. While Nancy is inclined to do an assignment as soon as she gets it, her brother Tom is **prone** to put it off until almost the last minute.

   ANSWER: **prone** means _____

8. The perpetrator could have been sentenced to ten years of imprisonment, but he was fined $50,000 and escaped **incarceration**.

   ANSWER: **incarceration** means _____

9. The child was **peevish** only because he was overtired. After his nap, he was not irritable.

   ANSWER: **peevish** means _____

10. On a beautiful day, I sometimes yield to the temptation of putting all my work aside and going to the beach. Today, however, I did not **succumb**.

    ANSWER: **succumb** means _____

Here are the fuller meanings of the words you have just defined. Study them.

clemency (*n.*)
klem′ ən sē

mercy; leniency; mildness of temper toward offenders
   ant. **harshness**

condone (*v.*)
kən dōn′

forgive; overlook; pardon; excuse

incarceration (*n.*)
in kär′ sər ā′ shən

imprisonment; confinement

peevish (*adj.*)
pēv′ ish

cross; irritable; ill-tempered; fretful

prone (*adj.*)
prōn

1. inclined; apt; likely
2. lying face downward

repugnant (*adj.*)
ri pug′ nənt

offensive to one's taste or feelings; objectionable; distasteful; disgusting

somber (*adj.*)
säm′ bər

1. dark and gloomy; dimly lighted
   ant. **bright**
2. depressing; melancholy
   ant. **cheerful**

spurn (v.) refuse with contempt; scorn; reject; decline
spurn   *ant.* **accept**

succumb (v.) 1. yield; give in to overpowering force; submit
sə kum′ 2. perish; die

sustain (v.) 1. withstand; endure
sə stān′ 2. support; keep going; maintain

EXERCISE 21.2: LESSON WORDS. Fill each blank below with the most appropriate boldfaced word from the left column, above.

1. The ex-convict had painful memories of his _____.

2. Thanks to penicillin, the patient did not _____ to pneumonia.

3. Some had asked the Governor to commute the convict's death sentence to life imprisonment as an act of _____.

4. Without nourishment, we would be unable to _____ life.

5. Storekeepers cannot remain in business long if they _____ shoplifting.

6. The skies are overcast. It is a(n) _____ day.

7. He gave us a(n) _____ reply. What can be irritating him?

8. When you lie on your stomach, you are in a(n) _____ position.

9. She dislikes that organization. If it offered her a chance to become a member, she would _____ it.

10. Some enjoy making fun of others, but I would find that _____.

RELATED WORDS. Learn the boldfaced **related words** in the middle column below, together with their meanings.

Lesson Words	Related Words	Meanings of Related Words
clemency (n.)	**inclement** (adj.)	stormy; rough; severe
condone (v.)	**condonable** (adj.)	justifiable; excusable
incarceration (n.)	**incarcerate** (v.)	imprison; confine

(Related words are continued on next page.)

New Words From Synonyms in the Context

peevish (adj.) ....**peeved** (adj.)		annoyed; irritated
..............**peevishness** (n.)		irritability; petulance
prone (adj.) ....**proneness** (n.)		inclination; propensity; tendency
repugnant (adj.).............**repugnance** (n.)		extreme dislike; aversion; loathing
somber (adj.) ....**somberness** (n.)		gloominess; dreariness
sustain (v.) ....**sustainable** (adj.)		bearable; tolerable; supportable
...............**sustenance** (n.)		food; nourishment

EXERCISE 21.3: RELATED WORDS. Fill each blank below with the most appropriate **related word** from the middle column, above. Do not use any of them more than once.

1. This room is bright and cheerful. That one has the _____ of a dungeon.

2. She is _____ because she is the only member of the chorus whose name was not on the program. It was omitted by mistake.

3. His _____ to pick quarrels with everyone is making him very unpopular.

4. In this case, lying was _____. If we had told the truth, it would have broken the youngster's heart.

5. She won't sell her vote. She has a(n) _____ to taking bribes.

6. A shortage of prison space made it difficult for the local government to _____ anyone.

7. The child kept whining because she couldn't have her way. It took a great deal of patience to put up with her _____.

8. I started with a burst of speed and quickly took the lead, but after a while I fell behind. My initial pace was not _____.

9. After a week of _____ weather, we finally got a pleasant day.

10. They are starved. They need some _____.

EXERCISE 21.4: BRAINTEASERS. Each sentence below contains a partially spelled word. Fill in whatever letters are missing.

1. Most of those who can stand on their heads cannot __ __ s t a i n themselves in that position for more than a few seconds.

2. Solitary confinement is the worst form of __ __ c a r __ __ __ __ __ __ __ .

3. Milly was __ __ e v e __ because she was given a small part in the play.

4. The game will be played in spite of the __ __ __ __ __ m e n __ weather.

5. I would seize that opportunity if I were you. Don't __ __ u r n it.

6. Taking something that belongs to another is not __ __ __ d o n __ __ __ __ .

7. As night approaches, the woods take on a(n) __ __ __ b e __ appearance.

8. We cannot trust people who are __ __ o n e to go back on their word.

9. Open the windows to rid the kitchen of __ __ __ __ __ __ a n t cooking odors.

10. She can remember faces but she has a(n) __ __ __ p e n s __ __ __ for forgetting names.

EXERCISE 21.5: ANALOGIES. Which lettered pair of words—**a**, **b**, **c**, or **d**—most nearly has the same relationship as the numbered pair? Circle the letter of your answer.

1. EDIBLE : SUSTENANCE
    a. ambiguous : clarity
    b. barren : fruit
    c. hysterical : amusement
    d. volatile : stability

2. INCARCERATION : LIBERTY
    a. calisthenics : stamina
    b. disease : vigor
    c. curiosity : knowledge
    d. suspicion : stigma

3. CHEERFUL : SOMBER
    a. indifferent : apathetic
    b. acrimonious : caustic
    c. uniform : identical
    d. articulate : speechless

4. UNPARDONABLE : CONDONED
    a. sustainable : tolerated
    b. mandatory : ignored
    c. alterable : changed
    d. lucid : comprehended

5. MERCILESS : CLEMENCY
    a. unprejudiced : bias
    b. shrewd : sagacity
    c. timid : trepidation
    d. avaricious : greed

New Words From Synonyms in the Context

Lesson 22. New Words From Antonyms in the Context

QUESTION: What does **frivolous** mean?

ANSWER: If we are given an unfamiliar word, like **frivolous**, all by itself, with no context, it is almost impossible to tell its meaning. However, if we were to meet **frivolous** in context, the context might give us a clue.

QUESTION: What does **frivolous** mean in the following context?

There are no serious objections to our plan. The few that have been mentioned are quite **frivolous**.

ANSWER: An obvious clue is **serious** because it is being contrasted with **frivolous**. If **serious** is the opposite of **frivolous**, then our problem is solved: **frivolous** must mean "not serious."

In this lesson, you will practice the skill of getting the meaning of an unfamiliar word, like **frivolous**, from a contrasting word or expression in the context.

EXERCISE 22.1: CONTEXT CLUES. Find the meaning of the boldfaced word in each passage below. Look for an antonym or contrasting word or expression as a clue.

First enter the clue, and then the meaning of the boldfaced word. The entries for the first two passages have been made as samples.

1. We were pleasantly surprised that the members of your committee were **pliable**. We had thought they would be hard to persuade.

    a. CLUE: __**Pliable** contrasts with **hard to persuade**.__

    b. MEANING: __**Pliable** means "easy to persuade."__

2. From its **inception** to its termination, the trial received nationwide press coverage.

    a. CLUE: __**Inception** is the opposite of **termination**.__

    b. MEANING: __**Inception** means "beginning."__

3. We are trying to **curtail** the animosity between the two sides, but you seem determined to prolong it.

    a. CLUE: _____

    b. MEANING: _____

4. Things may not go well at first, but don't give up. **Persevere**.
   a. CLUE: _____
   b. MEANING: _____

5. As a rule, we show **deference** for our elders. We do not treat them with disrespect.
   a. CLUE: _____
   b. MEANING: _____

6. Before making any alterations to a home, the owner should consider whether they will **enhance** or reduce its value.
   a. CLUE: _____
   b. MEANING: _____

7. Recently, she has been in poor health, but her physicians have told her she will soon be **hale** again.
   a. CLUE: _____
   b. MEANING: _____

8. Decent citizens show respect for the law. Criminals **flout** it.
   a. CLUE: _____
   b. MEANING: _____

9. If the mayor learns that some city officials have taken bribes, he will surely expose them. He will certainly not **shield** them.
   a. CLUE: _____
   b. MEANING: _____

10. Your efforts to get ahead have been effective. Mine have proved **futile**.
    a. CLUE: _____
    b. MEANING: _____

Here are the words you have just tried to define, together with their meanings. Study these meanings.

curtail (*v.*)   cut short; reduce; abridge
kər tāl′   *ant.* **prolong**; **extend**

deference (*n.*)   respect; yielding to the will or opinion of another; courteous
def′ ər əns   regard; honor
                         ant. **disrespect**

(*Related words are continued on next page.*)

New Words From Antonyms in the Context

enhance (v.) en hans′	make greater; increase; augment; improve *ant.* **reduce**	
flout (v.) flout	show contempt for; mock; scoff at; show disrespect for *ant.* **revere**; **respect**	
futile (adj.) fyoot′ ′l	ineffective; serving no useful purpose; useless; fruitless *ant.* **effective**; **fruitful**	
hale (adj.) hāl	healthy; well; vigorous; free from disease *ant.* **sickly**	
inception (n.) in sep′ shən	beginning; origin; start *ant.* **termination**	
persevere (v.) pur′ sə vir′	persist; continue in a course of action in spite of difficulty, opposition, or discouragement *ant.* **give up**	
pliable (adj.) plī′ ə bəl	1. easy to influence or persuade; yielding *ant.* **obstinate** 2. easily bent; flexible	
shield (v.) shēld	defend; protect; serve as a **shield** (protective cover) for *ant.* **expose**	

EXERCISE 22.2: LESSON WORDS. Fill each blank below with the most appropriate boldfaced word from the left column, above.

1. If you serve yourself before serving your guests, you are showing a lack of _____.

2. Despite their age, many elderly people are _____ and hearty.

3. Our president wanted to _____ the discussion, but several members objected because they still had a great deal to say.

4. It was hard for us to get them to change their minds. They are not so _____ as we had thought.

5. The police issue summonses to motorists who _____ the law.

6. I know how the fight began. I was present at its _____.

7. In a violent storm, an umbrella cannot really _____ you from the wind and the rain.

8. Heating the rolls for a few moments in the oven before serving them is a good way to _____ their flavor.

9. Obstacles are sure to arise as you pursue your goal in life, so only if you _____ do you have a chance of overcoming them.

10. Ponce de Leon spent many years in a(n) _____ search for the Fountain of Youth.

RELATED WORDS. Learn the boldfaced **related words** in the middle column below, together with their meanings.

Lesson Words	Related Words	Meanings of Related Words
curtail (v.)	**curtailment** (n.)	shortening; abridgment
deference (n.)	**defer** (v.)	give in to another's wishes out of respect or courtesy; yield
	deferential (adj.)	showing deference; respectful
enhance (v.)	**enhancement** (n.)	increase; augmentation
futile (adj.)	**futility** (n.)	ineffectiveness; uselessness
inception (n.)	**incipient** (adj.)	just starting to appear; in the early stages
persevere (v.)	**perseverance** (n.)	continued patient effort; steadfastness; persistence
	persevering (adj.)	showing perseverance; steadfast; persistent
pliable (adj.)	**pliability** (n.)	flexibility
shield (v.)	**windshield** (n.)	front window of an automobile, protecting its occupants from the wind and weather

EXERCISE 22.3: RELATED WORDS. Fill each blank with the most appropriate **related word** from the middle column, above. Do not use any of them more than once.

1. Many people lose patience and become discouraged when confronted by a difficult problem. They lack _____ .

2. Actors who become stars receive many benefits. One is an increase in their income. Another is the _____ of their popularity.

3. Should we sometimes speak out when our elders say things we believe are wrong, or should we always _____ to their opinions?

4. A dirty _____ reduces visibility.

5. If I had rested when I realized that I had a(n) _____ cold, my convalescence would have been much shorter.

6. The outdoor graduation ceremony was supposed to last until 4, but it was over by 3:30. Threatening weather forced the _____.

7. Neither of the disputants is willing to yield an inch. There is no _____ on either side.

8. Pierre can be _____. For example, he held the door for us this morning.

9. Most of the investigators have given up on the case. Only a few _____ ones are continuing to seek a solution.

10. Only when they saw the _____ of trying to put the fire out by themselves, did they summon the fire department. What poor judgment!

EXERCISE 22.4: BRAINTEASERS. Each sentence below contains a partially spelled word. Fill in whatever letters are missing.

1. Most of us are law-abiding, but there are always some who __ __ o u t the law.

2. When we came to see the patient, we decided to __ __ __ __ a i l our visit since we thought he might be tired, but he urged us to stay.

3. Show respect. Be __ __ __ __ r e n t __ __ __.

4. We stopped trying to convince them when we realized that our further efforts would be __ __ t i l e.

5. Charlotte's splendid performance in the debate is sure to __ __ __ a n __ __ her chances of reelection.

6. Our neighbor has been convalescing at home. He is still not so __ a l e as he normally is.

7. He gave up too easily. He showed a lack of __ __ __ e v e r __ __ __ __.

8. I shortened my essay, as my teacher had advised, but when I showed it to her she said that further __ __ r i d __ __ __ __ __ was necessary.

9. Some were __ __ a b l e. Others were hard to persuade.

10. A problem in its __ __ __ __ p i e __ __ stage is often harder to detect than one that has been in existence for some time.

EXERCISE 22.5: ANALOGIES. Which lettered pair of words—**a, b, c,** or **d**—most nearly has the same relationship as the numbered pair? Circle the letter of your answer.

1. DEFERENTIAL : COURTESY
    a. peevish : irritability
    b. pliable : obstinacy
    c. imperturbable : agitation
    d. craven : intrepidity

2. FLOUT : CONTEMPT
    a. sanction : disapproval
    b. humiliate : embarrassment
    c. resent : indignation
    d. dissent : agreement

3. HALE : DISEASE
    a. defective : imperfection
    b. culpable : guilt
    c. impure : contamination
    d. lucid : ambiguity

4. CURTAIL : PROLONG
    a. condone : pardon
    b. shield : expose
    c. supplant : supersede
    d. absolve : exonerate

5. PERSEVERE : PERSISTENT
    a. economize : lavish
    b. dominate : subservient
    c. generalize : definite
    d. equivocate : misleading

Lesson 23. Words of Chance and Fortune

The play *Julius Caesar* by William Shakespeare takes us to Rome in the year 44 B.C. Caesar, suspected of wanting to make himself dictator over his fellow Romans, has been warned by a **soothsayer** to beware the Ides of March (March 15th). When that day comes, Caesar's wife urges him to stay at home. There has been a violent thunderstorm during the night, and she has had a bad dream. These reasons convince her that it is not an **auspicious** day for her husband to appear in public. But Caesar, a soldier, has always been **venturesome**—he has not shrunk from risk. He believes that he can deal with anything that a new day may bring, be it good fortune or **adversity**, so he does not listen to his wife. Of course, he does not know that it is his **destiny** to be assassinated that day in the Roman Senate by some of his best friends.

This lesson deals with "words of chance and fortune." You have already met half of them in the above paragraph. They are good words to add to your vocabulary.

adversity (*n.*)
ad vur′ sə tē
    misfortune; trouble; misery; bad luck
      ant. **prosperity**

augury (*n.*)
ô′ gyo͞o rē
    omen; sign of something to come; indication; portent

auspicious (*adj.*)
ôs pish′ əs
    promising success; favorable; propitious
      ant. **inauspicious**; **ill-omened**

casually (*adv.*)
kazh′ o͞o ə lē
    in an unplanned manner; by chance; accidentally; fortuitously
      ant. **deliberately**

destiny (*n.*)
des′ tə nē
    what is bound to happen to any person or thing; a person's lot; fate; fortune

fortuitous (*adj.*)
fôr to͞o′ ə təs
    accidental; happening by chance; casual
      ant. **deliberate**

hazard (*v.*)
haz′ ərd
    risk; gamble; bet; venture

soothsayer (*n.*)
so͞oth′ sā′ ər
    person who claims to be able to foretell events; predictor; prophet

thrive (*v.*)
thrīv
    be fortunate; prosper; succeed; flourish
      ant. **languish**

venturesome (*adj.*)   inclined to take chances; adventurous; daring; bold
ven′ chər səm

EXERCISE 23.1: LESSON WORDS. Fill each blank below with the most appropriate boldfaced word from the left column, above.

1. Everyone thought the company would _____, but it soon had to go out of business.

2. After the first minute, we led by 4–0. It was a(n) _____ beginning for our team.

3. I met Ralph at the library. Neither of us had expected the other to be there. It was an entirely _____ encounter.

4. When Columbus sailed from Spain in 1492, little did he suspect that it was his _____ to discover a new world.

5. The mayor should not _____ our well-being by appointing an inexperienced person to the post of health commissioner.

6. The sun rose brightly, and we took that as a(n) _____ of continued fair weather.

7. Don't ask me to predict the outcome. I am not a(n) _____ .

8. He must be quite _____ if he wants to become a stunt flier.

9. True leaders do not lose their ability to reason when they meet with _____ .

10. We never know when our cousins will visit us. They drop in on us _____, whenever they happen to be in the neighborhood.

RELATED WORDS. Learn the boldfaced **related words** in the middle column below, together with their meanings.

Lesson Words	Related Words	Meanings of Related Words
adversity (*n.*)	**adverse** (*adj.*)	unfortunate; unlucky; unfavorable
augury (*n.*)	**augur** (*v.*)	be a sign of; give promise of; bode

(Related words are continued on next page.)

Words of Chance and Fortune

auspicious (*adj.*)..............**auspiciously** (*adv.*)		in a way that promises success; favorably
casually (*adv.*) ....**casual** (*adj.*)		1. happening by chance; not planned 2. not dressy; informal
................**casualty** (*n.*)		1. serious or fatal accident 2. person injured or killed in an accident
destiny (*n.*)....................**destined** (*adj.*)		1. bound for a certain destiny or fate; foreordained 2. bound for a certain destination
fortuitous (*adj.*) ....**fortuitously** (*adv.*)		accidentally; by chance; casually
hazard (*v.*) ....**haphazard** (*adj.*)		lacking plan or order; random; aimless; accidental
thrive (*v.*) ....**thriving** (*adj.*)		flourishing; prospering; successful
venturesome (*adj.*)...........**venture** (*v.*)		place in danger; risk; gamble; hazard

EXERCISE 23.2: RELATED WORDS. Fill each blank below with the most appropriate **related word** from the middle column, above. Do not use any of them more than once.

1. Many of the places that had been _____ communities in gold-mining days were later abandoned and became ghost towns.

2. Steve cannot afford to _____ any of his money on lotteries or horse races because he is saving for his college education.

3. Success, as a rule, does not drop _____ into a person's lap. If you want to get ahead, you must work hard and plan carefully.

4. As we were leaving for the picnic, we heard the low rumbling sound of distant thunder. It did not _____ well for our picnic.

5. On February 12, 1809, in a Kentucky log cabin, there was born a child who was _____ to become the 16th President of the United States.

6. The previous treasurer's _____ way of keeping track of the club's finances created chaos and confusion.

7. Sibyl's forearm was slightly bruised in the crash. Luckily, she was the only _____.

8. Formal dress is not required at today's party. You may come in _____ clothes.

9. The discussion was conducted under very _____ circumstances. It was extremely hot in the room, and the acoustics were poor.

10. Sally's career with the firm began _____. She was given a higher starting salary than she had expected.

EXERCISE 23.3: BRAINTEASERS. Each sentence below contains a partially spelled word. Fill in whatever letters are missing.

1. I regularly see my classmates in school, but I also encounter some of them _ _ _ _ a l l y when I shop or go bowling.

2. Employers do not choose employees in a h a p _ _ _ _ _ _ way. They try to hire those who have the best qualifications.

3. The day began _ _ _ _ _ _ _ _ _ _ s l y for me. My bus arrived late.

4. The roads were so icy that only the most _ _ _ _ _ _ s o m e motorists dared to drive to work.

5. This plant did not do well in the shade, so we placed it in the sun. Now, it is _ _ _ _ _ i n _.

6. Both belligerents are sick of the war. Each of them has suffered heavy destruction and thousands upon thousands of _ _ _ _ _ t i e s.

7. As _ _ v e r s e weather approached, many small vessels and pleasure craft sought the safety of the nearest harbor.

8. The fire marshals have not been able yet to determine whether the fire began f o r t _ _ _ _ _ _ _ _ or was deliberately started.

9. We cannot say what our future will be. We do not know our _ _ _ t i n y.

10. Some give up when trouble strikes, but others persevere and are ultimately able to triumph over a d _ _ _ _ _ _ _.

Words of Chance and Fortune

EXERCISE 23.4: ANALOGIES. Which lettered pair of words—**a**, **b**, **c**, or **d**—most nearly has the same relationship as the numbered pair? Circle the letter of your answer.

1. SPECULATOR : VENTURESOME
    - *a.* glutton : satiable
    - *b.* hermit : gregarious
    - *c.* coward : craven
    - *d.* pessimist : buoyant

2. INDIGENCE : ADVERSITY
    - *a.* evasion : candor
    - *b.* avarice : insatiability
    - *c.* lavishness : frugality
    - *d.* trembling : intrepidity

3. THRIVE : LANGUISH
    - *a.* absolve : exonerate
    - *b.* validate : authenticate
    - *c.* revere : respect
    - *d.* survive : perish

4. DESTINY : PREDICTABLE
    - *a.* energy : exhaustible
    - *b.* past : reversible
    - *c.* mood : alterable
    - *d.* reputation : assailable

5. AUSPICIOUS : SUCCESS
    - *a.* volatile : stability
    - *b.* ominous : failure
    - *c.* controversial : harmony
    - *d.* equivocal : misunderstanding

Lesson 24. Wordbuilding With Five Latin Roots

In this lesson, we will build some words with these Latin roots:

ROOT	MEANING
dele	destroy
firm	strong
lumin	light
turb	disturb
via	way

EXERCISE 24.1: WORDBUILDING. Complete each partially spelled word below by inserting the necessary root from the above list. The first insertion has been made as a sample.

1. During the power failure, we used candles to il__**lumin**__ate our apartment.

2. There are things we would like to forget, but it may not be easy to _____te them from our memory.

3. You worry too much. Every little problem seems to per_____ you.

4. The physicians and nurses made him walk soon after the operation, though he was so in_____ that he could hardly stand.

5. Follow the instructions exactly as given. You will have trouble assembling the bicycle if you de_____te from them.

6. There was some _____ulent weather yesterday. Tornados carved a path of destruction in several Midwestern states.

7. Occasionally, the dark road was lit up by the _____ous headlights of an oncoming vehicle.

8. By spending sensibly, you can ob_____te the need of borrowing money.

9. Sugary desserts have a _____terious effect. They cause cavities.

10. I told the proprietor that I had purchased the unsatisfactory merchandise at his store, and I showed him my register receipt to con_____ my claim.

Here are the words that you were asked to build, listed alphabetically and accompanied by fuller definitions. Learn those definitions.

confirm (*v.*)
kən furm′
1. strengthen; add firmness to
2. establish the truth of; verify; authenticate
   ant. **deny; contradict; invalidate**

delete (*v.*)
dē lēt′
erase; cross out; remove; eradicate

deleterious (*adj.*)
del′ ə tir′ ē əs
injurious; damaging to health; pernicious
   ant. **salutary**

deviate (*v.*)
dē′ vē āt′
depart from an established way or course of action; swerve; veer; stray

illuminate (*v.*)
i lōō′ mə nāt′
1. light up; supply with light
2. make clear; explain; elucidate

infirm (*adj.*)
in furm′
not strong in body or health; feeble; weak
   ant. **strong; hale**

luminous (*adj.*)
lōō′ mə nəs
1. giving off light; bright; radiant; brilliant
   ant. **dark**
2. very clear; easily understood; unambiguous; enlightening

obviate (*v.*)
äb′ vē āt′
prevent by taking action ahead of time; forestall; preclude; avert; make unnecessary

perturb (*v.*)
pər turb′
disturb greatly; disquiet; trouble the mind of; agitate
   ant. **pacify**

turbulent (*adj.*)
tur′ byōō lənt
1. causing turmoil or unrest; boisterous; unruly
2. full of wild disorder or violent motion; tempestuous
   ant. **calm; placid**

EXERCISE 24.2: LESSON WORDS. In each blank space below, write the most appropriate boldfaced word from the left column, above.

1. I didn't tell Mother the bad news because I knew it would _____ her.

2. Tonight will be clear. A full moon will _____ the sky.

3. A member objected to a sentence in the report of the last meeting, and the club voted to _____ it from the minutes.

122   Vocabulary for the High School Student, Book B

4. The police officers on duty called for reinforcements to help them control the _____ crowd.

5. The coach would neither _____ nor deny the rumor that he would resign.

6. There are not too many seats left, so let's buy our tickets now to _____ the possibility of our not getting to see the play.

7. You do not have to bring him his lunch. He is not so _____ that he cannot carry his own tray.

8. The store's policy is not to accept checks. It does not _____ from that policy.

9. Of all the objects we can see in the daytime, nothing is as _____ as the sun.

10. Some drinkers may not be aware of the _____ effects of consuming too much alcohol.

RELATED WORDS. Learn the boldfaced **related words** in the middle column below, together with their meanings.

Lesson Words	Related Words	Meanings of Related Words
confirm (*v.*)	**confirmation** (*n.*)	proof; verification; corroboration
delete (*v.*)	**deletion** (*n.*)	something crossed out; erasure
	indelible (*adj.*)	unerasable; lasting; permanent; unforgettable
deviate (*v.*)	**deviation** (*n.*)	departure from a normal course or normal behavior; divergence
	devious (*adj.*)	1. not in a straight path; roundabout; circuitous 2. not straightforward; deceiving; sly; cunning
illuminate (*v.*)	**illuminating** (*adj.*)	highly informative; enlightening
infirm (*adj.*)	**infirmity** (*n.*)	weakness; ailment; frailty

(Related words are continued on next page.)

Wordbuilding With Five Latin Roots

luminous (*adj.*)............	**luminary** (*n.*)	person of brilliant achievement; prominent person
perturb (*v.*)...............	**imperturbable** (*adj.*)	not easily excited; calm; cool
turbulent (*adj.*)...........	**turbulence** (*n.*)	commotion; wild disorder

EXERCISE 24.3: RELATED WORDS. Fill each blank below with the most appropriate **related word** from the middle column, above. Do not use any of the related words more than once.

1. The visitor made a(n) _____ impression on us. We shall never forget her.

2. His report provided a great deal of information. It was very _____.

3. No one will believe their accusations unless they can provide _____.

4. A jury is unlikely to be convinced by witnesses who are _____ in their responses.

5. Lloyd is easily upset, but his sister is _____.

6. Many suffer from hay fever. It is a common _____.

7. The leader of the discussion did not permit any _____ from the topic.

8. I was awakened by a commotion in the street, but it did not last, and I fell asleep again, without learning the cause of the _____.

9. Benjamin Franklin was regarded as a(n) _____ both here and abroad. He was one of the most brilliant persons of his times.

10. This is a messy _____. If you must erase something, can't you do it more neatly?

EXERCISE 24.4: BRAINTEASERS. Each sentence below contains a partially spelled word. Fill in whatever letters are missing.

1. Nothing seemed to worry him. He was i m p _ _ _ _ _ _ _ _ _ _.

2. You haven't offered any _ _ _ r o b _ _ _ _ _ _ _ _. Where is your proof?

3. _ _ l e t _ this sentence. It repeats what you have stated in the previous paragraph.

4. It was a(n) _ _ _ _ _ l e n t meeting. The presiding officer could not maintain order.

5. I had expected to get some help by reading my friend's notes, but they were not too i l l _ _ _ _ _ _ _ _ _ .

6. Sunbathing is not so _ _ _ _ t a r _ as was once thought. If done to excess, it can be deleterious.

7. Many suffer from arthritis. It is a common _ _ f i r m _ _ _ .

8. We may be able to _ _ _ _ s t a l l trouble by taking a few simple precautions.

9. One candidate was _ _ _ _ _ u s in answering questions that were put to her, making us think that she was not being frank.

10. The report we heard must be considered a rumor, unless there is evidence to _ _ t h e n _ _ _ _ _ it.

EXERCISE 24.5: ANALOGIES. Which lettered pair of words—**a**, **b**, **c**, or **d**—most nearly has the same relationship as the numbered pair? Circle the letter of your answer.

1. INDELIBLE : ERADICATE
    - *a.* conspicuous : see
    - *b.* illuminating : understand
    - *c.* repugnant : accept
    - *d.* condonable : forgive

2. DEVIOUS : STRAIGHTFORWARD
    - *a.* apathetic : indifferent
    - *b.* unscrupulous : conscientious
    - *c.* frugal : thrifty
    - *d.* destitute : indigent

3. IMPERTURBABLE : POISE
    - *a.* undiplomatic : tact
    - *b.* selfish : altruism
    - *c.* persevering : persistence
    - *d.* frail : endurance

4. NEARSIGHTEDNESS : INFIRMITY
    - *a.* memory : faculty
    - *b.* stamina : hardship
    - *c.* adversity : prosperity
    - *d.* insight : problem

5. DISSENTER : DEVIATE
    - *a.* optimist : mope
    - *b.* imitator : innovate
    - *c.* ingrate : appreciate
    - *d.* glutton : overeat

Wordbuilding With Five Latin Roots

Lesson 25. Review and Enrichment

EXERCISE 25.1: SYNONYMS. For the boldfaced word in each sentence below, find two synonyms. Choose all your synonyms from the list at the end of this exercise. The first two synonyms have been entered as samples.

1. This is the **inception** of a new era. ___beginning   start___
2. It was a(n) **luminous** explanation. _____
3. They are not too **venturesome**. _____
4. He has done little to **enhance** his prestige. _____
5. Few are completely satisfied with their **lot**. _____
6. Nourishment is needed to **sustain** life. _____
7. Some interpret a rainbow as a good **portent**. _____
8. Why are you so **peevish**? _____
9. The visitors were treated with **deference**. _____
10. This was a(n) **somber** occasion. _____
11. Both choices are equally **repugnant**. _____
12. I could not **delete** it from my memory. _____
13. Further efforts would be **futile**. _____
14. They did not **hazard** any of their own money. _____
15. Is it legal to **incarcerate** a suspect before trial? _____

LIST OF SYNONYMS

adventurous	destiny	imprison	remove
augment	disgusting	improve	respect
augury	distasteful	ineffective	risk
beginning	enlightening	irritable	start
confine	eradicate	maintain	support
cross	fate	melancholy	unambiguous
daring	fruitless	omen	venture
depressing	honor		

EXERCISE 25.2: ANTONYMS Replace each boldfaced word with an **antonym** from the list below.

1. It was a(n) **illuminating** reply. 1. _____
2. Shade has a(n) **deleterious** effect on some shrubs. 2. _____
3. These judges have a reputation for **clemency**. 3. _____
4. Why did you **spurn** the opportunity? 4. _____
5. They wanted to **prolong** the discussion. 5. _____
6. What she did is **uncondonable**. 6. _____
7. We are witnessing the **incipient** stage of a great drama. 7. _____
8. Her arrival at that moment was **deliberate**. 8. _____
9. It was a(n) **auspicious** beginning. 9. _____
10. We had no desire to **shield** them. 10. _____
11. They **revere** our customs and traditions. 11. _____
12. Neither of us was **pliable**. 12. _____
13. Everyone was in **casual** attire. 13. _____
14. It was a(n) **turbulent** scene. 14. _____
15. There is evidence to **contradict** his claim. 15. _____

LIST OF ANTONYMS

accept   fortuitous
ambiguous   harshness
confirm   ill-omened
curtail   justifiable
expose   obstinate
final   placid
flout   salutary
formal

Review and Enrichment

EXERCISE 25.3: SENTENCE COMPLETION. Two words are missing in each sentence below. Select those words from the following list, and enter them where they belong. Do not use any listed word more than once.

>casualty   incarcerate
>cheerful   persevere
>condone   somber
>destiny   soothsayer
>flout   succumb

1. If you _____, you have a good chance of success. Don't _____ to discouragement.

2. This room is _____, but with proper lighting it can be made quite _____.

3. To _____ someone without a trial is repugnant to us. We cannot _____ it.

4. Caesar did not want others to think that he was so gullible as to believe that a(n) _____ could foretell his _____.

5. Heed the safety regulations. If you _____ them, you may end up as a(n) _____.

Continue, as above, but select your words from the following list:

>adverse   imperturbable
>augury   obviate
>deletion   prone
>deviation   succumb
>haphazard   sustain

6. Harriet does not lose her poise when she encounters _____ conditions. She remains _____.

7. I have put the directions on the board to _____ the need of my having to repeat them. Please follow them without _____.

8. The patient is responding to medication. That is a good _____. We were afraid that he might _____.

9. I wrote without planning, in a(n) _____ way. As a result, I had to make one _____ after another.

10. Learn to float not only on your back, but also in a(n) _____ position. The water will _____ you.

EXERCISE 25.4: ROOTS. Fill each blank with the root from the following list:

ROOT	MEANING
dele	destroy
firm	strong
lumin	light
turb	disturb
via	way

1. Automobile exhaust has a _____terious effect on the air we breathe.

2. The peaceful crowd soon turned into a _____ulent mob.

3. Shoppers can ob_____te the need for carrying cash by using credit cards.

4. Jim used to catch colds easily, but he has overcome that in_____ity.

5. If you find any unnecessary commas, _____te them.

6. A birth certificate is generally accepted as legal con_____ation of a person's age.

7. Thank you for your il_____ating talk. We learned a great deal from it.

8. Some of my classmates make it a policy never to lend their notes to anyone, and they follow that policy without de_____tion.

9. Shakespeare was probably the greatest _____ary of his century.

10. The _____ulence of the winds makes this an inauspicious day to fly a kite.

EXERCISE 25.5: SPELLING. Enter the two missing letters. The first word has been completed as a sample.

1. suc **cu** mb
2. c____tail
3. fort____tous
4. dev____us
5. p____turb
6. in____pient
7. sh____ld
8. clemen____
9. repug____nt
10. pl____ble
11. per____vere
12. aug____y
13. elu____date
14. bril____ant
15. cor____boration
16. p____vish
17. condo____ble
18. incar____rate
19. cas____lly
20. turb____ent
21. cas____lty
22. h____hazard
23. ill-om____ed
24. sust____ance

EXERCISE 25.6: CONCISE WRITING. Each of the following sentences uses ten or more words to express a thought. Express that same thought in *no more than four words*.

1. Those who deliberately destroy or damage public property show contempt for the law.
   _____

2. Were there many people killed or injured in the accident?
   _____

3. The judge showed mildness of temper toward people who commit offenses.
   _____

4. The thing we admire about her is her sticking to her purpose and not giving up, in spite of difficulty, opposition, and discouragement.
   _____

5. The people who live next door to you were easy to persuade.
   _____

6. Donald is the sort of person who is not easily upset.
   _____

7. No departure from the established way of doing things was tolerated.
   _____

8. The voyage began in a way that gave promise of success.
   _____

9. Avoid topics that are offensive to people's tastes and feelings.
   _____

10. People who expect everything to turn out all right are inclined to take chances.
    _____

EXERCISE 25.7: CLOSE READING. Carefully read the following passages, and answer the questions below them.

PART ONE

When the Greeks are about to admit defeat because they cannot get through the walls of Troy, Odysseus—one of their heroes—proposes a plan. He would have carpenters construct a huge wooden horse in which he and some other Greeks would hide. The rest of the Greeks would disappear temporarily to suggest that they had gone home. The jubilant, unsuspecting Trojans would then open their gates and take in the wooden horse, and at night the Greek warriors would emerge from the hollow horse to set fire to Troy. The Greeks accept the plan of Odysseus, and everything turns out as he has predicted.

Everyone aboard the *Indomitable* likes Billy Budd, except Claggart, the master-at-arms, who has taken a dislike to him. Billy does his best to promote the welfare of his shipmates and to please the ship's officers. However, he has a strange weakness—he becomes tongue-tied when his feelings are deeply hurt. One day, when Claggart falsely accuses Billy in the captain's presence of plotting a mutiny, Billy is unable to speak, but he strikes Claggart a single blow, killing him. For further details, see *Billy Budd* by Herman Melville.

In the opening scene of *Macbeth* by William Shakespeare, three witches stop Macbeth as he is returning from battle, and one of them tells him that he will be King of Scotland.

QUESTIONS

1. Who suffers from an emotional infirmity? _____

2. Who is devious? _____

3. Who utters something extremely repugnant? _____

4. Who speaks of a person's destiny? _____

5. Who becomes a casualty? _____

PART TWO

A character in *Great Expectations* by Charles Dickens is embarrassed on her wedding day when the bridegroom fails to appear for the ceremony. Her name is Miss Havisham.

On his release from nineteen years of imprisonment, Jean Valjean is an outcast whom no one will have anything to do with. Tired and hungry, he knocks at the door of the Bishop of Digne. Madame Magloire, the bishop's housekeeper, is terrified by Valjean's appearance, but despite her fears and misgivings, Valjean is given food and shelter. During the night, Valjean runs off with the bishop's silverware. When he is brought back with his loot by three gendarmes to the bishop's home, the bishop tells them to let the suspect go, saying that he had given Valjean the silverware as a gift. Valjean is the main character in *Les Miserables* by Victor Hugo.

QUESTIONS

6. Who shields someone? _____

7. Who is a victim of incarceration? _____

8. Who is spurned and humiliated? _____

9. Who shows trepidation and perturbation? _____

10. Who shows clemency? _____

Lesson 26. New Words From Commonsense Context Clues

QUESTION: What does **diminutive** mean in the following sentence?

The inhabitants of Lilliput were so **diminutive** that Gulliver could easily hold several of them in the palm of his hand.

ANSWER: Common sense tells us that **diminutive**, in the above context, must mean "tiny" or "very small." If the Lilliputians had not been tiny, Gulliver would not have been able to hold several of them in the palm of his hand.

Note that we discovered the meaning of **diminutive** not from a particular word in the context, but from a commonsense view of the context as a whole. This lesson will give you practice in getting the meaning of unfamiliar words from **commonsense context clues**.

EXERCISE 26.1: CONTEXT CLUES. Find the meaning of the boldfaced word in each passage below by using a commonsense context clue. The meaning of the first boldfaced word has been entered as a sample.

1. Despite all our efforts, there are still some traces of poison ivy here. We have not been able to **extirpate** it.

    extirpate means ___completely destroy___

2. The mission was so dangerous that, when it was first described, no one was **audacious** enough to volunteer for it.

    audacious means _____

3. It was an exceptionally delicious Thanksgiving dinner, thanks to our grandmother's **culinary** skill.

    culinary means _____

4. Most employees preferred to work in a nonsmoking area to escape the **noxious** effects of tobacco smoke.

    noxious means _____

5. She is so **obdurate** that she will cling to her opinion even if you present overwhelming evidence to show that she is wrong.

    obdurate means _____

6. It is sometimes hard to distinguish between those who **simulate** friendship for you and those who are really your friends.

   simulate means _____

7. If we hire a **caterer**, our party will be much more expensive than if we provide the food ourselves.

   caterer means _____

8. When your rivals are seeking to outsmart you, you have to be especially **adroit** to survive.

   adroit means _____

9. The letters to the editor are full of **scathing** comments about the light sentence imposed on the convicted murderer.

   scathing means _____

10. You never ask others how they are, or how they are getting along, so why should any of them **manifest** interest in you?

    manifest means _____

Each word that you just tried to define is listed below with some of its meanings. Familiarize yourself with these meanings.

adroit (*adj.*)　　　　cleverly skillful; resourceful; dexterous
ə droit′　　　　　　　　　*ant.* **clumsy**

audacious (*adj.*)　　1. bold; daring; fearless; intrepid
ô dā′ shəs　　　　　　　　　*ant.* **circumspect**
　　　　　　　　　　　　2. too bold; impudent; insolent; brazen

caterer (*n.*)　　　　person who is in the business of providing food and other
kāt′ ər ər　　　　　　　necessary services for a social gathering

culinary (*adj.*)　　　having to do with cooking or the kitchen
kyo͞o′ lə ner′ ē

extirpate (*v.*)　　　pull up by the roots; destroy completely; exterminate;
ek′ stər pāt′　　　　　eradicate

manifest (*v.*)　　　make clear; show; reveal; demonstrate; evince
man′ ə fest′　　　　　　　*ant.* **conceal**

noxious (*adj.*)　　　harmful; unhealthful; injurious; unwholesome
näk′ shəs　　　　　　　　　*ant.* **wholesome; sanitary; innocuous**

134　Vocabulary for the HIGH SCHOOL STUDENT, Book B

obdurate (*adj.*)
äb′ dōōr it
unmoved by persuasion or pity; hardened in feelings; obstinate; unyielding; inflexible

scathing (*adj.*)
skā′ *thi*ŋ
very harsh; bitterly severe; caustic; searing

simulate (*v.*)
sim′ yōō lāt′
1. give a false indication of; pretend; feign
2. assume the appearance of; look or act like; imitate

EXERCISE 26.2: LESSON WORDS. Fill each blank below with the most appropriate boldfaced word from the left column, above.

1. Plastic can be made to assume the appearance of other products. For example, it can _____ leather.

2. Before the judge could award Betty the trophy, she snatched it from his hands. Wasn't that a(n) _____ thing for her to have done?

3. Anyone who is afraid of heights is unlikely to _____ much enthusiasm for mountain climbing.

4. The _____'s assistants not only prepared and delivered the banquet food, but they kept it warm until they were ready to serve it.

5. The champion will probably retain his title. He is too _____ to be outmaneuvered by the challenger.

6. Ignorance is so deeply rooted that it seems almost impossible to _____ it.

7. At the end of the dinner, the kitchen staff received a round of applause for their _____ skill.

8. After hearing herself bitterly denounced by her rival, the candidate responded with a(n) _____ attack on his record.

9. The _____ suspect continues to refuse to give his name or address or any other information about himself.

10. Two tenants overcome by _____ fumes were resuscitated by the firefighters.

RELATED WORDS. Learn the boldfaced **related words** in the middle column below, together with their meanings.

Lesson Words	Related Words	Meanings of Related Words
adroit (*adj.*)	**adroitly** (*adv.*)	shrewdly; skillfully
audacious (*adj.*)	**audaciously** (*adv.*)	boldly; insolently
	audacity (*n.*)	boldness; effrontery; insolence
caterer (*n.*)	**cater** (*v.*)	1. (followed by *to*) provide what is wanted or needed 2. provide food and service for
extirpate (*v.*)	**extirpation** (*n.*)	eradication; extermination
manifest (*v.*)	**manifestation** (*n.*)	indication; demonstration
noxious (*adj.*)	**innocuous** (*adj.*)	harmless; inoffensive
obdurate (*adj.*)	**obdurately** (*adv.*)	inflexibly; unyieldingly
scathing (*adj.*)	**unscathed** (*adj.*)	uninjured; wholly unharmed
simulate (*v.*)	**simulated** (*adj.*)	made to look genuine; fake; artificial *ant.* **genuine**

EXERCISE 26.3: RELATED WORDS. Fill each blank below with the most appropriate **related word** from the middle column, above. Do not use any of the related words more than once.

1. The attorney helped his client greatly by his shrewd cross-examination of the evasive witnesses. No one could have done it more _____.

2. You couldn't tell they were _____ pearls. They looked so real.

3. We do not know for certain whether the preservatives added to some foods are harmful or _____.

4. As we watched in trepidation, a lifeguard _____ dived into the treacherous water and brought the struggling swimmer to the shore.

5. Miraculously, the driver of the car that turned over escaped _____.

6. Most of the fashionable shops in the high-rent districts _____ to an affluent clientele.

7. One of the principal goals of the French Revolution was the _____ of totalitarian rule.

8. So long as both sides remain _____ committed to their selfish points of view, a compromise is unlikely.

9. Andy didn't have a long wait because he managed to squeeze in near the head of the line. I didn't have the _____ to do what he did.

10. A frown is a(n) _____ of disapproval.

EXERCISE 26.4: BRAINTEASERS. Each sentence below contains a partially spelled word. Fill in whatever letters are missing.

1. No _ _ _ _ _ _ s t a t i o n of pain or distress was observed.

2. These creatures cannot hurt anyone. They are i n n _ _ _ _ _ _.

3. Aren't oranges, bananas, and oatmeal _ h o l e _ _ _ _ foods?

4. The goal of medical research is to _ _ _ _ _ p a t _ disease.

5. She would never have the _ _ _ _ c i t y to come to a party to which she was not invited.

6. No one in the kitchen has greater _ _ _ i n _ _ _ skill than the chef.

7. The walls of the den are covered with panels of _ _ _ _ l a t e _ oak.

8. Wholesale lumber dealers do not _ a t e _ to retail customers.

9. Congratulations on your skill in dealing with this problem. You handled it _ _ _ _ i t _ _.

10. There was not a scratch on any of them. They returned _ _ _ c a t _ _ _.

EXERCISE 26.5: ANALOGIES. Which lettered pair of words—**a, b, c,** or **d**—most nearly has the same relationship as the numbered pair? Circle the letter of your answer.

1. CULINARY : COOKING
    - *a.* rural : city
    - *b.* histrionic : hysteria
    - *c.* acoustic : sound
    - *d.* manual : humanity

2. HYPOCRITE : FEIGN
    - *a.* glutton : gorge
    - *b.* successor : precede
    - *c.* dynamo : shirk
    - *d.* spendthrift : hoard

3. DIMINUTIVE : SMALL
    - *a.* frivolous : serious
    - *b.* rational : absurd
    - *c.* scathing : harsh
    - *d.* microscopic : enormous

4. OBDURATE : YIELD
    - *a.* pessimistic : brood
    - *b.* tenacious : deviate
    - *c.* articulate : speak
    - *d.* docile : obey

5. CLUMSY : ADROIT
    - *a.* lucid : unambiguous
    - *b.* redundant : repetitive
    - *c.* unfamiliar : novel
    - *d.* subservient : domineering

Lesson 27. Monosyllabic Words for Persons

Wouldn't you agree that a **person who is habitually in a bad mood and keeps complaining about everything** is not likely to have many friends?

There is a word that can take the place of all the thirteen boldfaced words in the above sentence. You will meet it in this lesson.

Note that each of our new words below is **monosyllabic**—it contains only one syllable—and that each of them stands for a person.

boor (*n.*) one who has bad manners; rude, insensitive person
boor

bore (*n.*) tiresome, uninteresting person or thing; cause of boredom
bôr

dupe (*n.*) one who is easily tricked or deceived; fool; gull
dyo͞op

grouch (*n.*) habitually irritable, fault-finding person; grumbler; crank
grouch

heir (*n.*) one who inherits or is legally entitled to inherit property
er

quack (*n.*) dishonest, unqualified person who pretends to be a physician; one who fraudulently pretends to have knowledge or skill in a particular field; charlatan
kwak

sage (*n.*) person respected for wisdom, breadth of knowledge, and sound judgment; savant; scholar
sāj

snob (*n.*) person who admires and tries to associate with people of wealth and position, while ignoring others as inferior; one who has an offensive sense of superiority
snäb

spouse (*n.*) one's partner in a marriage; husband or wife
spous

ward (*n.*) 1. person under the care of a guardian or court
wôrd 2. division of a hospital

EXERCISE 27.1: LESSON WORDS. In each blank space below, write the most appropriate boldfaced word from the left column of the preceding list.

1. The comedian made some people laugh, but most of the audience found him to be a(n) _____ .

2. Since the check was made out to Mr. and Mrs. Smith, he would not have been able to cash it without the signature of his _____ .

3. Nick never has a good word for anything we say or do. That's why we consider him a(n) _____ .

4. When I was younger, I was gullible. Now, I am no _____ .

5. "Please" and "thank you" are not in his vocabulary. He is obviously a(n) _____ .

6. Until the age of twenty-one, the orphan will be the _____ of a court or a legally appointed guardian.

7. The patients were astounded to learn that they had been treated by a(n) _____ whose medical license and diplomas were forgeries.

8. Valerie learned that her grandparents plan to name her in their will as their sole _____ .

9. Many sought to benefit from the experience and wisdom of the former President after his retirement from politics. He was regarded as a(n) _____ .

10. Your cousin looks down on our opinions and suggestions because she considers herself superior. We think she is a(n) _____ .

RELATED WORDS. Learn the boldfaced **related words** in the middle column below, together with their meanings.

Lesson Words	Related Words	Meanings of Related Words
boor (*n.*)	**boorish** (*adj.*)	rude; ill-mannered; insensitive
bore (*n.*)	**boredom** (*n.*)	state of being bored; tedium
dupe (*n.*)	**dupe** (*v.*)	deceive; trick

(*Related words are continued on next page.*)

grouch (*n.*)	**grouchy** (*adj.*)	ill-tempered; grumbling; peevish
heir (*n.*)	**disinherit** (*v.*)	keep from becoming an heir; deprive of an inheritance
....	**heirloom** (*n.*)	treasured possession handed down from generation to generation
quack (*n.*)	**quackery** (*n.*)	claims or pretensions of a quack; charlatanry
sage (*n.*)	**sagacious** (*adj.*)	wise; discerning; shrewd
spouse (*n.*)	**espouse** (*v.*)	support or embrace as a cause
ward (*n.*)	**wardrobe** (*n.*)	1. closet where clothes are kept 2. one's collection of clothes

EXERCISE 27.2: RELATED WORDS. Fill each blank below with the most appropriate **related word** from the middle column, above. Do not use any of the related words more than once.

1. This old sewing machine belonged to my great-grandmother. It is a family _____.

2. We give to the March of Dimes. It is a cause that we _____.

3. That child is _____. He always has something to grumble about.

4. There are several clothing sales going on. This is a good time to add to your _____.

5. Your _____ friends can use a few lessons in manners.

6. One of the functions of the American Medical Association is to investigate cases of suspected _____.

7. She refuses to read her composition because she thinks it is tiresome, and she does not want to subject others to _____.

8. They have tricked many people. Don't let them _____ you.

9. My speech would have been more effective if I had ended it sooner, but I was not _____ enough to realize that.

10. Wealthy parents have often threatened to _____ a child whose behavior they did not approve of.

EXERCISE 27.3: BRAINTEASERS. Each sentence below contains a partially spelled word. Fill in whatever letters are missing.

1. It is a good idea to wait for a clothing sale if you plan to add to your __ __ __ __ r o b e.

2. The new proprietor has a pleasant disposition. The former one was inclined to be __ __ o u c h __.

3. Health insurance provided by an employer usually protects not only the employee, but also the employee's __ __ __ u s __ and children.

4. One way to escape __ o r e __ __ __ is to have an interesting hobby.

5. A person who thinks that everyone else is inferior is probably a(n) __ n o __.

6. It was a tragic mistake for the elderly king to __ __ __ __ h e r __ __ his youngest daughter and leave all of his property to her evil sisters.

7. We were ashamed of his rudeness. He behaved like a b o o __.

8. The stranger who claimed to be an eminent professor of pharmacology was really a(n) __ __ __ __ __ t a n. He had been expelled from medical school.

9. The pickle dish, a valuable __ __ __ __ l o o m, fell and shattered into a thousand fragments.

10. A person of outstanding scholarship, learning, and wisdom is usually regarded as a(n) __ __ __ a n t.

EXERCISE 27.4: ANALOGIES. Which lettered pair of words—**a, b, c,** or **d**—most nearly has the same relationship as the numbered pair? Circle the letter of your answer.

1. BOOR : MANNERS
    - *a.* zealot : fervor
    - *b.* snob : vanity
    - *c.* savant : intellect
    - *d.* quack : ethics

2. WARDROBE : APPAREL
    - *a.* cabinet : doors
    - *b.* elevator : grain
    - *c.* furnace : fuel
    - *d.* courtroom : testimony

3. DUPE : GULLIBILITY
    - *a.* scapegoat : culpability
    - *b.* shirker : perseverance
    - *c.* extremist : moderation
    - *d.* equivocator : deviousness

4. SPOUSE : RELATIVE
    - *a.* child : adolescent
    - *b.* heir : benefactor
    - *c.* proprietor : entrepreneur
    - *d.* alien : citizen

5. WARD : HOSPITAL
    - *a.* college : university
    - *b.* hangar : aircraft
    - *c.* house : room
    - *d.* drama : theater

Lesson 28. Disyllabic Words for Persons

Do you know someone who believes that everything that people do is done only out of selfishness and self-interest, and that there is no generosity, honesty, or sincerity in the world?

There is a word for a person with such a sneering outlook. You will find it among the lesson words below.

Note that each new word below has two characteristics. One is that it is **disyllabic**—it is made up of two syllables—and the other is that it describes a person.

buffoon (*n.*)
bə foon′
person who amuses others by joking, clowning, or trying to be funny; clown; zany

cynic (*n.*)
sin′ ik
sneering, faultfinding person who believes that people do what they do only for selfish reasons

despot (*n.*)
des′ pət
person who rules with absolute power and authority; tyrant; oppressor; autocrat

felon (*n.*)
fel′ ən
person guilty of a major crime; criminal; malefactor

martyr (*n.*)
märt′ ər
person who chooses to suffer or die rather than give up his or her principles or beliefs

mason (*n.*)
mā′ sən
skilled worker who builds with stone, brick, concrete, and similar materials

mentor (*n.*)
men′ tôr′
wise, trusted adviser or guide; teacher; tutor; coach

mimic (*n.*)
mim′ ik
person who ridicules others by imitating their voices, gestures, and mannerisms; impersonator; imitator

stoic (*n.*)
stō′ ik
person who is indifferent to joy or grief and endures pain or misfortune calmly, without flinching

suitor (*n.*)
soot′ ər
1. person who petitions (sues) for something; plaintiff; petitioner
2. man who courts a woman, seeking to marry her

EXERCISE 28.1: LESSON WORDS. In each blank space below, write the most appropriate boldfaced word from the left column of the preceding list.

1. At the talent show, Milly did imitations of several singing stars. She is an excellent _____.

2. True Son could endure extreme heat or cold without complaining. He was a(n) _____.

3. The escaped _____ has a long criminal record.

4. Stop clowning. Why must you always act like a(n) _____?

5. Bassanio was not the only _____ that Portia had. Two others also sought her hand.

6. Who is the _____ who did the brickwork around the chimney?

7. Nathan Hale became a(n) _____ when he was hanged by the British as an American spy in the Revolutionary War.

8. At first, our new president tried to run the club like a(n) _____. He did not abide by our constitution.

9. Whenever the pianist won a prize, he never failed to express his gratitude to his first music teacher. She was a wonderful _____.

10. If you stop to think of the many people who unselfishly help others every day, you are not likely to become a(n) _____?

RELATED WORDS. Learn the boldfaced **related words** in the middle column below, together with their meanings.

Lesson Words	Related Words	Meanings of Related Words
buffoon (*n.*)	**buffoonery** (*n.*)	clowning; joking; jesting
cynic (*n.*)	**cynical** (*adj.*)	distrustful of human nature; sneering; sarcastic
despot (*n.*)	**despotic** (*adj.*)	autocratic; tyrannical
felon (*n.*)	**felony** (*n.*)	serious crime, such as murder, kidnapping, burglary, etc.

(*Related words are continued on next page.*)

Disyllabic Words for Persons

martyr (n.)	**martyrdom** (n.)	extreme suffering for adherence to one's beliefs; torture; death
mason (n.)	**masonry** (n.)	stonework; brickwork
mentor (n.)	**mentorship** (n.)	tutelage; coaching; training
mimic (n.)	**mimicry** (n.)	close imitation; mimicking
stoic (n.)	**stoical** (adj.)	indifferent to pain or pleasure; impassive; imperturbable
suitor (n.)	**suit** (n.)	1. lawsuit; case 2. petition; courtship

EXERCISE 28.2: RELATED WORDS. Fill each blank below with the most appropriate **related word** from the middle column, above. Do not use any related word more than once.

1. Captain Miles Standish wanted to marry Priscilla Mullens, but she denied his _____.

2. The people of France revolted against the _____ rule of the Bourbon monarchy.

3. Ernie does an excellent _____ of a dog's bark.

4. The modernization of the dwelling will require _____, carpentry, plumbing, and electrical work.

5. Though she must have been in pain, she gave no outward sign of it. She was remarkably _____.

6. We know you like to joke, but we have serious matters to discuss, so put aside your _____.

7. On Veterans' Day, we recall the _____ of those who died or were wounded while fighting for our country.

8. It is a mistake to assume the _____ view that no one can be trusted just because one person has tricked you.

9. My father taught me to swim. Under his _____, I learned to float and to do the crawl and the backstroke.

10. Hijacking is a(n) _____.

EXERCISE 28.3: BRAINTEASERS. Each sentence below contains a partially spelled word. Fill in whatever letters are missing.

1. The new dictator is even more __ __ s p o t __ __ than his predecessor.

2. Almost everything that Danny knows about dancing he has learned from his cousin Maria. She is his principal m e n __ __ __.

3. A(n) __ __ s o n prepares mortar by mixing cement and sand with water.

4. The customer plans to bring a(n) __ __ i t against the firm because it has refused to return her deposit.

5. The patriot who volunteered to go on the dangerous mission took the risk of becoming a m a r __ __ __.

6. To impersonate someone, you have to be skilled in __ __ __ __ c r y.

7. The patient was __ t o __ __ __ __. Despite the pain, he didn't even wince.

8. It was a horrible crime. A nationwide search is under way for the suspected __ __ __ __ f a c t __ __.

9. Some like practical jokes. I detest that sort of __ __ __ __ __ o n e __ __.

10. Throwing litter on the streets is a misdemeanor, not a(n) __ __ __ o n __.

EXERCISE 28.4: ANALOGIES. Which lettered pair of words—**a, b, c,** or **d**—most nearly has the same relationship as the numbered pair? Circle the letter of your answer.

1. MASON : CONSTRUCTION
    - *a.* tyrant : equality
    - *b.* vandal : destruction
    - *c.* boor : courtesy
    - *d.* glutton : moderation

2. MARTYR : SUFFER
    - *a.* stoic : weep
    - *b.* mimic : simulate
    - *c.* optimist : mope
    - *d.* spendthrift : economize

3. SUIT : COURTROOM
    - *a.* drama : stage
    - *b.* garment : wardrobe
    - *c.* vehicle : garage
    - *d.* kitchen : apartment

4. DESPOT : DEMOCRATIC
    - *a.* snob : conceited
    - *b.* assailant : belligerent
    - *c.* pessimist : cynical
    - *d.* bore : stimulating

5. BURGLARY : FELONY
   - a. suspicion : arrest
   - b. buffoonery : laughter
   - c. dime : coin
   - d. evasion : frankness

Lesson 29. Uncomplimentary Words

You would not like any of the new words in this lesson to be used to describe you or your behavior. All of them are uncomplimentary.

contentious (*adj.*)
kən ten′ shəs
    prone to argue; quarrelsome; belligerent; combative
        ant. **peaceable**

evasive (*adj.*)
ē vā′ siv
    tending to **evade** (get around or avoid someone or something by trickery or cleverness); shifty; elusive; equivocal
        ant. **direct**

imprudent (*adj.*)
im prood′ ′nt
    lacking discretion; not **prudent** (wise and cautious); indiscreet; rash
        ant. **prudent**

incoherent (*adj.*)
in′ kō hir′ ənt
    unable to think clearly and express oneself logically; rambling; confused; inarticulate
        ant. **coherent; articulate**

mendacious (*adj.*)
men dā′ shəs
    lying; deceitful; dishonest; untruthful
        ant. **veracious**

testy (*adj.*)
tes′ tē
    easily annoyed; irritably impatient; irascible; edgy

uncivil (*adj.*)
un siv′ əl
    rude; impolite; ill-mannered; boorish
        ant. **civil**

vacillating (*adj.*)
vas′ ə lāt′ iŋ
    constantly changing one's mind; indecisive; wavering

venal (*adj.*)
vēn′ əl
    easily bribed; open to corruption; purchasable; crooked; mercenary
        ant. **incorruptible**

verbose (*adj.*)
vər bōs′
    using or containing an unnecessary and wearisome amount of words; wordy
        ant. **concise**

EXERCISE 29.1: LESSON WORDS. In each blank space below, write the most appropriate boldfaced word from the left column of the preceding list.

1. It is _____ for a pedestrian to dash across a busy thoroughfare at the height of the rush hour, against the light.

2. You were going to vote for Amy, then you shifted your support to Tom, and now you are backing Pat. No one is more _____ than you.

3. My opponent is _____. Whenever he gets a question that he doesn't want to answer, he tries to change the topic.

4. The witness has been charged with making _____ statements under oath.

5. Dan bored us with his _____ explanations. Much of what he said was repetitious and unnecessary.

6. If one government employee is convicted of taking a bribe, we must not hastily assume that all public officials are _____.

7. Several players on the team used to quarrel not only with the manager but also with the owner. It was a(n) _____ ball club.

8. Courtesy pays. You cannot get very far if you are _____.

9. Her first remarks were _____. Obviously, my call had awakened her from a deep sleep.

10. One of the officials was so _____ that she raged at us when we asked for additional information.

RELATED WORDS. Learn the boldfaced **related words** in the middle column below, together with their meanings.

Lesson Words	Related Words	Meanings of Related Words
contentious (*adj.*)	**contend** (*v.*)	argue; maintain; assert
evasive (*adj.*)	**evade** (*v.*)	avoid by trickery or cleverness
imprudent (*adj.*)	**prudence** (*n.*)	discretion; shrewdness
incoherent (*adj.*)	**cohere** (*v.*)	stick together; adhere
mendacious (*adj.*)	**mendacity** (*n.*)	falsehood; practice of lying

(*Related words are continued on next page.*)

testy (*adj.*)......................**testiness** (*n.*)   irritability

uncivil (*adj.*)....................**incivility** (*n.*)   rudeness; discourtesy

vacillating (*adj.*) ....**vacillate** (*v.*)   keep changing one's mind; hesitate

venal (*adj.*)......................**vendor** (*n.*)   person who sells; seller

verbose (*adj.*)...................**verbosity** (*n.*)   wordiness

EXERCISE 29.2: RELATED WORDS. Fill each blank below with the most appropriate **related word** from the middle column, above. Do not use any of the related words more than once.

1. The escapee used clever disguises to try to _____ detection.

2. Did you ever buy lemonade from a street _____?

3. Be concise. Avoid _____.

4. The employees are asking for a raise. They _____ that their purchasing power has diminished.

5. When you repaired the broken dish, which adhesive did you use to make the parts _____?

6. This is an emergency. We must make a decision at once. It is no time to _____.

7. His _____ is getting worse. He is much more irritable now than he has ever been.

8. I felt that my informant was telling the truth. I did not suspect him of _____.

9. Decent people should be able to disagree without being rude to each other. There is no need for _____.

10. The secret would not have gotten out if I had had the _____ to keep it to myself.

EXERCISE 29.3: BRAINTEASERS. Each sentence below contains a partially spelled word. Fill in whatever letters are missing.

1. Except for one _ _ _ i l l _ _ _ _ _ member, everyone in the group quickly decided what to order for lunch.

2. We get along fine. Their ideas and ours __ __ h e r e perfectly.

3. The __ e n d __ __ from whom we bought the merchandise gave us a discount.

4. It was __ __ __ r u d e __ __ of the tenant to try to put out the fire by himself, instead of calling the fire department immediately.

5. There used to be fights and quarrels below deck before Billy Budd arrived, but his presence made the crew less __ __ __ t e n t __ __ __ __.

6. Little information could be gotten from the victims at first. The shock of the accident left them confused and __ __ __ __ __ __ r e n t.

7. The public expects reporters to give a(n) __ e r a __ __ __ __ account of the day's news.

8. When you spoke, I listened politely, without __ __ __ __ __ __ l i t __. Now, please listen to my side of the story with the same courtesy.

9. It is common for a(n) __ __ a s __ __ person to use equivocal language.

10. The person who ran the meeting yesterday was __ __ a s __ __ __ __ __. When I asked a question, he gave me a testy answer.

EXERCISE 29.4: ANALOGIES. Which lettered pair of words—**a, b, c,** or **d**—most nearly has the same relationship as the numbered pair? Circle the letter of your answer.

1. BOOR : UNCIVIL
    - *a.* dupe : prudent
    - *b.* bore : diverting
    - *c.* grouch : irritable
    - *d.* victim : omnipotent

2. EVASIVE : DIRECT
    - *a.* clumsy : adroit
    - *b.* avaricious : covetous
    - *c.* vindictive : vengeful
    - *d.* mandatory : essential

3. VENDOR : SELL
    - *a.* mentor : learn
    - *b.* defendant : sue
    - *c.* ward : protect
    - *d.* cynic : sneer

4. LIAR : MENDACITY
    - *a.* defector : loyalty
    - *b.* procrastinator : punctuality
    - *c.* charlatan : quackery
    - *d.* felon : innocence

5. VERBOSE : CONCISENESS
    - *a.* rude : incivility
    - *b.* vacillating : self-confidence
    - *c.* tactful : discretion
    - *d.* frank : candor

Lesson 30. Review and Enrichment

EXERCISE 30.1: SYNONYMS. For the boldfaced word in each sentence below, find two synonyms. Choose all your synonyms from the list at the end of this exercise. The first two synonyms have been entered as samples.

1. Don't be a(n) **fool**! ___dupe   gull___
2. They were **ill-mannered**. _____
3. Did he **show** any surprise? _____
4. She made a(n) **sarcastic** comment. _____
5. For a moment, he was **indecisive**. _____
6. It is hard to get along with a(n) **crank**. _____
7. They **contend** that we have not kept our word. _____
8. That was a(n) **rash** thing to have done. _____
9. Some know how to **pretend** friendship. _____
10. The main character is truly a(n) **clown**. _____
11. That was a(n) **wise** move. _____
12. Cynics would say that everyone is **crooked**. _____
13. Both sides were **obstinate**. _____
14. In court, the suspect was **imperturbable**. _____
15. What makes them so **irritable** today? _____

LIST OF SYNONYMS

argue	feign	maintain	stoical
boorish	grouch	manifest	testy
buffoon	grumbler	mercenary	uncivil
cynical	gull	obdurate	vacillating
discerning	impassive	sagacious	venal
dupe	imprudent	simulate	wavering
edgy	indiscreet	sneering	zany
evince	inflexible		

EXERCISE 30.2 ANTONYMS. Replace each boldfaced word with an **antonym** from the list below.

1. My brother is **discourteous** to strangers.   1. _____
2. The handbag is made of **simulated** leather.   2. _____
3. It was a(n) **incoherent** reply.   3. _____
4. Is there proof that the official is **incorruptible**? 4. _____
5. Was the witness **direct** in her testimony?   5. _____
6. The evidence was presented in a(n) **clumsy** way. 6. _____
7. Some leaders are too **audacious**.   7. _____
8. Next to us sat a(n) **contentious** fellow passenger. 8. _____
9. That was a(n) **prudent** step to take.   9. _____
10. Isn't this is a(n) **verbose** description?   10. _____

LIST OF ANTONYMS

adroit	concise	peaceable
articulate	evasive	rash
circumspect	genuine	venal
civil		

EXERCISE 30.3: SENTENCE COMPLETION. Two words are missing in each sentence below. Select those words from the following list, and enter them where they belong. Do not use any listed word more than once.

cater	evade	stoical
culinary	evince	vendor
cynical	martyr	wardrobe
espouse		

1. _____s are prepared to endure any suffering, rather than surrender the principles that they _____.

2. Most salespeople are honest. We do not share your _____ view that every _____ is a thief.

3. Indian braves did not _____ pain. They were trained to be _____.

Vocabulary for the High School Student, Book B

4. Since storage space is limited, we cannot _____ the chore of getting rid of the clothes in our _____ that no longer fit.

5. The person we have hired to _____ our banquet knows a great deal about _____ matters.

Continue, as above, but select your words from the following list:

    bore   imprudent
    effrontery   noxious
    exterminate quack
    feign   scathing
    felon   verbose

6. Many farmers use pesticides to _____ or control the _____ organisms that attack crops.

7. The town official is being denounced in _____ terms by those who accuse him of _____ use of public funds.

8. If you are _____, your audience may quickly lose interest in what you are saying, and they may consider you a(n) _____.

9. It is possible for a(n) _____ to _____ the learning and manner of a physician.

10. The _____ now in custody once had the _____ to try to rob the bank across the street from police headquarters.

EXERCISE 30.4: SPELLING. Enter the two missing letters. The first two words have been completed as samples.

1. d_i_min_u_tive
2. buff_oo_nery
3. f___l___ny
4. cat___r___r
5. p___vish
6. su___t___r
7. s___m___late
8. h___rloom
9. c___lin___ry
10. m___r___enary
11. iras___ble
12. c___n___cal
13. inc___h___rent
14. d___cerning
15. m___rt___r
16. s___ga___ious
17. st___cal
18. t___ran___ical
19. ext___pate
20. esp___se
21. indiscr___t
22. peac___ble
23. menda___ous
24. innoc___us
25. mimi___ing

EXERCISE 30.5: CONCISE WRITING. Each of the following sentences uses ten or more words to express a thought. Express that same thought in *no more than four words*.

1. They tend to get around others by trickery or cleverness.

2. Who was the person you hired to provide the food for your party?

3. The practice of telling lies is something that is not to be condoned.

4. A criminal who was convicted of a major crime has escaped.

5. Where is the closet in which the clothes that belong to you are kept?

6. He no longer had anything to do with his old friends, considering them to be beneath him, and he sought new acquaintances among those he regarded as upper-class, more cultured, and wealthier.

7. Mothers and fathers see that infants get what they need and want.

8. Pete is the sort of person that likes to amuse people by joking, clowning, and trying to be funny.

9. Find the division of the hospital where patients receive emergency treatment.

10. She believes that there is no sincerity in this world and that no one ever does anything for anyone else except for selfish reasons.

11. There were many men who sought the hand of Helen in marriage.

12. What were the reasons for which you kept changing your mind?

13. They needed someone who was skilled in working with brick, stone, and concrete.

14. Individuals who are continually grumbling and finding fault with others are not well-liked.

15. It was a treasured possession that had been handed down in the family from generation to generation.

EXERCISE 30.6: CLOSE READING. Carefully read the following passages, and answer the questions below them.

PART ONE

Hector embraced his tearful wife, Andromache, and his infant son, Astyanax. Then, he left to meet Achilles in combat, an encounter from which, as Homer reports in *The Iliad,* he did not return.

Dr. Manette was abducted and thrown into the Bastille, where he remained for eighteen years in solitary confinement, eventually losing his mind. Because he was a survivor of that infamous prison, the people of Paris had a special place for him in their hearts. Dr. Manette is a character in *A Tale of Two Cities* by Charles Dickens.

Montresor was insane with desire for revenge on Fortunato, who had insulted him. He therefore lured Fortunato to the vaults below the Montresor palace, on the pretext of going to taste some new wine, and got him drunk. Then, using mortar, stones, and a trowel, Montresor walled Fortunato into a crypt and left him there for eternity. This tale is told by Edgar Allan Poe in *The Cask of Amontillado* with remarkable conciseness.

QUESTIONS

1. Who was a victim of mendacity? _____
2. Who was considered a martyr? _____
3. Who committed a felony? _____
4. Who lost a spouse? _____
5. Who avoided verbosity? _____
6. Who did some masonry? _____

PART TWO

Squire Trelawney hired Long John Silver to be ship's cook on a voyage to bring back buried pirate treasure. The squire was so overwhelmed by Silver's engaging personality that he did not bother to check into his past, and therefore he could not have known that Silver had been a pirate. Trelawney and Silver are characters in *Treasure Island* by Robert Louis Stevenson.

When Mr. Shimerda bought his house from Mr. Krajiek, he was greatly overcharged. Krajiek also sold him a pair of bony old horses and a team of oxen for much more than they were worth. These incidents occur in *My Antonia,* by Willa Cather.

Captain William Bligh used merciless floggings to enforce discipline aboard H.M.S. *Bounty*. Bligh is a character in *Mutiny on the Bounty* by Charles Nordhoff and James Norman Hall.

QUESTIONS

7. Who was a vendor? _____

8. Who was a despot? _____

9. Who assumed culinary responsibilities? _____

10. Who was a felon? _____

11. There are two dupes in the above questions 7–10. Who was one of them?
    _____

12. Who was the other? _____

Lesson 31. Polysyllabic Words for Persons

When young Jim Hawkins went on deck to get an apple before turning in for the night, he had to climb into the apple barrel, as it was practically empty. There, lulled by the gentle swaying of the ship, he must have fallen asleep for a moment, and he was about to climb out when a heavy man sat down near the barrel, shaking it as he leaned his broad shoulders against it. That man, as Jim could tell by his voice, was Long John Silver, the ship's cook. The very first words that Silver spoke terrified Jim, convincing him to remain hidden in the barrel. Jim learned that Silver and the others in the conversation were actually pirates, and that they were planning to seize the treasure-laden ship and murder the captain and Jim's friends the moment Silver gave the signal. Jim and Long John Silver are characters in *Treasure Island* by Robert Louis Stevenson.

Among the lesson words below, three are relevant to the above paragraph. Two of them tell who Silver really was, and one describes Jim. Examine the new words to see if you can identify those three.

Note that our new lesson words are **polysyllabic**—every one of them has three or more syllables.

conspirator (*n.*) — person who takes part in a **conspiracy** (plot); plotter
kən spir′ ət ər

deputy (*n.*) — person appointed with authority to act as a substitute or assistant for another or others; agent; proxy
dep′ yōō tē

disciple (*n.*) — person who follows a teacher or a doctrine; pupil; follower; adherent
di sī′ pəl

eavesdropper (*n.*) — person who secretly listens to the private conversation of others
ēvz′ dräp′ ər

impostor (*n.*) — person who assumes someone else's identity to deceive others; fraud; charlatan; deceiver
im päs′ tər

intellectual (*n.*) — highly intelligent person; one who relies on the power of the mind rather than on emotions or feelings
in′ tə lek′ chōō əl

litigant (*n.*) — person engaged in a lawsuit
lit′ i gənt

maverick (*n.*)
mav′ ər ik

one who does not go along with the ideas of a party or group, but takes an independent stand; nonconformist

nonentity (*n.*)
nän′ en′ tə tē

mediocre person; person of little or no achievement or distinction

veterinarian (*n.*)
vet′ ər ə ner′ ē ən

one who is professionally trained and authorized to treat the diseases and injuries of animals

EXERCISE 31.1: LESSON WORDS. In each blank space below, write the most appropriate boldfaced word from the left column of the preceding list.

1. The tenant and the landlord want to settle their dispute out of court, if possible. Neither of them wishes to become a(n) _____.

2. A sheriff's _____ is empowered to make arrests.

3. Cassius was not the only _____. Brutus, too, was involved in the plot.

4. The position of editor in chief of a large publication requires a person of talent and experience. It cannot be filled by a(n) _____.

5. If the person who said he was a telephone company employee had no identification, we would have suspected he was a(n) _____.

6. The instructions for assembling the bookshelves are easy to follow. You don't have to be a(n) _____ to understand them.

7. Our dog has had medical attention from a(n) _____ since puppyhood.

8. Whenever we praise the chef, he gives all the credit to his mother because she taught him his culinary skills. He is her _____.

9. It would be indiscreet for us to discuss confidential matters in a public place, where a(n) _____ might be lurking.

10. Eight members are for the dues increase, six are against it, and one _____ insists that there should be no dues at all.

RELATED WORDS. Learn the boldfaced **related words** in the middle column below, together with their meanings.

Lesson Words	Related Words	Meanings of Related Words
conspirator (*n.*)	**conspiracy** (*n.*)	act of conspiring; plot; intrigue
	conspire (*v.*)	agree secretly to do something wrong; plot; scheme
deputy (*n.*)	**deputize** (*v.*)	appoint as deputy
disciple (*n.*)	**discipline** (*n.*)	training that teaches self-control and obedience to rules
	disciplinarian (*n.*)	person who enforces discipline
eavesdropper (*n.*)	**eavesdrop** (*v.*)	listen secretly to the private conversation of others
impostor (*n.*)	**impose on** (*v.*)	deceive by false representation; cheat; defraud
intellectual (*n.*)	**intellect** (*n.*)	reason; great mental power
litigant (*n.*)	**litigation** (*n.*)	process of carrying on a lawsuit; lawsuit
veterinarian (*n.*)	**veterinary** (*adj.*)	having to do with the medical treatment of animals

EXERCISE 31.2: RELATED WORDS. Fill each blank below with the most appropriate **related word or expression** from the middle column, above. Do not use any of them more than once.

1. Under certain conditions, a judge may permit government investigators to _____ on the telephone conversations of suspected criminals.

2. Gwen loves animals. She plans to study _____ medicine.

3. Consumers are victimized when dealers _____ to fix prices.

4. At present, the company is not suing anyone, or being sued. It is not involved in _____ .

Polysyllabic Words for Persons 161

5. Most problem drivers know the rules of safe driving, but they fail to obey them. They lack _____.

6. Did the proprietor _____ anyone to take charge of the business in her absence?

7. The swindler will be unable to _____ people for a while. He is in jail.

8. Why does he assume that he is the target of a(n) _____? There is not a shred of evidence that anyone is plotting against him.

9. A person of your _____ should have no difficulty with higher mathematics.

10. Occasionally, when a player disregards the regulations, the coach has to assume the role of a(n) _____.

EXERCISE 31.3: BRAINTEASERS. Each sentence below contains a partially spelled word. Fill in whatever letters are missing.

1. We hold him in low esteem. To us, he is a n o n e _ _ _ _ _ .

2. One _ _ _ _ _ a n t hired a new attorney.

3. If important business prevents the mayor from addressing us at commencement, she will _ _ p u t _ _ _ someone to speak for her.

4. On a crowded bus, it is almost impossible not to _ _ _ _ _ d r o p on your fellow passengers.

5. Did the suspect act alone, or did he _ _ _ s p i r e with others to commit the crime?

6. Not one of the parties in the election campaign appeals to Marjorie, so she is going to organize a party of her own. She is a(n) _ _ _ _ r i c k.

7. The proprietor of the animal hospital is a(n) _ _ _ _ _ i n _ _ _ _ _ .

8. Every shareholder may vote, either in person or by _ _ o x _ .

9. When Aristotle was seventeen, he went to study under Plato, and he became Plato's most famous _ i s _ _ _ _ _ .

10. The person claiming to be a duke was obviously a(n) _ _ p o s t _ _ .

EXERCISE 31.4: ANALOGIES. Which lettered pair of words—**a, b, c,** or **d**—most nearly has the same relationship as the numbered pair? Circle the letter of your answer.

1. MAVERICK : NONCONFORMITY
    - *a.* boor : civility
    - *b.* zealot : indolence
    - *c.* nonentity : mediocrity
    - *d.* grouch : agreeability

2. LITIGATION : COURT
    - *a.* bullfight : arena
    - *b.* felon : incarceration
    - *c.* wardrobe : furniture
    - *d.* curb : sidewalk

3. DISCIPLE : MENTOR
    - *a.* conductor : orchestra
    - *b.* mountain climber : guide
    - *c.* pilot : airplane
    - *d.* summer : autumn

4. IMPOSTOR : IDENTITY
    - *a.* pickpocket : wallet
    - *b.* shoplifter : arrest
    - *c.* intruder : eviction
    - *d.* eavesdropper : conversation

5. CONSPIRACY : SECRECY
    - *a.* plant : sunlight
    - *b.* avarice : generosity
    - *c.* rumor : fact
    - *d.* malice : benevolence

Polysyllabic Words for Persons

Lesson 32. Complimentary Words

Here are words you may feel proud to have others use in describing you or your behavior. All of them are complimentary.

analytical (*adj.*)
an′ ə lit′ i kəl
good in **analyzing** (breaking up a complex problem into its parts to examine it); logical; analytic

erudite (*adj.*)
er′ yoo dīt′
having or showing a great deal of knowledge acquired through reading and study; learned; scholarly
    ant. **illiterate**

genial (*adj.*)
jēn′ yəl
friendly, cheerful, and sympathetic; cordial; amiable; gracious

humane (*adj.*)
hyoo mān′
showing kindness, mercy, and consideration for other human beings or animals; humanitarian; altruistic
    ant. **inhumane**

impeccable (*adj.*)
im pek′ ə bəl
free from defect or blame; flawless; faultless; irreproachable

judicious (*adj.*)
joo dish′ əs
showing or exercising sound judgment; sensible; wise; discreet
    ant. **injudicious; unwise**

objective (*adj.*)
əb jek′ tiv
free from prejudice or personal feelings for or against someone or something; unbiased; detached; fair
    ant. **subjective; biased**

personable (*adj.*)
pur′ sən ə bəl
pleasing in appearance and manner; handsome; attractive

resilient (*adj.*)
ri zil′ yənt
1. capable of quickly recovering or adjusting after misfortune or illness; buoyant; flexible
2. capable of springing back to original shape after being stretched, bent, or compressed; elastic

self-possessed (*adj.*)
self′ pə zest′
having or showing control over one's feelings and actions, especially in tense situations; calm; cool; serene

EXERCISE 32.1: LESSON WORDS. In each blank space below, write the most appropriate boldfaced word from the left column of the preceding list.

1. Both candidates have _____ records. There is nothing in their past for which they can be reproached.

2. To write encyclopedia articles, a person has to be _____.

3. After losing three games in a row, the Bruins have bounced back and are again leading the league. They are a(n) _____ team.

4. A(n) _____ neighbor has been caring for the stray dog and is trying to locate its owner.

5. Unlike the protesting players, who could not control their emotions, the umpire seemed remarkably _____.

6. It is helpful for an actor to be _____, since good looks are an asset on stage.

7. Customers get a friendly welcome from the _____ proprietor when they enter that store. They like to shop there.

8. Before selecting a movie, read what the critics have said about it. Their reviews may help you to make a(n) _____ choice.

9. Gwen gets the meaning of difficult passages by reading and rereading them many times, sentence by sentence. She has a(n) _____ mind.

10. The mother resigned as a judge of the contest in which her son was competing. She felt she could not be _____.

RELATED WORDS. Learn the boldfaced **related words** in the middle column below, together with their meanings.

Lesson Words	Related Words	Meanings of Related Words
analytical (*adj.*)	**analysis** (*n.*)	careful, detailed examination
erudite (*adj.*)	**erudition** (*n.*)	extensive knowledge; scholarship; learning
genial (*adj.*)	**congenial** (*adj.*)	having the same interests or tastes; compatible

(*Related words are continued on next page.*)

Complimentary Words

humane (adj.)	**humanely** (adv.)	compassionately; sympathetically
impeccable (adj.)	**impeccably** (adv.)	faultlessly; without a flaw
judicious (adj.)	**injudicious** (adj.)	unwise; indiscreet
	.... **judiciously** (adv.)	wisely; with sound judgment
objective (adj.)	**objectivity** (n.)	impartiality; absence of bias
resilient (adj.)	**resilience** (n.)	elasticity; flexibility
self-possessed (adj.)	**self-possession** (n.)	calmness; composure; equanimity

EXERCISE 32.2: RELATED WORDS. Fill each blank below with the most appropriate **related word** from the middle column, above. Do not use any of the related words more than once.

1. We were not _____. Each of us had different interests and tastes.

2. She is wise. You may be sure she will act _____.

3. When we ask him a question, he tells us much more than we need to know. He obviously wants to impress us with his _____.

4. This material is known for its _____. It does not wrinkle.

5. A(n) _____ of the well water showed that it contained no harmful impurities.

6. International law requires that prisoners of war should be treated _____.

7. This is a biased report. It lacks _____.

8. Even the calmest witnesses may lose their _____ when they are subjected to cross-examination.

9. I asked my instructor if I could change my topic when I realized that I had made a(n) _____ choice.

10. No one could possibly find fault with the way she handled her role. She played it _____.

EXERCISE 32.3: BRAINTEASERS. Each sentence below contains a partially spelled word. Fill in whatever letters are missing.

1. They were indiscreet, but you acted _ _ _ _ _ _ _ s l y.

2. Our rivals will soon recover from the shock. They are _ _ _ _ l i e _ _ .

3. He was not so self-possessed as we had thought. It was difficult for him to maintain his _ _ _ _ _ s u r e.

4. We helped them when they were suffering because it was the _ _ m a n e thing to do.

5. That news story is unreliable. It lacks o b j e c t _ _ _ _ _ .

6. When asked how he had become so _ _ _ _ i t _ , he replied, "By reading."

7. I was afraid the announcer might mispronounce some of the names, but she read all of them _ _ _ _ _ _ a b l y.

8. Before going out, he checked his appearance in the mirror to make sure that he looked _ _ _ s o n _ _ _ _ .

9. To solve the problem, be a n _ _ _ _ _ _ _ _ . Try breaking it up into its parts.

10. A faultfinder seldom has anything _ _ _ _ l i m e _ _ _ _ _ to say.

EXERCISE 32.4: ANALOGIES. Which lettered pair of words—**a, b, c,** or **d**—most nearly has the same relationship as the numbered pair? Circle the letter of your answer.

1. SAVANT : ERUDITION
    - *a.* potentate : helplessness
    - *b.* maverick : independence
    - *c.* snob : superiority
    - *d.* conspirator : openness

2. SELF-POSSESSION : ASSET
    - *a.* verbosity : handicap
    - *b.* health : liability
    - *c.* discourtesy : felony
    - *d.* vacillation : decision

3. SUBJECTIVE : BIAS
    - *a.* inanimate : life
    - *b.* lucid : obscurity
    - *c.* pure : contamination
    - *d.* humane : compassion

4. OBJECTIVE : PREJUDICED
    - *a.* erudite : illiterate
    - *b.* gullible : injudicious
    - *c.* contentious : combative
    - *d.* corruptible : venal

5. CREASED : RESILIENCE
   - a. sanctioned : approval
   - b. impeccable : perfection
   - c. creative : originality
   - d. futile : effectiveness

Lesson 33. Wordbuilding With Four Latin Roots

In this lesson, we will build some words with these Latin roots:

ROOT	MEANING
cord	heart
medi	middle
rog	ask
surge	rise

EXERCISE 33.1: WORDBUILDING. Complete each partially spelled word below by inserting the necessary root from the above list. The first insertion has been made as a sample.

1. The results were neither very good nor very bad. They were just ___**medi**___ocre.

2. It was a warm, _____ial greeting, spoken from the heart.

3. Did anyone **inter**_____**ate** you? What questions were you asked?

4. The meeting was friendly, except for a clash between two members who had **dis**_____**ant** views about whether we should hire a caterer.

5. In a revolution, those who support the government are known as loyalists. Those who rise in revolt are called rebels or **in**_____**nts**.

6. Reading about life in a _____**eval** castle can teach us a great deal about the Middle Ages.

7. The director asked Thelma to take his place, and she is here to speak for him as his **sur**_____**ate**.

8. When two people have stopped speaking to each other, they sometimes send each other messages through the _____**um** of a third person.

9. The flames seem to have died down, but there is fear that they may **re**_____. The firefighters are still on the scene.

10. The new ruler's claims are unlawful. He is trying to **ar**_____**ate** to himself powers not given to him by the constitution.

Here are the words that you were asked to build, listed alphabetically and accompanied by fuller definitions. Learn those definitions.

arrogate (*v.*)
ar′ ə gāt′
claim or seize without right or justification; appropriate; usurp
    ant. **renounce**; **yield**

cordial (*adj.*)
kôr′ jəl
warm and sincere; hearty; amiable; genial

discordant (*adj.*)
dis kôrd′ ′nt
not in accord; conflicting; disagreeing; clashing

insurgent (*n.*)
in sʉr′ jənt
one who rises in revolt against established authority; rebel

interrogate (*v.*)
in ter′ ə gāt′
ask questions of; examine (someone) by questioning; quiz

medieval (*adj.*)
mē′ dē ē′ vəl
having to do with the **Middle Ages** (A.D. 500 to 1500), the period of European history between ancient and modern times

mediocre (*adj.*)
mē′ dē ō′ kər
of low, middle, or ordinary quality; barely acceptable; not good enough

medium (*n.*)
mē′ dē əm
1. means through which something is done, conveyed, or transmitted; agency; channel; instrumentality
2. something in a middle position or condition

resurge (*v.*)
ri sʉrj′
sweep back; surge again; rise again

surrogate (*n.*)
sʉr′ ə git
person appointed to act for another; deputy; substitute

EXERCISE 33.2: LESSON WORDS. In each blank space below, write the most appropriate boldfaced word from the left column, above.

1. Shelly and I cannot agree. We have _____ views.

2. The senior coach is empowered to act as the manager's _____ whenever the manager is absent or incapacitated.

3. We would not have gone to see that movie if we had known that the critics considered it _____ .

4. Joan of Arc (1412–1431) was a(n) _____ heroine.

5. Food prices have dropped quite a bit since the drought, but there are signs that they may _____ .

6. The two were once bitter rivals. Now, they are on _____ terms.

7. The attorneys for both sides have the right to _____ all witnesses who testify.

8. Only the treasurer may sign checks for our organization. It would be illegal for any other officer to _____ that authority.

9. Local merchants use our community newspaper as a(n) _____ for advertising.

10. The despot warned that any _____ who did not surrender at once would be severely dealt with.

RELATED WORDS. Learn the boldfaced **related words** in the middle column below, together with their meanings.

Lesson Words	Related Words	Meanings of Related Words
arrogate (*v.*)	**arrogance** (*n.*)	excessive pride; haughtiness *ant.* **humility**
cordial (*adj.*)	**cordiality** (*n.*)	warm, friendly feeling; amiability
discordant (*adj.*)	**discord** (*n.*)	conflict; dissension; strife *ant.* **concord**; **harmony**
insurgent (*n.*)	**insurrection** (*n.*)	revolt; rebellion; uprising
interrogate (*v.*)	**interrogative** (*adj.*)	conveying a question
	interrogation (*n.*)	questioning; cross-examination
mediocre (*adj.*)	**mediocrity** (*n.*)	lack of distinction; inferiority
medium (*n.*)	**media** (*n. pl.*)	channels of communicating with the general public
resurge (*v.*)	**resurrect** (*v.*)	raise from the dead; bring back to life, use, or attention
	resurrection (*n.*)	coming back into use after disuse or decay; revival; restoration

Wordbuilding With Four Latin Roots

EXERCISE 33.3: RELATED WORDS. Fill each blank below with the most appropriate **related word** from the middle column of the preceding list. Do not use any of the related words more than once.

1. An important event draws the attention of TV, radio, newspapers, and magazines. All the _____ are eager to report it.

2. A(n) _____ sentence ends with a question mark.

3. Run-down buildings are being repaired and modernized. A shopping mall has been constructed. The neighborhood is undergoing a(n) _____ .

4. The despot used force to suppress the _____ .

5. She is so convinced of her superiority that she doesn't think any of us have anything important to say. We cannot stand her _____ .

6. Hasn't there been enough strife? When will the _____ end?

7. Our host and hostess greeted us with _____ . They were delighted to see us.

8. They will ask you just one or two questions. You will not be subjected to a lengthy _____ .

9. No state in our nation may _____ the practice of whipping criminals because the Constitution forbids cruel and unusual punishment.

10. The legislator's record doesn't appeal to voters. In the past four years, he has done nothing of distinction. It is a record of _____ .

EXERCISE 33.4: BRAINTEASERS. Each sentence below contains a partially spelled word. Fill in whatever letters are missing.

1. Books were scarce in __ __ d i e __ __ __ times.

2. Money is a m e __ __ __ __ for exchanging goods and services.

3. A(n) __ __ __ u r g e __ __ is dissatisfied with the Establishment.

4. We have some d i s c __ __ __ __ __ relatives who are always bickering among themselves.

5. Was the reporter the only one who asked you questions or did somebody else __ __ __ __ __ __ g a t e you?

6. An arrogant person lacks __ __ __ __ l i t __.

7. It was an important conference, but the commissioner was too busy to attend, so he sent a(n) __ __ p u t __.

8. The visitors met with a cold, formal reception on the grounds of the home team. There was no __ __ __ d i a l __ __ __.

9. The identity of the conspirators who plotted the __ __ __ __ __ __ __ __ __ o n remains a mystery.

10. H a r m __ __ __ has been restored. The conflict has been resolved.

EXERCISE 33.5: ANALOGIES. Which lettered pair of words—**a**, **b**, **c**, or **d**—most nearly has the same relationship as the numbered pair? Circle the letter of your answer.

1. ANTAGONIST : CORDIAL
   - *a.* bore : tiresome
   - *b.* dupe : astute
   - *c.* cynic : distrustful
   - *d.* snob : conceited

2. QUERIES : INTERROGATION
   - *a.* compliments : condemnation
   - *b.* rebukes : commendation
   - *c.* bribes : corruption
   - *d.* flaws : perfection

3. MEDIOCRITY : DISTINCTION
   - *a.* intrepidity : valor
   - *b.* imprudence : discretion
   - *c.* resilience : elasticity
   - *d.* perjury : mendacity

4. NEWS : MEDIA
   - *a.* roads : traffic
   - *b.* wires : electricity
   - *c.* vehicles : passengers
   - *d.* blood : arteries

5. USURPER : ARROGATE
   - *a.* stoic : flinch
   - *b.* impostor : impersonate
   - *c.* shirker : participate
   - *d.* spendthrift : economize

Wordbuilding With Four Latin Roots

Lesson 34. "Little" Words

You already know quite a few "little" words. One such word is **gradually,** which means "little by little." Another is **nonentity** (a person of "little" or no achievement or distinction). A third is **unreasonable** (having or showing "little" or no sense or judgment). Any word with "little," "small," "tiny," etc., in its definition may be called a "little" word. Here are some useful ones to add to your vocabulary.

cursory (*adj.*)
kur′ sə rē

done in a hurry, with little attention to details; hasty; superficial
    ant. **painstaking**

extemporaneous (*adj.*)
eks′ tem′ pə rā′ nē əs

spoken or performed with little or no advance preparation; improvised; impromptu
    ant. **memorized**

ignoramus (*n.*)
ig nə rā′ məs

person who knows little; ignorant person; dunce

impecunious (*adj.*)
im′ pi kyōō′ nē əs

having little or no money; poor; penniless; indigent
    ant. **affluent**

iota (*n.*)
ī ōt′ ə

very small quantity; insignificant amount; particle; ounce; smidgen
(In the Greek alphabet, **iota** is the name for *i*—a relatively small letter.)

lukewarm (*adj.*)
lōōk′ wôrm′

1. barely warm; tepid
    ant. **boiling**
2. having or showing little enthusiasm, eagerness, or warmth; indifferent; halfhearted

minimize (*v.*)
min′ ə mīz′

1. make as small as possible; reduce to a minimum
2. make (someone or something) appear small or unimportant; belittle; disparage
    ant. **magnify; maximize**

paucity (*n.*)
pô′ sə tē

insufficiency; scarcity; dearth; smallness of quantity

piecemeal (*adv.*)
pēs′ mēl′

piece by piece; in small amounts; little by little; gradually

piecemeal (*adj.*)   done one piece at a time; accomplished in a fragmentary way; gradual
pēs' mēl'

trivia (*n. pl.*)   matters of very little importance or significance; trifles; trivialities
triv' ē ə

EXERCISE 34.1: LESSON WORDS. In each blank space below, write the most appropriate boldfaced word from the left column of the preceding list.

1. There are very important matters to discuss. Let us not waste our time on _____ .

2. Almost all who were present eagerly supported your idea. Only one or two were _____ about it.

3. When I was called upon, I was so surprised that I didn't know what to say. I must have looked like a(n) _____ .

4. If we put up the decorations _____ , we will waste a great deal of time.

5. The story that was going around was just a rumor. There was not one _____ of truth in it.

6. You should not expect to get the full meaning of a complicated passage after just one _____ reading.

7. Roger is inclined to _____ the injury he sustained by calling it just a scratch. Actually, it required a couple of stitches.

8. The visitor was a(n) _____ unemployed relative who came to borrow some money.

9. There is a(n) _____ of fresh vegetables in the wintertime, and those that are available are quite expensive.

10. Susan's talk was the best. It seemed like a(n) _____ speech, but she told me afterwards that she had memorized it.

"Little" Words

RELATED WORDS. Learn the boldfaced **related words** in the middle column below, together with their meanings.

Lesson Words	Related Words	Meanings of Related Words
cursory (*adj.*)	**cursorily** (*adv.*)	hurriedly; superficially
	discursive (*adj.*)	wandering from topic to topic; rambling; digressive
extemporaneous (*adj.*)	**extemporaneously** (*adv.*)	in an impromptu manner
	extemporize (*v.*)	improvise; speak or perform extemporaneously
ignoramus (*n.*)	**ignore** (*v.*)	take no notice of; overlook; disregard
impecunious (*adj.*)	**pecuniary** (*adj.*)	financial; involving money
lukewarm (*adj.*)	**lukewarmly** (*adv.*)	without enthusiasm; tepidly; halfheartedly
minimize (*v.*)	**diminutive** (*adj.*)	exceptionally small; tiny
	minimal (*adj.*)	least possible; smallest
trivia (*n. pl.*)	**triviality** (*n.*)	unimportant matter; trifle

EXERCISE 34.2: RELATED WORDS. Fill each blank below with the most appropriate **related word** from the middle column, above. Do not use any of the related words more than once.

1. The person who found my wallet said my thanks were enough. He refused to take any _____ reward.

2. We were greeted so _____ that we felt we were not really welcome.

3. When my mother was called upon to make a few remarks, she had to _____ because she had not prepared a speech.

4. Most modern vehicles do not overtax the energy of the driver and can be operated with _____ effort.

5. The price was a few pennies more than expected, but we paid it. There was no sense in making a fuss about a(n) _____.

6. Some speakers have a tendency to be _____. They keep rambling from the topic.

7. Cathy raised her hand to indicate that she wanted to say something, but the presiding officer chose to _____ her.

8. Some ants are so _____ that they are barely visible.

9. When making a report, plan your talk. Do not speak _____ because you might omit something that you really wanted to say.

10. I didn't read that article with the attention it deserved. I went through it too _____.

EXERCISE 34.3: BRAINTEASERS. Each sentence below contains a partially spelled word. Fill in whatever letters are missing.

1. Many good jobs remain unfilled because there is a(n) __ __ __ c i t y of qualified applicants.

2. We greeted you, but you were silent. Why did you __ __ n o r __ us?

3. His fault is that he is __ __ __ c u r s __ __ __. He does not stick to the topic.

4. The mosquitoes that were biting us were so __ __ __ __ n u t __ __ __ that it was hard to see them.

5. In the Depression, many i m p __ __ __ __ __ __ __ employees used to walk to and from their jobs because they could not afford the bus fare.

6. The work took a long time because it was done p i e __ __ __ __ __ __ .

7. Let's move on to something important. We have already spent too much time on a(n) __ __ __ v i a l __ __ __ .

8. We never belittled you. Why did you __ __ __ __ __ r a g e us?

9. The water is still __ __ __ __ __ a r m. How long does it take to boil?

10. Each contestant was handed a topic in a sealed envelope and asked to talk about it __ __ __ __ __ __ __ r a n __ __ __ __ __ for a minute.

"Little" Words

EXERCISE 34.4: ANALOGIES. Which lettered pair of words—**a, b, c,** or **d**—most nearly has the same relationship as the numbered pair? Circle the letter of your answer.

1. PECUNIARY : MONEY
    - *a.* mercantile : trade
    - *b.* urban : agriculture
    - *c.* venal : honesty
    - *d.* rustic : congestion

2. IGNORAMUS : KNOWLEDGE
    - *a.* sage : erudition
    - *b.* stoic : pain
    - *c.* mentor : guidance
    - *d.* beginner : experience

3. CURSORY : PAINSTAKING
    - *a.* inordinate : excessive
    - *b.* subjective : biased
    - *c.* subservient : domineering
    - *d.* fearless : intrepid

4. DIMINUTIVE : SMALL
    - *a.* enthusiastic : zealous
    - *b.* large : enormous
    - *c.* meticulous : careful
    - *d.* judicious : indiscreet

5. LUKEWARM : APATHY
    - *a.* vain : humility
    - *b.* greedy : cupidity
    - *c.* industrious : indolence
    - *d.* mediocre : excellence

Lesson 35. Review and Enrichment

EXERCISE 35.1: SYNONYMS. For the boldfaced word in each sentence below, find two synonyms. Choose all your synonyms from the list at the end of this exercise.

1. We did not **overlook** you intentionally. _____
2. Exercise can make us more **personable**. _____
3. She thought there was a(n) **plot** to oust her. _____
4. Who was chosen as his **deputy**? _____
5. There isn't a(n) **particle** of difference between them. _____
6. Is the **revolt** gaining support? _____
7. His record is **flawless**. _____
8. You have a(n) **amiable** personality. _____
9. They are trying to **impose on** us. _____
10. Gold has often been a(n) **means** of exchange. _____
11. The leader had many a devoted **follower**. _____
12. There is a(n) **dearth** of indoor tennis courts. _____
13. Was he the true heir, or just a(n) **fraud**? _____
14. Several **clashing** opinions were expressed. _____
15. Stop worrying. Try to be **calm**. _____

LIST OF SYNONYMS

adherent	discordant	instrumentality	rebellion
attractive	disregard	insurrection	scarcity
charlatan	genial	intrigue	self-possessed
cheat	gracious	iota	serene
conflicting	handsome	irreproachable	smidgen
conspiracy	ignore	medium	substitute
defraud	impeccable	paucity	surrogate
disciple	impostor		

179

EXERCISE 35.2: ANTONYMS. Replace each boldfaced word with an **antonym** from the list below.

1. It was a(n) **painstaking** inspection.   1. _____
2. Some were truly **illiterate**.   2. _____
3. There is **discord** in the staff.   3. _____
4. Two of the prison guards were **inhumane**. 4. _____
5. He is inclined to **disparage** his achievements. 5. _____
6. Apparently, they are **affluent**.   6. _____
7. It was a(n) **wise** choice.   7. _____
8. They conducted themselves with **arrogance**. 8. _____
9. That tea was made with **boiling** water.   9. _____
10. We have been presented with **objective** evidence. 10. _____

LIST OF ANTONYMS

altruistic	humility
biased	impecunious
cursory	injudicious
erudite	magnify
harmony	tepid

EXERCISE 35.3: SENTENCE COMPLETION. Two words are missing in each sentence below. Select those words from the following list, and enter them where they belong. Do not use any listed word more than once.

disparage	litigant
eavesdrop	media
equanimity	nonentity
humane	objective
interrogation	veterinarian

1. At one time during his lengthy _____, the witness became enraged, but he quickly recovered his _____.

180   Vocabulary for the High School Student, Book B

2. The American people depend on the _____ for _____ reporting of the news.

3. One of the new commissioner's jealous rivals once _____d him by calling him a(n) _____.

4. When the _____ and her attorney were conferring, she was worried that someone in the courtroom might _____ on them.

5. Being a(n) _____ person, the _____ hates to see animals suffer.

Continue, as above, but select your words from the following list:

> arrogate   medieval
> illiterate   minimal
> impromptu   minimize
> indiscreet   piecemeal
> insurrection   renounce

6. Most of the people in _____ times were _____ because very few books were then available.

7. Many government officials do not make _____ statements to the press because they are afraid of saying something _____.

8. The crafty dictator promised to _____ certain powers that he had _____d to himself, but he did not keep his word.

9. This renovation would have caused _____ inconvenience if it had been done all at once, instead of _____.

10. At first, the despot was inclined to _____ the revolt, not realizing that it was a full-scale _____.

EXERCISE 35.4: ROOTS. Fill each blank with the required root from the following list:

ROOT	MEANING
cord	heart
medi	middle
rog	ask
surge	rise

Review and Enrichment 181

1. The leader of the in_____nts has vowed to continue the uprising.

2. A magazine that refuses to serve as a _____um for advertising may have difficulty in meeting its expenses.

3. We cannot endure his ar_____ance. He is too proud.

4. They greeted us lukewarmly, without _____iality.

5. Superior students should be grateful if teachers refuse to accept _____ocre work from them.

6. On most points we agree; on a few, we are not in ac_____.

7. The heat wave has abated somewhat in the past twenty-four hours, but it is expected to re_____.

8. Try to begin a paragraph once in a while with an inter_____ative sentence.

9. The partners have designated a senior employee to act as their sur_____ate when they are not on the premises.

10. The only dis_____ant note in the hearing was some bickering between the commissioner's deputy and a member of the audience.

EXERCISE 35.5: SPELLING. Enter the two missing letters. The first two words have been completed as samples.

1. prej_u_di_c_e
2. finan_ci_al
3. s___r___ne
4. d___p___tize
5. p___city
6. ___s___rp
7. c___ng___nial
8. intrig___
9. c___rs___ry
10. imp___st___r
11. ___vesdrop
12. res___l___ent
13. h___m___lity
14. p___cemeal
15. anal___t___cal
16. lit___g___nt
17. veter___arian
18. sm___dg___n
19. dis___ur___ive
20. extempora___ous
21. m___v___rick
22. m___nim___l
23. med___val
24. injud___c___ous
25. impr___vi___e
26. disagr___ing
27. dis___ipl___narian
28. equ___n___mity
29. cord___lity
30. inte___lect___al

EXERCISE 35.6: CONCISE WRITING. Each of the following sentences uses ten or more words to express a thought. Express that same thought in *no more than four words*.

1. Stop worrying over things that are of very little importance or significance.

2. I never secretly listen in on the private conversations that other people are having.

3. Sherlock Holmes was good at breaking down a complex problem into its component parts to determine what it was all about.

4. Some investigations are carried out in a great hurry, with little attention to details.

5. The conclusions that he reached showed a lack of sound judgment.

6. Instead of going along with the ideas of the rest of her group, Dolores is inclined to take an independent stand.

7. There are people who are inconsiderate and cruel not only to their fellow human beings, but also to animals.

8. Most of the time, we express ourselves with little or no advance preparation.

9. They make everything that we achieve seem as small as possible.

10. Those who rise in revolt against the established order risk retaliation.

11. We studied the history of a period known as the Middle Ages.

12. As a result of all the reading and study that she has done, the instructor has a great deal of knowledge.

Review and Enrichment

13. The two of them have the same interests and tastes.
   _____

14. Pat has shown remarkable ability to recover quickly from a setback or illness.
   _____

15. Those who act as judges must be free of prejudice and personal bias.
   _____

EXERCISE 35.7: CLOSE READING. Carefully read the following passages, and answer the questions below them.

PART ONE

On November 8, 63 B.C., in the Roman Senate, Cicero accused Catiline of plotting to overthrow the government.

In 871 A.D., Alfred the Great began his twenty-year reign over Wessex, an Anglo-Saxon kingdom in England.

The Olympic Games, held every fourth summer in ancient Greece beginning about 776 B.C., were discontinued after about a thousand years. In 1896, thanks largely to the efforts of Pierre de Coubertin, a Frenchman, the Olympic Games were revived.

King Oliver (1885–1938) was a jazz musician and band leader who did a great deal to popularize Dixieland, a style of jazz that originated in New Orleans. Louis Armstrong (1900–1971)—who was to win international fame as a jazz trumpeter, composer, and band leader—joined King Oliver's group in 1922. Oliver is credited with having had a major influence on Armstrong's career.

QUESTIONS

1. Who lived in medieval times? _____

2. Who was a disciple? _____

3. Who was charged with conspiracy? _____

4. Who resurrected something? _____

5. Who was a mentor? _____

PART TWO

Gulliver was shipwrecked on the shores of Lilliput, where the inhabitants were less than six inches in height. The Emperor of Lilliput, who was taller than any of his subjects by the breadth of Gulliver's fingernail, asked Gulliver many questions about the land he had come from. *Gulliver's Travels* was written by Jonathan Swift (1667–1745).

During the Revolutionary War, those Americans who remained loyal to George III of England were known as Loyalists, or Tories.

Jabez Stone could not extricate himself from poverty, but after making a contract with the devil, he prospered for ten years. When the devil came to collect his due, Stone retained Daniel Webster as his attorney in an attempt to invalidate the contract. A jury ruled in Stone's favor. *The Devil and Daniel Webster* was written by Stephen Vincent Benét (1898–1943).

QUESTIONS

6. Who had been impecunious? _____

7. Who refused to join an insurrection? _____

8. Who was interrogated? _____

9. Who was a loser in litigation? _____

10. Who surpassed others by a smidgen? _____

Lesson 36. Loanwords Ending in <u>US</u>

English is rich in loanwords—words "borrowed" or adopted from other languages. Actually, the term **loanwords** is misleading because English has no intention of ever returning these words. They are a part of our language.

All the loanwords in this lesson were taken from Latin, and in English they have kept exactly the same spelling as they had in Latin. Note that every one of them ends in **us**.

animus (*n.*)　　　　strong hatred; enmity; animosity; antagonism
an′ ə məs　　　　　　*ant.* **favor**

consensus (*n.*)　　general agreement; opinion held by most of those concerned
kən sen′ səs

focus (*n.*)　　　　1. central point; center of interest or activity
fō′ kəs　　　　　　　2. position in which an object must be viewed clearly

hiatus (*n.*)　　　　break in the continuity of something; missing part; gap;
hī āt′ əs　　　　　　　interruption

humus (*n.*)　　　　dark substance essential for fertility formed in the soil by
hyoō′ məs　　　　　　decomposition of plant and animal matter; organic part of the soil

impetus (*n.*)　　　driving force that stimulates activity; stimulus; impulse;
im′ pə təs　　　　　　incentive; goad

onus (*n.*)　　　　　burden; load; difficult task; unpleasant responsibility
ō′ nəs

status (*n.*)　　　　1. position one holds in relation to others; rank; standing
stat′ əs　　　　　　　2. high position; distinction; prestige

terminus (*n.*)　　　1. end; finishing point; boundary; extremity
tur′ mə nəs　　　　　2. either end of a transportation line; terminal

virus (*n.*)　　　　　1. disease-causing substance or organism so tiny that it
vī′ rəs　　　　　　　　　cannot be seen with an ordinary microscope
　　　　　　　　　　　2. anything that corrupts a person's character or mind

EXERCISE 36.1: LOANWORDS. In each blank space below, write the most appropriate boldfaced word from the left column of the preceding list.

1. When Milly blew out the candles on her birthday cake, she was the _____ of attention.

2. I believe the treasurer should resign, but few others share that view. The _____ is that he is doing a good job.

3. The next stop is the _____. All passengers will have to get off.

4. Hardly anyone had heard of Terry until one of her stories appeared in a national magazine. That was when she first achieved _____.

5. You should not antagonize your neighbors, since you depend on them. You need their favor, not their _____.

6. That soil is poor for growing things because it contains very little _____.

7. The _____ of supervising an unruly child is too great for most baby-sitters to bear.

8. Scientists believe that some colds are caused by a(n) _____.

9. The news that his cousins were coming for a visit was the _____ that made Joe clean up his room.

10. A power failure occurred in the evening from 9:07 to 9:11. During that brief _____, we were in total darkness.

RELATED WORDS. Learn the boldfaced **related words** in the middle column below, together with their meanings.

Lesson Words	Related Words	Meanings of Related Words
animus (*n.*)	**magnanimous** (*adj.*)	generous in forgiving insult or injury; not petty; greathearted
consensus (*n.*)	**sentiment** (*n.*)	attitude; feeling; opinion
focus (*n.*)	**focal** (*adj.*)	of or at a focus; central

(*Related words are continued on next page.*)

Loanwords Ending in US

humus (n.)	**exhume** (v.)	dig up; disinter; remove from a grave
	posthumous (adj.)	1. occurring after one has died 2. published after the author's death 3. born after the father's death
impetus (n.)	**impetuous** (adj.)	acting or done suddenly and forcefully with little thought; impulsive; rash; precipitate ant. **careful**; **planned**
	impetuosity (n.)	impetuous act; rashness
onus (n.)	**exonerate** (v.)	free from blame or responsibility; relieve of a task or obligation ant. **blame**; **incriminate**
	onerous (adj.)	burdensome; troublesome
terminus (n.)	**terminate** (v.)	conclude; close; finish ant. **initiate**
virus (n.)	**viral** (adj.)	of or caused by a virus

EXERCISE 36.2: RELATED WORDS. Fill each blank below with the most appropriate **related word** from the middle column, above. Do not use any of them more than once.

1. Blanche needs an assistant. Her duties are too _____.

2. Jerry Cruncher did a great deal of digging to _____ a body, but to his astonishment he found only an empty casket.

3. We have some unfinished business to _____.

4. The flu is a(n) _____ infection.

5. Look before you leap. Don't be _____.

6. The defendant is blameless. The jury should _____ her.

7. *A Moveable Feast* is a(n) _____ work by Ernest Hemingway. It appeared after his death.

8. The bride and groom were the _____ attraction at the wedding reception. Others received scant attention.

9. Now that we have told you what we think of this matter, we would like to hear your _____.

10. The prisoner is known for _____. In one escape attempt, he jumped out of a window without realizing he was on an upper story.

EXERCISE 36.3: BRAINTEASERS. Each sentence below contains a partially spelled word. Fill in whatever letters are missing.

1. As cornstalks decompose in the fields, they become h u m __ __.

2. A colonel has higher __ t a t __ __ than a lieutenant.

3. How do most people feel about the issue? What is the __ o n __ __ __ __ __ __?

4. David Copperfield was a p o s t __ __ __ __ __ child. His father died shortly before he was born.

5. If your dog is not in __ __ __ u s when you take his picture, the snapshot will be poor.

6. We are glad to be rid of that o n e __ __ __ __ chore.

7. A drunken driver crashed through the fence enclosing the property, leaving a noticeable __ __ a t __ __.

8. Andy sometimes rushes into action without thinking. He cannot always control his __ __ p e t __ __ __ __ __ __ __.

9. Ben Gunn was able to __ __ s i n __ __ __ the treasure that Flint had buried.

10. The firm could have dismissed the employee who made the costly error, but it was __ __ __ __ a n __ __ __ __ __ and forgave him.

EXERCISE 36.4: ANALOGIES. Which lettered pair of words—**a, b, c,** or **d**—most nearly has the same relationship as the numbered pair? Circle the letter of your answer.

1. PROMOTION : STATUS
   a. exercise : stamina
   b. failure : morale
   c. education : ignorance
   d. malnutrition : resistance

2. BURDEN : ONEROUS
   a. rebuke : complimentary
   b. virus : innocuous
   c. foreboding : ominous
   d. stone : buoyant

3. ANIMUS : FEUD
    - *a.* forethought : impetuosity
    - *b.* conciseness : verbosity
    - *c.* hiatus : inactivity
    - *d.* moderation : gluttony

4. MAVERICK : CONSENSUS
    - *a.* disciplinarian : obedience
    - *b.* insurgent : authority
    - *c.* eavesdropper : information
    - *d.* conspirator : plot

5. MAGNANIMOUS : FORGIVE
    - *a.* frank : equivocate
    - *b.* illiterate : read
    - *c.* envious : covet
    - *d.* frugal : waste

Lesson 37. Loanwords Ending in *IUM*

English has borrowed, without change, a substantial number of Latin words ending in **ium**. Many—like **auditorium**, **gymnasium**, and **stadium**—are quite familiar, but there are other **ium** words that also deserve to be in your vocabulary. Here are a few.

aquarium (*n.*)
ə kwer' ē əm

1. public building for the study and exhibition of live water animals and plants
2. glass-sided tank or artificial pond for keeping living water animals and plants

compendium (*n.*)
kəm pen' dē əm

brief but comprehensive summary of a subject; condensed account of a field of knowledge; abstract; abridgment

delirium (*n.*)
di lir' ē əm

1. violent excitement or emotion; wild enthusiasm; frenzy
  ant. **apathy**
2. mental disturbance characterized by delusions or hallucinations

equilibrium (*n.*)
ē' kwi lib' rē əm

1. balance between opposing weights or forces
2. mental or emotional stability; poise

millennium (*n.*)
mi len' ē əm

period of a thousand years

odium (*n.*)
ō' dē əm

disgrace and hatred to which one is subjected for doing something despicable; ignominy; opprobrium
  ant. **honor**

premium (*n.*)
prē' mē əm

1. something offered free as an inducement for buying; reward; prize
2. sum in addition to the regular price or wages; bonus
3. very high value

sanitarium (*n.*)
san' ə ter' ē əm

1. health resort
2. institution for the care and treatment of invalids and convalescents

solarium (*n.*)
sō ler' ē əm

glass-enclosed room for sunbathing; sun-room

tedium (*n.*)
tē' dē əm

wearisomeness; boredom; monotony

EXERCISE 37.1: LOANWORDS. In each blank space below, write the most appropriate boldfaced word from the left column of the preceding list.

1. If you buy the toothpaste on sale today, you will get a free toothbrush as a(n) _____.

2. In a(n) _____, one can enjoy the warmth of the sun in winter without going outdoors.

3. The article she read in the encyclopedia is a(n) _____ of medieval history.

4. Some lengthy radio commercials have been broadcast so many times that it is absolute _____ for us to have to listen to them again.

5. The two teams are evenly matched now, but if one of them were to lose a key player, the _____ between them would be upset.

6. Visitors to the _____ can enjoy close views of a fascinating variety of marine life.

7. The once-popular legislator never recovered from the _____ that he was subjected to for taking a bribe.

8. The Middle Ages cover about a(n) _____ of European history.

9. Thanks to modern drug therapy, tuberculosis patients can be treated at home. They do not have to convalesce in a(n) _____.

10. The news that World War II had ended threw untold millions of war-sick people into a(n) _____ of joy.

RELATED WORDS. Learn the boldfaced **related words** in the middle column below, together with their meanings.

Lesson Words	Related Words	Meanings of Related Words
aquarium (*n.*) .... **aquatic** (*adj.*)		living or growing in water; taking place in or on water
compendium (*n.*) .... **compendious** (*adj.*)		of or like a compendium; concise; succinct

(Related words are continued on next page.)

delirium (*n.*) .... **delirious** (*adj.*)   wildly enthusiastic; frenzied
ant. **apathetic**

equilibrium (*n.*) .... **equilibrate** (*v.*)   balance; bring into or be in equilibrium

millennium (*n.*) .... **millimeter** (*n.*)   one-thousandth of a meter; 0.039 inch

odium (*n.*) .... **odious** (*adj.*)   hateful; repugnant; disgusting; detestable
ant. **lovable**; **attractive**

sanitarium (*n.*) .... **sanitize** (*v.*)   make sanitary; free from dirt or germs

solarium (*n.*) .... **solar** (*adj.*)   having to do with the sun; produced by or coming from the sun

.... **solstice** (*n.*)   either of the two times a year when the sun reaches its farthest point from the equator

tedium (*n.*) .... **tedious** (*adj.*)   tiresome because of length; dull and wearisome; boring
ant. **exciting**; **lively**

EXERCISE 37.2: RELATED WORDS. Fill each blank below with the most appropriate **related word** from the middle column, above. Do not use any of them more than once.

1. The _____ cells in this battery convert sunlight into electrical energy.

2. A meter (39.37 inches) is a thousand times as long as a(n) _____.

3. Two of the _____ events in the Olympic Games are canoeing and kayaking.

4. Anyone who makes a long speech runs the risk of becoming _____.

5. As the curtain went down on the first act of the opera, the _____ audience sprang to its feet and cheered wildly.

6. An electric dishwasher must use water that is hot enough to _____ the dishes, glassware, and silverware.

7. Hit-and-run drivers are _____ criminals.

Loanwords Ending in IUM

8. The Nineteenth Amendment, which granted women the right to vote, helped to _____ their status with that of men.

9. About June 22, the sun reaches its farthest point north of the equator. That day, known as the summer _____, is the beginning of summer in the northern hemisphere.

10. The report on skiing dealt only with cross-country skiing. It was not a(n) _____ treatment of the sport.

EXERCISE 37.3: BRAINTEASERS. Each sentence below contains a partially spelled word. Fill in whatever letters are missing.

1. The patient benefited greatly from his stay in the _ _ _ _ t a r _ _ _ _.

2. We doubt any structure built today can last a m i l l _ _ _ _ _ _.

3. Before beginning to do research, read a(n) _ _ _ _ e n d _ _ _ of your topic in a good encyclopedia.

4. The hotel converted a portion of its top story into a s o _ _ _ _ _ _ _.

5. Water polo is a(n) _ _ _ a t _ _ sport.

6. Some were delirious with enthusiasm. Others remained _ p a t h _ _ _ _.

7. Inspectors found a crack about a(n) _ _ _ l i m e _ _ _ wide.

8. By breaking his promise, he brought a great deal of _ _ _ r o b _ _ _ _ on himself.

9. In judging an employee, most employers look for reliability and efficiency. They also put a p r e _ _ _ _ on honesty and courtesy.

10. Shoplifting is _ _ _ _ _ _ a n t. It cannot be condoned.

EXERCISE 37.4: ANALOGIES. Which lettered pair of words—**a, b, c,** or **d**—most nearly has the same relationship as the numbered pair? Circle the letter of your answer.

1. CENTURY : MILLENNIUM
   a. nickel : quarter
   b. dime : dollar
   c. inch : foot
   d. quart : gallon

2. FELON : OPPROBRIUM
   - *a.* vandal : commendation
   - *b.* equivocator : trust
   - *c.* scapegoat : sympathy
   - *d.* benefactor : ingratitude

3. STUMBLE : EQUILIBRIUM
   - *a.* vacillate : indecision
   - *b.* eavesdrop : information
   - *c.* equivocate : evasion
   - *d.* panic : equanimity

4. VARIETY : TEDIUM
   - *a.* humus : fertility
   - *b.* seatbelt : injury
   - *c.* inflammation : swelling
   - *d.* sunburn : itching

5. METER : MILLIMETER
   - *a.* one : thousand
   - *b.* ton : pound
   - *c.* thousand : one
   - *d.* yard : inch

Lesson 38. Loanwords Ending in <u>OR</u>

If we could resurrect one or two literate inhabitants of ancient Rome and show them the following English words, they would recognize all of them as commonly used Latin words. English, a modern language, has appropriated these words without any change in spelling. Note that each of them ends in **or**.

clangor (*n.*)
klaŋ′ ər
loud resounding noise, as from two heavy pieces of metal struck together; repeated clanging; din

fervor (*n.*)
fʉr′ vər
1. great warmth of feeling; ardor; passion
2. intensity of expression; enthusiasm; zeal
   ant. **apathy**

furor (*n.*)
fyoo′ rôr′
1. fit of anger; rage
2. outburst of public indignation; uproar

pallor (*n.*)
pal′ ər
lack of natural color; paleness, as from fear, sickness, or death; wanness

rancor (*n.*)
raŋ′ kər
bitter, deep-seated hate or ill will; malice; animosity; antipathy

rigor (*n.*)
rig′ ər
1. harshness; strictness; severity; inflexibility
2. severe or harsh circumstance; hardship

splendor (*n.*)
splen′ dər
1. great brightness; brilliance
2. richness; splendid surroundings; magnificence; grandeur
   ant. **squalor**

squalor (*n.*)
skwäl′ ər
filthiness resulting from neglect or poverty; sordidness; wretchedness; misery; degradation
   ant. **splendor**

torpor (*n.*)
tôr′ pər
loss or slowing of the power of motion or sensation; sluggishness; inactivity; stupor; lethargy
   ant. **activity; animation**

tremor (*n.*)
trem′ ər
1. trembling; shaking; vibration
2. involuntary shaking of the body; shudder; shiver

EXERCISE 38.1: LOANWORDS. In each blank space below, write the most appropriate boldfaced word from the left column of the preceding list.

1. The patient seems to be recovering. His _____ is diminishing.

2. Changing places with a pauper, the prince gave up the _____ of the royal palace for the wretched life of a beggar on London's streets.

3. A long strike by sanitation workers could endanger the health of the community and force it to live in _____.

4. They are still bitter enemies. Their _____ has not subsided.

5. A strong earth _____ was felt moments before the volcano erupted.

6. The Pilgrims, who had intended to land in Virginia, not Massachusetts, were unprepared for the _____s of a New England winter.

7. The _____ of the Liberty Bell was last heard in 1846. A serious crack prevents the famous bell from being sounded.

8. The disclosure that the official had misused public funds for his personal benefit created such a(n) _____ that he had to resign.

9. As the woodchuck crawls into its underground burrow in the fall to begin its long winter sleep, it shows signs of _____.

10. Emily spoke of the new play with such _____ that we regretted we had not gone with her to see it.

RELATED WORDS. Learn the boldfaced **related words** in the middle column below, together with their meanings.

Lesson Words	Related Words	Meanings of Related Words
fervor (*n.*)	**effervescent** (*adj.*)	bubbling; lively; high-spirited; exuberant
	fervid (*adj.*)	full of fervor; impassioned; ardent
furor (*n.*)	**infuriate** (*v.*)	enrage; anger; madden; incense
pallor (*n.*)	**appalling** (*adj.*)	frightful; horrible; shocking *ant.* **reassuring**

(*Related words are continued on next page.*)

..................**pall** (v.)		become tiresome; bore; lose effectiveness
..................**pallid** (adj.)		pale; wan; ashen
rancor (n.) ....**rancorous** (adj.)		full of rancor; malicious; hateful; spiteful
squalor (n.) ....**squalid** (adj.)		dirty; filthy; sordid; wretched ant. **splendid**
torpor (n.) ....**torpid** (adj.)		sluggish; inactive; lethargic ant. **energetic; active**
tremor (n.) ....**tremulous** (adj.)		trembling; quivering; timid

EXERCISE 38.2: RELATED WORDS. Fill each blank below with the most appropriate **related word** from the middle column, above. Do not use any of them more than once.

1. The losses at the Battle of Gettysburg (July 1–3, 1863) were _____. 40,000 Confederate and Union soldiers were killed.

2. In comparison with a computer, which provides answers with amazing speed, the human brain seems _____.

3. Soda water is _____.

4. That letter must have contained bad news because, after reading it, he turned _____.

5. People were tracking in so much mud from outdoors that the lobby had to be mopped every few hours to keep it from becoming _____.

6. Some have very short tempers. It does not take much to _____ them.

7. Repetition causes boredom. Even the most hilarious joke begins to _____ after you have heard it for the fifth time.

8. She began in a(n) _____ voice—she was obviously nervous—but she quickly gained poise and confidence.

9. That individual is the most _____ person we know. He has a deep-seated and long-lasting bitterness against many people.

10. According to legend, Captain John Smith was spared when Pocahontas made a(n) _____ last-minute plea for his life.

EXERCISE 38.3: BRAINTEASERS. Each sentence below contains a partially spelled word. Fill in whatever letters are missing.

1. At first, they bubbled over with enthusiasm. Now, they are considerably less _ _ _ _ _ _ _ c e n t.

2. In France, before the French Revolution, ordinary people were treated inhumanely, while the privileged classes lived in _ _ l e n d _ _.

3. The sinking of the *Titanic* was a(n) _ _ _ a l l _ _ _ disaster.

4. Hercules accomplished the difficult task of cleaning the _ _ _ _ l i d Augean stables.

5. We shivered, our teeth chattered, and our hands were _ _ e m u _ _ _ _.

6. The r a n _ _ _ that these former foes once had for each other took long to subside.

7. After taking the medicine, I felt torpid, and my family noticed that I was not so _ _ _ g e t _ _ as usual.

8. Right after the accident, the victim was as _ a l l _ _ as a ghost.

9. From the _ _ _ _ _ o r we heard, we could tell that some of our friends were pitching horseshoes in the back yard.

10. A stern disciplinarian enforces rules with _ _ _ o r.

EXERCISE 38.4: ANALOGIES. Which lettered pair of words—**a, b, c,** or **d**—most nearly has the same relationship as the numbered pair? Circle the letter of your answer.

1. SUNSHINE : SPLENDOR
    - *a.* tornado : destruction
    - *b.* drought : agriculture
    - *c.* fog : traffic
    - *d.* precipitation : reservoirs

2. PALLOR : ILLNESS
    - *a.* stupor : alertness
    - *b.* tremor : trepidation
    - *c.* vigor : frailty
    - *d.* rigor : leniency

3. RANCOROUS : HATE
    - *a.* impetuous : plan
    - *b.* loyal : defect
    - *c.* infallible : err
    - *d.* persistent : persevere

4. POLLUTER : SQUALOR
   a. coward : valor
   b. idler : inefficiency
   c. quack : candor
   d. dynamo : torpor

5. APPALLING : HORRIFY
   a. gratifying : displease
   b. complimentary : irk
   c. tedious : pall
   d. disparaging : compliment

Lesson 39. Loanwords Ending in UM

One reason English excels is that it has always been ready to adopt useful words from other languages. These borrowings have helped to make our language the wonderful medium that it is for communicating ideas and shades of meaning.

In this lesson, we will be dealing with loanwords from Latin that end in **um**. Two of the most familiar words in this category are **maximum** and **minimum**. Here are a few more that should be in your vocabulary:

album (*n.*)
al′ bəm
1. (literally, "something white") book of blank pages for mounting photographs or stamps, or for collecting autographs; collection
2. book-like container for phonograph records; set of recordings

decorum (*n.*)
di kôr′ əm
socially acceptable conduct; propriety and good taste in behavior, dress, and manners; appropriateness; politeness

factotum (*n.*)
fak tōt′ əm
someone hired to do all sorts of work; handy, versatile person

forum (*n.*)
fôr′ əm
1. ancient Roman public square or marketplace where legislatures and courts met
2. public meeting place for open discussion; opportunity for open discussion
3. medium for the expression of ideas

modicum (*n.*)
mäd′ i kəm
small amount; moderate quantity; bit; particle

momentum (*n.*)
mō men′ təm
force or speed of a moving object; impetus

optimum (*n.*)
äp′ tə məm
best or most favorable amount, degree, or condition

optimum (*adj.*)
äp′ tə məm
best; most favorable

quorum (*n.*)
kwôr′ əm
minimum number of members that must be present at a meeting before it can transact business legally

rostrum (*n.*)
räs′ trəm

platform on which a person stands while delivering a speech; stage

stratum (*n.*)
strat′ əm

any of several layers (as of earth, rock, or other material) lying one upon the other; level; section

EXERCISE 39.1: LOANWORDS. In each blank space below, write the most appropriate boldfaced word from the left column of the preceding list.

1. She was nervous as she mounted the _____ to begin her speech.

2. I was embarrassed at not being able to handle that simple problem. Anyone with a(n) _____ of common sense could have seen how to solve it.

3. We will soon need a new family photograph _____. The one we have is almost full.

4. The garden has about six inches of topsoil. If you dig below that, you will reach a(n) _____ of rock and sand.

5. By publishing letters to the editor, a newspaper or magazine provides its readers with a(n) _____.

6. The school board meeting was postponed because only four members appeared, and five are required for a(n) _____.

7. If all planes were required to wait for _____ weather conditions before taking off, air traffic would be seriously affected.

8. Anyone who comes to a banquet in a jogging suit and sneakers has no regard for _____.

9. As the unoccupied vehicle rolled downhill, it gained _____.

10. Our caretaker is a(n) _____. Besides keeping the premises neat, he can do painting, plumbing, carpentry, and electrical repairs.

RELATED WORDS. Learn the boldfaced **related words** in the middle column below, together with their meanings.

Lesson Words	Related Words	Meanings of Related Words
album (*n.*)	**albumen** (*n.*)	white of an egg
decorum (*n.*)	**decorous** (*adj.*)	proper; in good taste; becoming; seemly *ant.* **indecorous; blatant**
factotum (*n.*)	**artifact** (*n.*)	object made by a human being—especially a simple, primitive tool, weapon, or ornament
	factor (*n.*)	1. one who transacts business for another; broker; agent 2. one of the causes contributing to a result or situation; element; ingredient 3. one of two or more numbers multiplied together to form a product
forum (*n.*)	**forensics** (*n.*)	art or study of argumentative discussion; debate; argumentation
modicum (*n.*)	**immoderate** (*adj.*)	too much; extreme; exceeding reasonable limits *ant.* **reasonable; moderate**
	moderate (*v.*)	1. make or become less strong or less extreme; restrain 2. preside over (a debate or discussion); act as moderator of
momentum (*n.*)	**momentous** (*adj.*)	very important; crucial; serious *ant.* **trivial**

(*Related words are continued on next page.*)

stratum (*n.*)	.........**prostrate** (*adj.*)	lying face down or flat on one's back; completely overcome; exhausted; weak; unable to rise
	.........**substratum** (*n.*)	layer lying under another; underlying support; foundation

EXERCISE 39.2: RELATED WORDS. Fill each blank below with the most appropriate **related word** from the middle column, above. Do not use any of them more than once.

1. The stone ax we saw in the museum is a(n) prehistoric _____.

2. On reaching the shore, the swimmer lay on the beach, _____ with fatigue.

3. The numbers 2 and 7 are _____s of 14.

4. Rose is a better debater than Arlo. He is not good at _____.

5. Dad's diet does not permit him to have the yolk of eggs. He eats only the _____.

6. Mother used to use _____ amounts of salt. Now, she is forbidden to have any of it.

7. That structure has an excellent foundation. It rests on a(n) _____ of rock.

8. The American astronauts' landing on the moon on July 16, 1969, was one of the twentieth century's most _____ events.

9. After reaching the peak of its fury just before 6 P.M., the storm began to _____.

10. If you have something to tell me about the acting, wait until the scene ends. It would not be _____ to talk during the performance.

EXERCISE 39.3: BRAINTEASERS. Each sentence below contains a partially spelled word. Fill in whatever letters are missing.

1. The berries are ripening. This is the _ _ _ _ m u m time to pick them.

2. Calm down. Try to m o d e _ _ _ _ your temper.

3. The only part of the egg used in making meringue is the _ _ _ _ m e n.

4. One _ _ _ _ o r to consider in making a purchase is quality. Another is price.

5. Only seven members have arrived. Three more are needed for a(n) _ _ o r _ _.

6. Several erudite specialists will speak at the _ _ r u m.

7. When we awake, we rise from a(n) _ _ _ _ _ _ a t _ position.

8. Will the next speaker please come up to the _ _ _ _ r u m?

9. The anti-pollution campaign has made progress in some areas, but in others it is losing _ o m e n _ _ _.

10. It would be i n _ _ _ _ _ _ _ _ for a host or a hostess to eat before their guests have been served.

EXERCISE 39.4: ANALOGIES. Which lettered pair of words—*a, b, c,* or *d*—most nearly has the same relationship as the numbered pair? Circle the letter of your answer.

1. PAGE : ALBUM
    - *a.* cover : book
    - *b.* core : apple
    - *c.* story : edifice
    - *d.* hub : wheel

2. BOOR : DECORUM
    - *a.* stoic : endurance
    - *b.* nonentity : status
    - *c.* mansion : splendor
    - *d.* luminary : prestige

3. GOOD : OPTIMUM
    - *a.* better : superior
    - *b.* worse : inferior
    - *c.* greater : maximum
    - *d.* small : minimum

4. MODERATE : MOMENTUM
    - *a.* accelerate : speed
    - *b.* pall : effectiveness
    - *c.* convalesce : health
    - *d.* equivocate : deception

5. MODICUM : PLETHORA
    - *a.* paucity : abundance
    - *b.* glut : scarcity
    - *c.* smidgen : iota
    - *d.* excess : surplus

Lesson 40. Review and Enrichment

EXERCISE 40.1: SYNONYMS. For the boldfaced word in each sentence below, find two synonyms. Choose all your synonyms from the list at the end of this exercise.

1. There was a slight **vibration**. _____
2. This **burden** is more than they can bear. _____
3. Luck is always a(n) **element** in competition. _____
4. Maintain your **poise**. _____
5. Insults **anger** us. _____
6. **Animosity** destroys relationships. _____
7. There was a(n) **break** in the flow of information. _____
8. She is good in **argumentation**. _____
9. Is there a(n) **reward** for working overtime? _____
10. Some object to the **severity** of the new regulations. _____
11. In one **section**, the excavators found a few artifacts. _____
12. He turned **pale**. _____
13. Fame is a(n) **stimulus** that makes many strive harder. _____
14. The **rage** over the fare increase is abating. _____
15. The program offers a(n) **concise** account of the news. _____

LIST OF SYNONYMS

antipathy	forensics	ingredient	rigor
balance	furor	layer	shaking
bonus	gap	load	stratum
compendious	harshness	onus	succinct
debate	hiatus	pallid	tremor
enrage	impetus	premium	uproar
equilibrium	incense	rancor	wan
factor	incentive		

EXERCISE 40.2: ANTONYMS. Replace each boldfaced word with an **antonym** from the following list.

LIST OF ANTONYMS

animus impetuous
appalling momentous
exonerate squalor
fervor tedious
immoderate torpid

1. The outlook is **reassuring.** 1. _____
2. Did they **incriminate** anybody? 2. _____
3. It was a(n) **planned** move. 3. _____
4. I felt **energetic.** 4. _____
5. Something **trivial** is coming up for discussion. 5. _____
6. Their demands are **reasonable.** 6. _____
7. What have they done to earn his **favor?** 7. _____
8. It was a(n) **lively** meeting. 8. _____
9. There was considerable **apathy** in the audience. 9. _____
10. Reporters described the **splendor** of the scene. 10. _____

EXERCISE 40.3: SENTENCE COMPLETION. Two words are missing in each sentence below. Select those words from the following list, and enter them where they belong. Do not use any listed word more than once.

factor odious
focus optimum
humus status
indecorous terminus
momentum viral

1. The official no longer has any _____ with the voters, now that his _____ misdeeds have been exposed.

2. Rest was an important _____ in her early recovery from a(n) _____ infection.

3. For _____ results, farmers need abundant rainfall and a soil rich in _____ .

Review and Enrichment

4. As the train left the _____, it gained _____.

5. It is _____ for anyone at a social gathering to insist on being the sole _____ of attention.

Continue, as above, but select your words from the following list:

> appalling   impetuous   sentiment
> consensus   modicum   solarium
> decorum   premium   splendor
> forum

6. If you are an independent thinker, your _____s may often differ from the _____.

7. By insisting on fair play and _____, the moderator prevented the _____ from turning into a shouting match.

8. There was not much sunlight in the rest of the house, but the _____ was filled with _____.

9. People who put a(n) _____ on planning are unlikely to choose a(n) _____ person as their leader.

10. If the team had received a(n) _____ of support from the fans, its record would probably not have been so _____.

EXERCISE 40.4: SPELLING. Enter the two missing letters. The first three words have been completed as samples.

1. prem__iu__m
2. en__e__rg__e__tic
3. pal__lo__r
4. grand____r
5. m____d____cum
6. h____tus
7. ma____animous
8. t____rp____r
9. brill____nce
10. impet____sity
11. ex____n____rate
12. od____us
13. solsti____
14. ap____al____ing
15. mil____meter
16. ran____rous
17. mill____n____ium
18. post____mous
19. wret____edness
20. cons____n____us
21. fac____tum
22. efferve____ent
23. an____m____sity
24. leth____gic
25. ____bumen
26. d____l____rium
27. magnif____ence
28. ingred____nt
29. tr____m____lous
30. compend____us

EXERCISE 40.5: CONCISE WRITING. Each of the following sentences uses ten or more words to express a thought. Express that same thought in *no more than four words*.

1. We did not have the required number of members present for holding a meeting.

2. What is the opinion that is held by most of those who are concerned?

3. People who have to beg to keep from starving live in wretched surroundings.

4. Bruce is generous in forgiving those who injure or insult him.

5. Is it in the position in which it has to be to be viewed clearly?

6. She acted suddenly and forcefully, without thinking of what she was doing.

7. The loud resounding noise woke me up from my sleep.

8. What was the cause of that outburst of public indignation?

9. I felt a slowdown in the functioning of my senses and in my power of motion.

10. The demands that they have been making are beyond the limits of reason.

11. Those who run for office need a medium for expressing their ideas.

12. She enjoys sports that involve activity in or on the water.

13. What is the position he holds in relation to others?

14. This is the place where a speaker stands when addressing an audience.

_____

15. He entered an institution for the care and treatment of convalescents.

_____

EXERCISE 40.6: CLOSE READING. Carefully read the following passages, and answer the questions below them.

PART ONE

The Sleeping Beauty—in a tale by Charles Perrault—remained under a spell that kept her from waking until a certain Prince came, broke the spell, and married her.

When Jean Valjean was arrested for stealing the Bishop's silverware, the Bishop told the authorities that he had given Valjean the silverware as a gift, and they released the suspect. The Bishop and Jean Valjean are characters in *Les Miserables* by Victor Hugo.

The innkeeper Chicot agreed to pay Mother Magloire fifty crowns a month, with the understanding that he would inherit her farm, but he soon regretted the agreement because it seemed she might outlive him. He therefore introduced her to brandy, which she was too frugal to buy for herself, giving her large quantities without charge. Eventually, she fell intoxicated in the snow and died. Chicot and Mother Magloire are characters in *The Little Cask* by Guy De Maupassant.

Emily Dickinson (1830–1886), one of America's most talented and creative poets, was unknown to the public until the 20th century, when her works began to appear in print.

QUESTIONS

1. Who was magnanimous? _____

2. Who was found prostrate? _____

3. Who gained posthumous recognition? _____

4. Who emerged from torpor? _____

5. Who, of those mentioned above, was the most odious? _____

PART TWO

Demosthenes (384–322 B.C.) overcame a weak voice and other serious speech defects to become one of the world's greatest orators.

About the year 999, on a voyage from Norway to Greenland, Leif Ericsson was—according to one source—blown off course to an unknown land, where he found grapes, wheat, and trees he had never before seen. Ericsson then returned to Greenland. Many believe that the unknown land he visited was the North American continent.

Unlike the majority of his fellow Americans, who wanted the Thirteen Colonies to remain loyal to the British crown, Samuel Adams (1722–1803) favored independence.

Heinrich Schliemann (1822–1890) had a strong suspicion that Troy, the city made famous by Homer's *Iliad,* was not just a myth. Relying on clues from the *Iliad,* Schliemann began digging in 1870 in a mound at Hissarlik, Turkey. Within this mound, more than fifty feet deep and containing the remains of several settlements going back to 3000 B.C., Schliemann found the ruins of Homer's Troy.

QUESTIONS

6. Who exhumed something? _____

7. Who rejected a consensus? _____

8. Who lived about a millennium ago? _____

9. Who went through one stratum after another? _____

10. Who studied forensics? _____

Dictionary of the Words Taught in This Book

abound — amateur

abound (*v.*) 1. be present in great quantities; be plentiful 2. be filled; teem 62

abridgment (*n.*) shortening; curtailment; abstract; compendium 113, 191

absolute (*adj.*) 1. (as in **absolute** monarch) free from all restraint; not limited by a constitution, parliament, or congress 2. (as in **absolute** honesty) complete; perfect 93

absolve (*v.*) free from guilt or blame; acquit; exonerate 94

abstract (*n.*) condensation; compendium; abridgment 191

absurd (*adj.*) ridiculous; silly; preposterous 59

accomplice (*n.*) one who participates with another in wrongdoing or in a crime; partner in crime; confederate 26

accord (*n.*) agreement; peace 7

acknowledge (*v.*) admit to be true; confess; avow 35

acknowledgment (*n.*) admission; avowal 37

acoustic (*adj.*) having to do with hearing or sound; designed for absorbing sound 89

acoustics (*n. pl.*) 1. science that deals with sound 2. qualities of a room, auditorium, or theater that determine how clearly sounds can be heard there; sound-producing qualities 88

acquit (*v.*) absolve; exonerate 94

acrimonious (*adj.*) bitter in speech or manner; caustic; biting 58

acrimony (*n.*) sharpness or bitterness of words, manner, or feeling; asperity 57

adaptable (*adj.*) many-sided; versatile 31

adhere (*v.*) stick; cling; cohere 150

adherent (*n.*) follower; disciple; supporter 159

adroit (*adj.*) cleverly skillful; resourceful; dexterous 134

adroitly (*adv.*) shrewdly; skillfully 136

adverse (*adj.*) unfortunate; unlucky; unfavorable 117

adversity (*n.*) misfortune; trouble; misery; bad luck 116

affiliated (*adj.*) closely associated 58

affluence (*n.*) wealth 3

affluent (*adj.*) wealthy; rich; prosperous; in possession of an abundance of money or property 1

agent (*n.*) one who acts for another; proxy; deputy 159

aggression (*n.*) unprovoked attack; warlike act; encroachment by one nation on the territory of another 6

aggressor (*n.*) person or nation that attacks first 8

agile (*adj.*) capable of moving quickly and easily; nimble; spry 31

agility (*n.*) nimbleness 32

agitate (*v.*) disturb; bother; perturb 122

ailment (*n.*) disease; infirmity 123

album (*n.*) 1. (literally, "something white") book of blank pages for mounting photographs or stamps, or for collecting autographs; collection 2. booklike container for phonograph records; set of recordings 201

albumen (*n.*) white of an egg 203

alienate (*v.*) make unfriendly; disunite; estrange 68

altruistic (*adj.*) charitable; humane 164

amateur (*n.*) one who engages in an activity for pleasure rather than for money; person who lacks professional skill; nonprofessional 26

amateurish

amateurish (*adj.*) inexpert; unskillful 28

ambiguous (*adj.*) unclear; equivocal; unintelligible 37, 127

ameliorate (*v.*) make better; improve; become more tolerable 16

amelioration (*n.*) improvement 18

amiable (*adj.*) good-natured; genial 164

analysis (*n.*) careful, detailed examination 165

analytic (*adj.*) analytical 164

analytical (*adj.*) good in **analyzing** (breaking up a complex problem into its parts to examine it); logical; analytic 164

animation (*n.*) spirit; dash; life 196

animosity (*n.*) enmity; hostility; animus 186

animus (*n.*) strong hatred; enmity; animosity; antagonism 186

annul (*v.*) cancel; erase; revoke 66

antagonism (*n.*) enmity; animosity; animus 186

antipathy (*n.*) enmity; animosity; rancor 196

apathetic (*adj.*) uninterested; unconcerned; indifferent 53

apathy (*n.*) lack of emotion or feeling; lack of interest; unconcern; indifference 51

appalling (*adj.*) frightful; horrible; shocking 197

appease (*v.*) placate 8

apprehend (*v.*) 1. take into custody; arrest; capture 2. grasp the meaning of; perceive 3. anticipate with anxiety or fear; dread 66

apprehension (*n.*) 1. arrest 2. fear that something may go wrong; misgiving; foreboding 67

apprehensive (*adj.*) fearful; worried; anxious 67

appropriate (*v.*) make oneself the owner of something without

assume

permission or right; take possession of; annex; steal 16

aptitude (*n.*) ability; faculty 83

aquarium (*n.*) 1. public building for the study and exhibition of live water animals and plants 2. glass-sided tank or artificial pond for keeping living water animals and plants 191

aquatic (*adj.*) living or growing in water; taking place in or on water 192

ardent (*adj.*) burning with enthusiasm; fervent; zealous; impassioned 40

ardor (*n.*) great warmth of feeling; zeal 41

arduous (*adj.*) hard to accomplish; difficult 31

arrogance (*n.*) excessive pride; haughtiness 171

arrogate (*v.*) claim or seize without right or justification; appropriate; usurp 170

arson (*n.*) malicious burning of property 41

arsonist (*n.*) one who maliciously burns or tries to burn a building or other property; incendiary 40

articulate (*adj.*) smooth-spoken; fluent; eloquent 149

artifact (*n.*) object made by a human being—especially a simple, primitive tool, weapon, or ornament 203

artificial (*adj.*) false; simulated 136

asperity (*n.*) harshness; acrimony 57

assail (*v.*) attack with blows or words 8

assailant (*n.*) person who **assails** (violently attacks with blows or words); attacker 6

assert (*v.*) maintain; argue; contend 150

assume (*v.*) 1. take for granted; suppose to be a fact; postulate;

assume   boorish

presuppose   2. take upon oneself; undertake   66

assumption (*n.*)   supposition; something that is taken for granted   68

astute (*adj.*)   shrewd; clever; crafty   1

astuteness (*n.*)   cleverness   3

audacious (*adj.*)   1. bold; daring; fearless; intrepid   2. too bold; impudent; insolent; brazen   134

audaciously (*adv.*)   boldly; insolently   136

audacity (*n.*)   boldness; effrontery; insolence   136

augment (*v.*)   increase; enhance; enlarge   112

augur (*v.*)   be a sign of; give promise of; bode   117

augury (*n.*)   omen; sign of something to come; indication; portent   116

auspicious (*adj.*)   promising success; favorable; propitious   116

auspiciously (*adv.*)   in a way that promises success; favorably   118

authenticate (*v.*)   confirm; validate   80

authority (*n.*)   power to act, command, or judge   85

authorize (*v.*)   1. give someone **authority** (power or influence to do something); empower   2. give permission for; approve; sanction   83

autocrat (*n.*)   absolute ruler; tyrant; despot   144

autonomous (*adj.*)   self-governing; sovereign   84

avarice (*n.*)   excessive desire to gain and hoard wealth; greed for riches; cupidity   51

avaricious (*adj.*)   too eager for riches; greedy; covetous   53

aversion (*n.*)   dislike; repugnance   108

avert (*v.*)   prevent; forestall; obviate   122

avow (*v.*)   admit; acknowledge   35

axiom (*n.*)   statement accepted by all as true; self-evident truth; established rule or principle; maxim; truism   93

axiomatic (*adj.*)   universally accepted as true   94

ballistics (*n. pl.*)   science dealing with the firing of bullets, rockets, and missiles   88

becoming (*adj.*)   decorous; proper; seemly   203

belittle (*v.*)   detract from; minimize; disparage   174

belligerence (*n.*)   fondness for fighting; pugnacity   8

belligerent (*adj.*)   fond of fighting; warlike; quarrelsome; pugnacious   6

belligerent (*n.*)   nation engaged in a war; person involved in a fight; warrior   6

benevolence (*n.*)   inclination to do good to others; good will; kindliness; generosity   51

benevolent (*adj.*)   disposed to do good; kind; generous   53

bias (*n.*)   prejudice   3

biased (*adj.*)   favoring one side too much; partial; prejudiced   1

blatant (*adj.*)   shameless; brazen; impudent   203

bode (*v.*)   foreshadow; augur   117

boisterous (*adj.*)   disorderly; turbulent; unruly   122

bonanza (*n.*)   source of great and sudden wealth; place of great abundance; gold mine   62

bonus (*n.*)   something in addition to what is due or expected   191

boor (*n.*)   one who has bad manners; rude, insensitive person   139

boorish (*adj.*)   rude; ill-mannered; insensitive   140

Dictionary of the Words Taught in This Book

bore (*n.*) tiresome, uninteresting person or thing; cause of boredom   139

boredom (*n.*) state of being bored; tedium   140

brazen (*adj.*) bold; insolent; audacious   134

bribe (*n.*) money or a favor given or promised to a person to persuade that person to do something dishonest or illegal   35

bribery (*n.*) giving or taking of a bribe   37

buffoon (*n.*) person who amuses others by joking, clowning, or trying to be funny; clown; zany   144

buffoonery (*n.*) clowning; joking; jesting   145

buoyant (*adj.*) bouncy; resilient   164

calisthenics (*n. pl.*) systematic exercises for developing a healthy, strong, and trim body; light gymnastics   88

candid (*adj.*) frank; outspoken; sincere   37

candor (*n.*) honesty in saying what one really thinks; frankness; outspokenness   35

casual (*adj.*) 1. happening by chance; not planned   2. not dressy; informal   118

casually (*adv.*) in an unplanned manner; by chance; accidentally; fortuitously   116

casualty (*n.*) 1. serious or fatal accident   2. person injured or killed in an accident   118

cater (*v.*) 1. (followed by *to*) provide what is wanted or needed   2. provide food and service for   136

caterer (*n.*) person who is in the business of providing food and other necessary services for a social gathering   134

caustic (*adj.*) 1. burning or destroying flesh; corrosive   2. severely critical; sarcastic; sharp; biting   40

caustically (*adv.*) very critically; sarcastically   42

cessation (*n.*) end; termination   80

charlatan (*n.*) impostor; quack   139

circuitous (*adj.*) not direct; roundabout; devious   123

circumspect (*adj.*) cautious; wary   134

civil (*adj.*) courteous; polite   149

clangor (*n.*) loud resounding noise, as from two heavy pieces of metal struck together; repeated clanging; din   196

clemency (*n.*) mercy; leniency; mildness of temper toward offenders   106

clog (*v.*) fill; congest; obstruct   62

cloy (*v.*) weary by too much of something pleasant; disgust   63

cloying (*adj.*) disgusting or distasteful because of excess; too sweet; too sentimental   62

cohere (*v.*) stick together; adhere   150

coherent (*adj.*) logically ordered; consistent; articulate   149

combative (*adj.*) quarrelsome; belligerent; contentious   149

combustible (*adj.*) able to catch or be set on fire and burn easily; inflammable; ignitable   12

combustion (*n.*) act or process of burning   13

commandeer (*v.*) take as one's own; arrogate; usurp   68

commercial (*adj.*) having to do with trade or commerce; mercantile   31

commiseration (*n.*) pity; sympathy; compassion   51

commotion (*n.*) wild disorder; turbulence   124

compassion

compassion (*n.*) sympathy and sorrow for the sufferings and misfortunes of others, accompanied by a desire to help them; pity; commiseration; empathy 51

compassionate (*adj.*) deeply sympathetic; pitying; tender 53

compatible (*adj.*) agreeable; congenial 165

compendious (*adj.*) of or like a compendium; concise; succinct 192

compendium (*n.*) brief but comprehensive summary of a subject; condensed account of a field of knowledge; abstract; abridgment 191

complicity (*n.*) partnership in wrongdoing or in a crime 28

complimentary (*adj.*) expressing esteem or admiration; favorable 164

composure (*n.*) calmness; equanimity; self-possession 166

comprehend (*v.*) 1. take into the mind; understand 2. take in; include; comprise 68

comprehensive (*adj.*) taking in a great deal; dealing with all or many of the relevant details; inclusive; encompassing 66

comprise (*v.*) include; comprehend 68

conceit (*n.*) self-admiration; vanity 52

conceited (*adj.*) having too high an opinion of oneself; vain 53

concise (*adj.*) expressed with brevity 62, 149

concord (*n.*) harmony; agreement 171

condonable (*adj.*) justifiable; excusable 107

condone (*v.*) forgive; overlook; pardon; excuse 106

confederate (*n.*) accomplice 26

convalescence

confine (*v.*) imprison; incarcerate 107

confirm (*v.*) 1. strengthen, add firmness to 2. establish the truth of; verify; authenticate 122

confirmation (*n.*) proof; verification; corroboration 123

conflagration (*n.*) huge destructive fire; holocaust; inferno 40

congenial (*adj.*) having the same interests or tastes; compatible 165

congest (*v.*) fill to excess; overcrowd; clog 62

congested (*adj.*) filled too full; overcrowded 63

congestion (*n.*) overcrowding 63

conscience (*n.*) sense of right and wrong 3

conscientious (*adj.*) 1. always trying to do what is right; controlled by **conscience** (a sense of right and wrong that governs behavior); honest; scrupulous 2. careful; painstaking; meticulous 1

consensus (*n.*) general agreement; opinion held by most of those concerned 186

conspiracy (*n.*) act of conspiring; plot; intrigue 161

conspirator (*n.*) person who takes part in a **conspiracy** (plot); plotter 159

conspire (*v.*) agree secretly to do something wrong; plot; scheme 161

contend (*v.*) argue; maintain; assert 150

contentious (*adj.*) prone to argue; quarrelsome; belligerent; combative 149

convalesce (*v.*) gradually recover strength and health after sickness; improve; recuperate 80

convalescence (*n.*) gradual recovery of strength and health after an illness; period of recuperation 79

convalescent — despotic

convalescent (*n.*) person recovering from an illness 191
copious (*adj.*) plentiful; abundant; ample 62
copiously (*adv.*) abundantly; plentifully 64
cordial (*adj.*) warm and sincere; hearty; amiable; genial 170
cordiality (*n.*) warm, friendly feeling; amiability 171
corroboration (*n.*) proof; verification; confirmation 123
corrosive (*adj.*) caustic; sarcastic 40
corrupt (*adj.*) influenced by bribes; dishonest; evil; mercenary 35
courtship (*n.*) social activities leading to engagement and marriage 146
crank (*n.*) faultfinder; grumbler; grouch 139
craven (*adj.*) cowardly 79
credulous (*adj.*) too ready to believe; gullible 2
cross-examination (*n.*) thorough questioning; interrogation; grilling 171
crucial (*adj.*) critical; acute 203
culinary (*adj.*) having to do with cooking or the kitchen 134
cupidity (*n.*) greed; avarice 51
cursorily (*adv.*) hurriedly; superficially 176
cursory (*adj.*) done in a hurry, with little attention to details; hasty; superficial 174
curtail (*v.*) cut short; reduce; abridge 111
curtailment (*n.*) shortening; abridgment 113
cynic (*n.*) sneering, faultfinding person who believes that people do what they do only for selfish reasons 144
cynical (*adj.*) distrustful of human nature; sneering, sarcastic 145

dauntless (*adj.*) brave; fearless; intrepid 79
dearth (*n.*) inadequate supply; scarcity; paucity 174
debilitate (*v.*) weaken 16
decorous (*adj.*) proper; in good taste; becoming; seemly 203
decorum (*n.*) socially acceptable conduct; propriety and good taste in behavior, dress, and manners; appropriateness; politeness 201
defer (*v.*) give in to another's wishes out of respect or courtesy; yield 113
deference (*n.*) respect; yielding to the will or opinion of another; courteous regard; honor 111
deferential (*adj.*) showing deference; respectful 113
delete (*v.*) erase; cross out; remove; eradicate 122
deleterious (*adj.*) injurious; damaging to health; pernicious 122
deletion (*n.*) something crossed out; erasure 123
delirious (*adj.*) widely enthusiastic; frenzied 193
delirium (*n.*) 1. violent excitement or emotion; wild enthusiasm; frenzy 2. mental disturbance characterized by delusions or hallucinations 191
deplete (*v.*) empty completely or partially; use up; exhaust 64
deputize (*v.*) appoint as deputy 161
deputy (*n.*) person appointed with authority to act as a substitute or assistant for another or others; agent; proxy 159
deride (*v.*) ridicule; mock; taunt 57
despot (*n.*) person who rules with absolute power and authority; tyrant; oppressor; autocrat 144
despotic (*adj.*) autocratic; tyrannical 145

destined

destined (*adj.*) 1. bound for a certain destiny or fate; foreordained 2. bound for a certain destination   118
destiny (*n.*) what is bound to happen to any person or thing; a person's lot; fate; fortune   116
destitute (*adj.*) lacking necessary things, such as food, shelter, or clothing; extremely poor; impoverished; indigent   2
destitution (*n.*) extreme poverty; indigence   3
detached (*adj.*) neutral; aloofly objective   164
deteriorate (*v.*) worsen   16
deviate (*v.*) depart from an established way or course of action; swerve; veer; stray   122
deviation (*n.*) departure from a normal course or normal behavior; divergence   123
devious (*adj.*) 1. not in a straight path; roundabout; circuitous 2. not straightforward; deceiving; sly; cunning   123
dexterous (*adj.*) skilled; adroit; handy   134
digressive (*adj.*) departing from a subject or topic; discursive   176
diminutive (*adj.*) exceptionally small; tiny   133, 176
din (*n.*) loud confused noise; racket; clangor   196
disable (*v.*) incapacitate   16
disassemble (*v.*) dismantle   66
discernible (*adj.*) perceptible   12
discerning (*adj.*) wise; sagacious   53
disciple (*n.*) person who follows a teacher or a doctrine; pupil; follower; adherent   159
disciplinarian (*n.*) person who enforces discipline   161
discipline (*n.*) training that teaches self-control and obedience to rules   161

dominate

discord (*n.*) conflict; dissension; strife   171
discordant (*adj.*) not in accord; conflicting; disagreeing; clashing   170
discretion (*n.*) prudence; forethought   149
discursive (*adj.*) wandering from topic to topic; rambling; digressive   176
disinherit (*v.*) keep from becoming an heir; deprive of an inheritance   141
disinter (*v.*) remove from a grave; exhume   188
disinterested (*adj.*) free from selfish motives; unbiased; impartial   35
dismantle (*v.*) take apart; disassemble   66
disparage (*v.*) belittle; minimize; depreciate   174
dispensable (*adj.*) capable of being dispensed with; unessential   12
dissension (*n.*) conflict; strife; discord   171
distinction (*n.*) eminence; renown; prestige   186
disyllabic (*adj.*) made up of two syllables   144
divergence (*n.*) deviation; departure from a topic or subject   123
docile (*adj.*) 1. capable of being easily instructed; teachable; obedient; tractable 2. lacking in independence; submissive   31
docility (*n.*) submissiveness   32
doctrine (*n.*) principle; body of principles   159
dominant (*adj.*) most important; most powerful   85
dominate (*v.*) 1. rule by superior power; control; govern 2. rise high above; tower over; overlook from a superior elevation   83

Dictionary of the Words Taught in This Book

domineering (adj.) tyrannical; dictatorial 85
ant. **subservient**

dramatics (n. pl.) art of acting; histrionics 88

dregs (n. pl.) worthless residue; sediment 59

drudge (n.) one who does hard, boring, or disagreeable work 26

drudgery (n.) disagreeable, dull, or hard work 28

dupe (n.) one who is easily tricked or deceived; fool; gull 139

dupe (v.) deceive; trick 140

durable (adj.) able to exist for a long time; lasting 31

dynamic (adj.) energetic; forceful; vigorous 85

dynamics (n. pl.) 1. science that makes it possible to determine or predict the motion of bodies acted on by forces 2. all the forces at work in any activity; driving forces 88

dynamite (n.) powerful explosive 89

dynamo (n.) 1. machine for generating electricity; generator 2. forceful, energetic, hardworking person; go-getter; powerhouse 83

eavesdrop (v.) listen secretly to the private conversation of others 161

eavesdropper (n.) person who secretly listens to the private conversation of others 159

edgy (adj.) tense; irritable; irascible 149

effervescent (adj.) bubbling; lively; high-spirited; exuberant 197

effrontery (n.) shameless boldness; insolence; audacity 136

element (n.) ingredient; factor 203

elevation (n.) height 83

elucidate (v.) throw light upon; explain; make clear; clarify 79

elusive (adj.) not easily pinned down; evasive 149

embarrass (v.) humiliate 16

empathy (n.) sympathy; compassion 51

encompassing (adj.) inclusive; comprehensive 66

enhance (v.) make greater; increase; augment; improve 112

enhancement (n.) increase; augmentation 113

enlightening (adj.) increasing knowledge; illuminating; luminous 122

enmity (n.) deep-seated dislike; antagonism; animus 186

enterprise (n.) 1. initiative; ambition 2. risky undertaking; business venture 51, 68

enterprising (adj.) willing to undertake new projects; venturesome 53

entrepreneur (n.) person who organizes, manages, and takes the risks of a business undertaking 66

environment (n.) all the surrounding conditions that affect the development and behavior of a person, plant, or animal; surroundings 93

environs (n. pl.) district around a city; surroundings; vicinity 94

equanimity (n.) calmness; composure; self-possession 166

equilibrate (v.) balance; bring into or be in equilibrium 193

equilibrium (n.) 1. balance between opposing weights or forces 2. mental or emotional stability; poise 191

equivocal (adj.) having two or more meanings; ambiguous 37

equivocate (v.) use language that has a double meaning in order to mislead; hedge 35

eradicate (v.) uproot; exterminate; delete 122

erudite   faculty

erudite (*adj.*) having or showing a great deal of knowledge acquired through reading and study; learned; scholarly   164

erudition (*n.*) extensive knowledge; scholarship; learning   165

espouse (*v.*) support or embrace as a cause   141

the Establishment (*n.*) controlling group; group of powerful leaders who represent the established order of society; ruling inner circle of a nation or institution   83

estrange (*v.*) alienate; disunite   68

ethical (*adj.*) morally right; conforming to **ethics** (recognized rules for right conduct); upright; honorable   35, 89

ethics (*n. pl.*) set of moral principles or values governing the behavior of an individual or group; recognized rules for right conduct   88

evade (*v.*) avoid by trickery or cleverness   150

evasion (*n.*) avoidance; runaround; lack of candor   35

evasive (*adj.*) tending to **evade** (get around or avoid someone or something by trickery or cleverness); shifty; elusive; equivocal   149

evince (*v.*) show; manifest   134

exclude (*v.*) shut out; bar; expel   95 *ant.* admit; include

exclusive (*adj.*) 1. keeping all others from a part or share 2. disposed to deny admission to outsiders   93

exclusively (*adv.*) only; solely   95

exhaust (*n.*) spent gas escaping from an engine   13

exhaustible (*adj.*) capable of being **exhausted** (used up completely)   12

exhaustion (*n.*) extreme weariness; fatigue   13

exhaustive (*adj.*) thorough; leaving nothing out   13

exhume (*v.*) dig up; disinter; remove from a grave   188

exonerate (*v.*) free from blame or responsibility; relieve of a task or obligation   188

extemporaneous (*adj.*) spoken or performed with little or no advance preparation; improvised; impromptu   174

extemporaneously (*adv.*) in an impromptu manner   176

extemporize (*v.*) improvise; speak or perform extemporaneously   176

exterminate (*v.*) wipe out; eradicate; extirpate   134

extirpate (*v.*) pull up by the roots; destroy completely; exterminate; eradicate   134

extirpation (*n.*) eradication; extermination   136

extravagant (*adj.*) lavish   2

extremity (*n.*) end; border; terminal point   186

exuberant (*adj.*) abounding in vitality; effervescent   197

facile (*adj.*) 1. capable of being easily done; easy; effortless 2. arrived at without due effort; superficial   31

facilitate (*v.*) make easier; make less difficult; simplify   16, 32

facility (*n.*) ease; skill   18

factor (*n.*) 1. one who transacts business for another; broker; agent 2. one of the causes contributing to a result or situation; element; ingredient 3. one of two or more numbers multiplied together to form a product   203

factotum (*n.*) someone hired to do all sorts of work; handy, versatile person   201

faculty (*n.*) 1. power or ability to do a particular thing; special aptitude; skill; knack 2. one of the powers of

Dictionary of the Words Taught in This Book   223

faculty   futility

the mind—for example, the **faculty** of memory, the **faculty** of reason, etc. 3. teaching staff of a school, college, or university   83

feasible (*adj.*)   capable of being done   12

feign (*v.*)   pretend; simulate   135

felon (*n.*)   person guilty of a major crime; criminal; malefactor   144

felony (*n.*)   serious crime, such as murder, kidnapping, burglary, etc.   145

fervent (*adj.*)   intense; ardent; impassioned   42

fervid (*adj.*)   full of fervor; impassioned; ardent   197

fervor (*n.*)   1. great warmth of feeling; ardor; passion   2. intensity of expression; enthusiasm; zeal   40, 196

filial (*adj.*)   befitting a son or daughter; expected from a son or daughter   57

flagrant (*adj.*)   glaring   40

flammable (*adj.*)   easily set on fire; inflammable; combustible   40

flinch (*v.*)   recoil; quail; wince   144

flourish (*v.*)   succeed; prosper; thrive   116

flout (*v.*)   show contempt for; mock; scoff at; show disrespect for   112

focal (*adj.*)   of or at a focus; central   187

focus (*n.*)   1. central point; center of interest or activity   2. position in which an object must be viewed clearly   186

foreboding (*n.*)   apprehension; misgiving   67

forensics (*n.*)   art or study of argumentative discussion; debate; argumentation   203

foreordained (*adj.*)   destined   118

forestall (*v.*)   prevent; avert; obviate   122

fortuitous (*adj.*)   accidental; happening by chance; casual   116

fortuitously (*adv.*)   accidentally; by chance; casually   118

forum (*n.*)   1. ancient Roman public square or marketplace where legislatures and courts met   2. public meeting place for open discussion; opportunity for open discussion   3. medium for the expression of ideas   201

fragile (*adj.*)   capable of being easily broken or damaged; delicate; frail   31

fragment (*n.*)   part broken off   32

frailty (*n.*)   physically weak condition; infirmity   123

fraternal (*adj.*)   of a brother; involving brothers; brotherly; like a brother; friendly   57

fraternity (*n.*)   1. brotherly feeling; brotherliness   2. men's or boys' social club   59

frenzy (*n.*)   furor; delirium   191

fretful (*adj.*)   irritable; peevish   106

frivolous (*adj.*)   not serious; silly   110

frugal (*adj.*)   sparing; thrifty; not wasteful   2

frugality (*n.*)   thrifty management; thrift   3

frustrate (*v.*)   make ineffectual; cause to have no effect; block; thwart   16

frustration (*n.*)   disappointment; defeat   18

fugitive (*n.*)   person who flees or tries to escape from danger, justice, etc.; runaway   26

furor (*n.*)   1. fit of anger; rage   2. outburst of public indignation; uproar   196

futile (*adj.*)   ineffective; serving no useful purpose; useless; fruitless   112

futility (*n.*)   ineffectiveness; uselessness   113

general (adj.) 1. having to do with all, nearly all, or most of a group; common; widespread 2. lacking in details; indefinite; not specific 93

generalize (v.) 1. make vague or indefinite statements 2. derive a broad conclusion from particular instances 95

genial (adj.) friendly, cheerful, and sympathetic; cordial; amiable; gracious 164

genuine (adj.) real; true; unquestionable 136

glare (v.) stare angrily 42

glaring (adj.) shining so brightly as to hurt the eyes; too obvious to escape notice; flagrant 40

glut (n.) excessive quantity; oversupply; plethora; surfeit 62

glutton (n.) person who overeats; voracious eater 53, 64

gluttony (n.) habit of eating or drinking too much 51

goad (n.) stimulus; incentive; impetus 186

gorge (v.) satiate; cloy; glut 62

gracious (adj.) sociable; cordial; genial 164

grandeur (n.) splendor; majesty 196

grave (adj.) serious; likely to cause great harm or damage; threatening 59

gravity (n.) seriousness; severity; danger; threat 57

grouch (n.) habitually irritable, fault-finding person; grumbler; crank 139

grouchy (adj.) ill-tempered; grumbling; peevish 141

gull (n.) fool; dupe 139

gullibility (n.) capability of being easily fooled 3

gullible (adj.) easily deceived or cheated; credulous 2

hale (adj.) healthy; well; vigorous; free from disease 112

hallucination (n.) delusion; mirage 191

haphazard (adj.) lacking plan or order; random; aimless; accidental 118

harmony (n.) unity; concord 171

haughtiness (n.) excessive pride; arrogance 171

hazard (v.) risk; gamble; bet; venture 116

hedge (v.) evade; equivocate 35

heir (n.) one who inherits or is legally entitled to inherit property 139

heirloom (n.) treasured possession handed down from generation to generation 141

hiatus (n.) break in the continuity of something; missing part; gap; interruption 186

histrionic (adj.) having to do with actors or acting 90

histrionics (n. pl.) 1. art of acting; dramatics 2. artificial, showy display of emotion; theatricality 88

holocaust (n.) great destruction of life by fire 42

humane (adj.) showing kindness, mercy, and consideration for other human beings or animals; humanitarian; altruistic 164

humanely (adv.) compassionately; sympathetically 166

humanitarian (adj.) charitable; humane 164

humble (adj.) unassuming 68

humiliate (v.) make someone feel ashamed; lower someone's pride or dignity; degrade; embarrass 16

humiliating (adj.) degrading 18

humility (n.) freedom from arrogance or vanity; unpretentiousness 52, 171

humus (*n.*) dark substance essential for fertility formed in the soil by decomposition of plant and animal matter; organic part of the soil 186

hypocrisy (*n.*) pretense of being what one is not 37

hypocrite (*n.*) one who only pretends to have—but really does not have—desirable beliefs, principles, or attitudes; pretender 36

hypocritical (*adj.*) insincere 37

hysteria (*n.*) uncontrollable outburst of emotion or fear 90

hysterical (*adj.*) 1. irrational because of emotional shock or fear 2. extremely comical; very funny 90

hysterics (*n. pl.*) fit of uncontrollable laughing or weeping 88

identical (*adj.*) same; exact 93

ignitable (*adj.*) burnable; combustible 42

ignite (*v.*) 1. set on fire; cause to burn; kindle 2. catch on fire; start burning 40

ignominy (*n.*) disgrace; shame; odium 191

ignoramus (*n.*) person who knows little; ignorant person; dunce 174

ignore (*v.*) take no notice of; overlook; disregard 176

illiterate (*adj.*) unable to read or write; uneducated 164

illuminate (*v.*) 1. light up; supply with light 2. make clear; explain; elucidate 122

illuminating (*adj.*) highly informative; enlightening 123

immature (*adj.*) juvenile; childish 31

immoderate (*adj.*) too much; extreme; exceeding reasonable limits; excessive 53, 203

immoral (*adj.*) bad; evil; morally wrong 35

immortalize (*v.*) make imperishable; perpetuate 17

impartial (*adj.*) not favoring one side more than the other; free of **bias** (prejudice); not partial 2

impartiality (*n.*) freedom from bias 3

impassioned (*adj.*) showing intense feeling; ardent; fervent 40

impassive (*adj.*) not showing passion or feeling; stoical 146

impeccable (*adj.*) free from defect or blame; flawless; faultless; irreproachable 164

impeccably (*adv.*) faultlessly; without a flaw 166

impecunious (*adj.*) having little or no money; poor; penniless; indigent 174

imperative (*adj.*) necessary; essential; indispensable 12

imperceptible (*adj.*) not discernible 12

impersonator (*n.*) actor; mime 144

imperturbable (*adj.*) incapable of being **perturbed** (agitated or disturbed); not easily excited; calm; cool 12, 124

impetuosity (*n.*) impetuous act; rashness 188

impetuous (*adj.*) acting or done suddenly and forcefully with little thought; impulsive; rash; precipitate 188

impetus (*n.*) driving force that stimulates activity; stimulus; impulse; incentive; goad 186

implacable (*adj.*) unable to be **placated** (made peaceful); unappeasable; unrelenting; unforgiving 6

implacably (*adv.*) unrelentingly 8

impose on (*v.*) deceive by false representation; cheat; defraud 161

impostor (*n.*) person who assumes someone else's identity to deceive

impostor

others; fraud; charlatan; deceiver 159
impotent (*adj.*) powerless; weak 83
impracticable (*adj.*) incapable of being put into practice; unworkable; impractical; impossible 12
impromptu (*adj.*) extemporaneous; spur-of-the-moment; offhand 174
improvised (*adj.*) impromptu; offhand; extemporaneous 174
imprudent (*adj.*) lacking discretion; not **prudent** (wise and cautious); indiscreet; rash 149
impudent (*adj.*) insolent; bold; audacious 134
impulse (*n.*) stimulus; goad; spur 186
impulsive (*adj.*) rash; hasty; impetuous 188
inalienable (*adj.*) incapable of being taken away; not transferable 66
inarticulate (*adj.*) unable to speak clearly and effectively; incoherent 149
incapacitate (*v.*) make unable or unfit; deprive of **capacity** (ability to do something); disable 16
incapacity (*n.*) lack of ability; unfitness 18
incarcerate (*v.*) imprison; confine 107
incarceration (*n.*) imprisonment; confinement 106
incendiary (*n.*) arsonist 40
incense (*v.*) anger; madden; infuriate 197
incentive (*n.*) stimulus; incitement; impetus 186
inception (*n.*) beginning; origin; start 112
incipient (*adj.*) just starting to appear; in the early stages 113
incivility (*n.*) rudeness; discourtesy 151
inclement (*adj.*) stormy; rough; severe 107

initiate

inclusive (*adj.*) comprehensive 66
incoherent (*adj.*) unable to think clearly and express oneself logically; rambling; confused; inarticulate 149
incombustible (*adj.*) incapable of being burned 12
incorruptible (*adj.*) incapable of being bribed 37
incriminate (*v.*) accuse; charge with involvement in a crime 188
indecisive (*adj.*) hesitant; uncertain; vacillating 149
indecorous (*adj.*) not in good taste; unbecoming; unseemly 203
indelible (*adj.*) unerasable; lasting; permanent; unforgettable 123
indifference (*n.*) unconcern; apathy 51
indigent (*adj.*) extremely poor; destitute; impecunious 1, 174
indiscreet (*adj.*) lacking discretion; unwise; imprudent 149
indispensable (*adj.*) incapable of being done without; necessary; imperative; essential 12
indomitable (*adj.*) unconquerable; unyielding 85
inducement (*n.*) something that influences or persuades; lure 191
inferno (*n.*) conflagration; holocaust 40
infirm (*adj.*) not strong in body or health; feeble; weak 122
infirmity (*n.*) weakness; ailment; frailty 123
inflexible (*adj.*) stubborn; unyielding; obdurate 135
infuriate (*v.*) enrage; anger; madden; incense 197
ingredient (*n.*) element; component; factor 203
inhumane (*adj.*) barbarous; cruel; inhuman 164
initiate (*v.*) begin 79

Dictionary of the Words Taught in This Book

initiative

initiative (*n.*) ambition; enterprise 51
injudicious (*adj.*) unwise; indiscreet 166
innocuous (*adj.*) harmless; inoffensive 136
innovative (*adj.*) tending to introduce new methods or ideas; original; creative; inventive 79
innovator (*n.*) one who introduces something new; inventor; originator 80
inordinate (*adj.*) beyond reasonable limits; immoderate; excessive 62
inordinately (*adv.*) excessively; immoderately 64
insatiable (*adj.*) incapable of being **satiated** (satisfied); always wanting more; unsatisfiable 12, 64
insensitive (*adj.*) unresponsive; tactless 139
insight (*n.*) wisdom; sagacity 52
insincere (*adj.*) hypocritical 37
insolent (*adj.*) bold; brazen; audacious 134
instrumentality (*n.*) agency; channel; medium 170
insuperable (*adj.*) unconquerable; invincible 6
insurgent (*n.*) one who rises in revolt against established authority; rebel 170
insurmountable (*adj.*) impassable; unconquerable 6
insurrection (*n.*) revolt; rebellion; uprising 171
intact (*adj.*) untouched; with nothing missing or damaged 32
intellect (*n.*) 1. great mental power; high intelligence; brainpower 2. person of high intelligence 83, 161
intellectual (*adj.*) requiring intelligence and clear thinking 85
intellectual (*n.*) highly intelligent person; one who relies on the power

irreproachable

of the mind rather than on emotions or feelings 159
intelligible (*adj.*) understandable; lucid 80
interminable (*adj.*) having or seeming to have no end or limit; ceaseless; continual; perpetual 79
interrogate (*v.*) ask questions of; examine (someone) by questioning; quiz 170
interrogation (*n.*) questioning; cross-examination 171
interrogative (*adj.*) conveying a question 171
intimidate (*v.*) make **timid** (fearful); frighten; scare; discourage from acting by threats or violence 6
intrepid (*adj.*) brave; not afraid; fearless; bold; dauntless 79
intrepidity (*n.*) bravery; fearlessness; valor 80
intrigue (*n.*) plot; conspiracy 161
invalid (*adj.*) unfounded; null and void 79
invalid (*n.*) one too sick to care for oneself 191
invalidate (*v.*) deprive of legal force; abolish; nullify 80
invigorate (*v.*) make strong; give **vigor** (strength) to; fill with life and energy; enliven; strengthen 16
invincibility (*n.*) unconquerability 8
invincible (*adj.*) incapable of being **vanquished** (conquered, defeated, or subdued); insuperable; insurmountable 6
involuntary (*adj.*) done or occurring against one's will 196
iota (*n.*) very small quantity; insignificant amount; particle; ounce; smidgen 174
irascible (*adj.*) easily angered; edgy; testy 149
irreproachable (*adj.*) blameless; faultless; impeccable 164

irrevocable — maternal

irrevocable (*adj.*) impossible to undo; unalterable 68

judicious (*adj.*) showing or exercising sound judgment; sensible; wise; discreet 164
judiciously (*adv.*) wisely; with sound judgment 166
juvenile (*adj.*) having to do with young persons; suitable for the young; immature; childish 31

kindle (*v.*) set fire to; ignite 42
kindling (*n.*) bits of dry wood or other easily lighted material for starting a fire 40
knack (*n.*) ability; skill; faculty 83

languish (*v.*) fail; deteriorate; weaken 116
lavish (*adj.*) too free in giving or spending; extravagant; prodigal 2
lavishness (*n.*) extravagance 3
leniency (*n.*) mercifulness; clemency 106
lethargic (*adj.*) sluggish; torpid 198
lethargy (*n.*) deficiency in activity or alertness; torpor; stupor 196
litigant (*n.*) person engaged in a lawsuit 159
litigation (*n.*) process of carrying on a lawsuit; lawsuit 161
loanword (*n.*) word borrowed or adopted from another language 186
lot (*n.*) fate; destiny 116
lucid (*adj.*) clear; easy to understand; intelligible 80
lukewarm (*adj.*) 1. barely warm; tepid 2. having or showing little enthusiasm, eagerness, or warmth; indifferent; halfhearted 174
lukewarmly (*adv.*) without enthusiasm; tepidly; halfheartedly 176

luminary (*n.*) person of brilliant achievement; prominent person 124
luminous (*adj.*) 1. giving off light; bright; radiant; brilliant 2. very clear; easily understood; unambiguous; enlightening 122

magnanimous (*adj.*) generous in forgiving insult or injury; not petty; greathearted 187
magnify (*v.*) make greater in size or importance 174
malefactor (*n.*) criminal; felon; evildoer 144
malevolence (*n.*) ill will; spitefulness 51
malice (*n.*) deep-seated meanness; desire to inflict injury on others or do mischief; spite 52
malicious (*adj.*) spiteful 53
mandatory (*adj.*) required 105
manifest (*v.*) make clear; show; reveal; demonstrate; evince 134
manifestation (*n.*) indication; demonstration 136
marine (*adj.*) 1. of the sea; inhabiting, found in, or produced by the sea; oceanic 2. having to do with navigation or shipping; nautical 57
maritime (*adj.*) on, near, or bordering on the sea 59
martyr (*n.*) person who chooses to suffer or die rather than give up his or her principles or beliefs 144
martyrdom (*n.*) extreme suffering for adherence to one's beliefs; torture; death 146
mason (*n.*) skilled worker who builds with stone, brick, concrete, and similar materials 144
masonry (*n.*) stonework; brickwork 146
maternal (*adj.*) characteristic of a mother; motherly 57

Dictionary of the Words Taught in This Book

matrimony (*n.*) marriage 59
maverick (*n.*) one who does not go along with the ideas of a party or group, but takes an independent stand; nonconformist 160
maxim (*n.*) axiom; truism; rule 93
maximize (*v.*) make the most of; overstress 174
meager (*adj.*) smaller than what is normal; scanty 62
media (*n. pl.*) channels of communicating with the general public 171
medieval (*adj.*) having to do with the **Middle Ages** (A.D. 500 to 1500), the period of European history between ancient and modern times 170
mediocre (*adj.*) of low, middle, or ordinary quality; barely acceptable; not good enough 170
mediocrity (*n.*) lack of distinction; inferiority 171
medium (*n.*) 1. means through which something is done, conveyed, or transmitted; agency; channel; instrumentality 2. something in a middle position or condition 170
melancholy (*adj.*) sad; depressing; somber 106
mendacious (*adj.*) lying; deceitful; dishonest; untruthful 149
mendacity (*n.*) falsehood; practice of lying 150
mentor (*n.*) wise, trusted adviser or guide; teacher; tutor; coach 144
mentorship (*n.*) tutelage; coaching; training 146
mercantile (*adj.*) having to do with trade or merchants; commercial 31
mercenary (*adj.*) serving merely for pay or gain; greedy 7
mercenary (*n.*) soldier serving for pay in a foreign army 6
merchandise (*n.*) goods bought and sold; wares 32

meter (*n.*) unit of length measuring approximately 39.37 inches 193
meticulous (*adj.*) painstaking; extremely careful about small details; scrupulous; fussy 66
meticulously (*adv.*) very carefully; painstakingly; scrupulously 68
millennium (*n.*) period of a thousand years 191
millimeter (*n.*) one-thousandth of a meter; 0.039 inch 193
mimic (*n.*) person who ridicules others by imitating their voices, gestures, and mannerisms; impersonator; imitator 144
mimicry (*n.*) close imitation; mimicking 146
mingle (*v.*) mix; socialize 95
minimal (*adj.*) least possible; smallest 176
minimize (*v.*) 1. make as small as possible; reduce to a minimum 2. make (someone or something) appear small or unimportant; belittle; disparage 174
mock (*v.*) ridicule; deride; taunt 57
moderate (*v.*) 1. make or become less strong or less extreme; restrain 2. preside over (a debate or discussion); act as moderator of 203
moderation (*n.*) avoidance of excesses or extremes in behavior or expression; restraint; temperance 52
moderator (*n.*) one who presides over a discussion 203
modicum (*n.*) small amount; moderate quantity; bit; particle 201
momentous (*adj.*) very important; crucial; serious 203
momentum (*n.*) force or speed of a moving object; impetus 201
monosyllabic (*adj.*) containing only one syllable 139

monotony (*n.*) boredom; tedium 191

nautical (*adj.*) having to do with navigation; marine 57
necessitate (*v.*) make necessary; require; demand 16
nimble (*adj.*) agile; spry 31
noncombustible (*adj.*) incombustible 12
nonconformist (*n.*) dissenter; maverick 160
nonentity (*n.*) mediocre person; person of little or no achievement or distinction 160
nonflammable (*adj.*) not flammable; incombustible 42
nonprofessional (*n.*) amateur 26
novel (*adj.*) new; unusual; strange 80
novelty (*n.*) 1. something new or unusual; innovation 2. newness 79
noxious (*adj.*) harmful; unhealthful; injurious; unwholesome 134
nullify (*v.*) abolish; invalidate 80

obdurate (*adj.*) unmoved by persuasion or pity; hardened in feelings; obstinate; unyielding; inflexible 135
obdurately (*adv.*) inflexibly; unyieldingly 136
objectionable (*adj.*) offensive; repugnant 106
objective (*adj.*) free from prejudice or personal feelings for or against someone or something; unbiased; detached; fair 164
objectivity (*n.*) impartiality; absence of bias 166
obliterate (*v.*) make nonexistent; erase; efface; blot out; delete; remove all traces of; destroy completely 17

obviate (*v.*) prevent by taking action ahead of time; forestall; preclude; avert; make unnecessary 122
odious (*adj.*) hateful; repugnant; disgusting; detestable 193
odium (*n.*) disgrace and hatred to which one is subjected for doing something despicable; ignominy; opprobrium 191
omen (*n.*) sign of something to come; portent; augury 116
omnipotence (*n.*) power over all; unlimited authority 85
omnipotent (*adj.*) all-powerful; having unlimited power, authority, or influence 59
omnipresent (*adj.*) ubiquitous; universal; present everywhere 95
omniscient (*adj.*) 1. knowing all things; perceiving all things 2. having extensive knowledge, awareness, or understanding 57
onerous (*adj.*) burdensome; troublesome 188
onus (*n.*) burden; load; difficult task; unpleasant responsibility 186
opprobrium (*n.*) disgrace; infamy; odium 191
optimum (*adj.*) best; most favorable 201
optimum (*n.*) best or most favorable amount, degree, or condition 201
organic (*adj.*) derived from living organisms 186
organism (*n.*) living being 186
orthopedics (*n. pl.*) branch of surgery that deals with problems of the spine, bones, and joints 88
orthopedist (*n.*) surgeon specializing in orthopedics 90

pacify (*v.*) restore to a tranquil condition; soothe; appease 122
painstaking (*adj.*) careful; meticulous; scrupulous 174

pall / plaintiff

pall (*v.*) become tiresome; bore; lose effectiveness 198
pallid (*adj.*) pale; wan; ashen 198
pallor (*n.*) lack of natural color; paleness, as from fear, sickness, or death; wanness 196
palpable (*adj.*) touchable; tangible; tactile 31
partial (*adj.*) favoring one side more than the other; biased 2
paternal (*adj.*) characteristic of a father; fatherly 57
patrimony (*n.*) property inherited from one's father or ancestor; heritage 59
paucity (*n.*) insufficiency; scarcity; dearth; smallness of quantity 174
pecuniary (*adj.*) financial; involving money 176
pediatrician (*n.*) physician specializing in pediatrics 90
pediatrics (*n. pl.*) branch of medicine dealing with the development, care, and illnesses of children 88
peer (*n.*) person or thing that is of equal standing with another; equal 26
peerless (*adj.*) unrivaled; without equal 28
peeved (*adj.*) annoyed; irritated 108
peevish (*adj.*) cross; irritable; ill-tempered; fretful 106
peevishness (*n.*) irritability; petulance 108
perceptible (*adj.*) able to be **perceived** (noticed through one or more of the senses); detectable; discernible 12
perception (*n.*) knowledge; understanding 13
perceptive (*adj.*) having keen insight; observant 13
perjurer (*n.*) one who swears falsely 37
perjury (*n.*) willful telling of a lie while under oath; false swearing 36
pernicious (*adj.*) deadly; exceedingly harmful; deleterious 122
perpetual (*adj.*) everlasting 18
perpetually (*adv.*) forever 18
perpetuate (*v.*) make **perpetual** (lasting forever or for a long time); cause to continue or be remembered; immortalize 17
perseverance (*n.*) continued patient effort; steadfastness; persistence 113
persevere (*v.*) persist; continue in a course of action in spite of difficulty, opposition, or discouragement 112
persevering (*adj.*) showing perseverance; steadfast; persistent 113
persist (*v.*) continue despite discouragement; persevere 112
personable (*adj.*) pleasing in appearance and manner; handsome; attractive 164
perturb (*v.*) disturb greatly; disquiet; trouble the mind of; agitate 13, 122
pervade (*v.*) spread through all parts of; extend throughout 93
pervasive (*adj.*) tending to spread throughout; thoroughly penetrating 95
petition (*n.*) suit; plea 146
petty (*adj.*) small-minded 187
petulance (*n.*) irritability; peevishness 108
piecemeal (*adj.*) done one piece at a time; accomplished in a fragmentary way; gradual 175
piecemeal (*adv.*) piece by piece; in small amounts; little by little; gradually 174
placate (*v.*) make peaceful; appease 8
placid (*adj.*) calm; quiet; tranquil 122
plaintiff (*n.*) one who sues; petitioner 144

plethora (n.) excess; oversupply; glut 62
pliable (adj.) 1. easy to influence or persuade; yielding 2. easily bent; flexible 112
pliability (n.) flexibility 113
poise (n.) balance; equilibrium 191
polysyllabic (adj.) containing three or more syllables 159
portent (n.) foreshadowing; omen; augury 116
posthumous (adj.) 1. occurring after one has died 2. published after the author's death 3. born after the father's death 188
postulate (v.) assume; presuppose 66
potency (n.) effectiveness; strength 85
potent (adj.) 1. having or exercising great power; mighty
  ant. **weak; impotent**
  2. achieving or bringing about a particular result; effective 83
potentate (n.) one who has great power; ruler; monarch 85
potential (n.) power or skill that may be developed; possibility; promise 84
practicable (adj.) feasible 12
precipitate (adj.) abrupt; sudden; impetuous 188
preclude (v.) prevent; forestall; obviate 122
premium (n.) 1. something offered free as an inducement for buying; reward; prize 2. sum in addition to the regular price or wages; bonus 3. very high value 191
preposterous (adj.) foolish; ridiculous; absurd 59
prestige (n.) status; rank; stature 186
prodigal (adj.) lavish 2
prodigality (n.) extravagance; lavishness 51

prodigious (adj.) amazing; wonderful; marvelous 28
prodigy (n.) one who has extraordinary talent or ability; marvel; wonder 26
prolong (v.) extend; draw out; protract 110
prominent (adj.) well-known; distinguished 124
prone (adj.) 1. inclined; apt; likely 2. lying face downward 106
proneness (n.) inclination; propensity; tendency 108
propensity (n.) inclination; tendency; proneness 108
prophecy (n.) prediction 28
prophesy (v.) predict; foretell 28
prophet (n.) one who foretells or predicts; predictor 26
propitious (adj.) favorable; auspicious 116
proprietor (n.) owner of a store or business 18
propriety (n.) decorum; decency 201
prosperity (n.) success; good fortune 116
prostrate (adj.) lying face down or flat on one's back; completely overcome; exhausted; weak; unable to rise 204
proxy (n.) agent; deputy 159
prudence (n.) discretion; shrewdness 150
prudent (adj.) wise and cautious 149
pugilism (n.) boxing 8
pugilist (n.) prizefighter; boxer; person who fights with fists 7
pyromania (n.) uncontrollable impulse to start destructive fires 42
pyromaniac (n.) one who has an uncontrollable, insane impulse to set things on fire 40

Dictionary of the Words Taught in This Book

quack (*n.*) dishonest, unqualified person who pretends to be a physician; one who fraudulently pretends to have knowledge or skill in a particular field; charlatan 139

quackery (*n.*) claims or pretensions of a quack; charlatanry 141

quivering (*adj.*) shaking; trembling; tremulous 198

quorum (*n.*) minimum number of members that must be present at a meeting before it can transact business legally 201

radiant (*adj.*) bright; luminous 122

rambling (*adj.*) wandering off the topic; discursive 176

rancor (*n.*) bitter, deep-seated hate or ill will; malice; animosity; antipathy 196

rancorous (*adj.*) full of rancor; malicious; hateful; spiteful 198

random (*adj.*) aimless; haphazard 118

rash (*adj.*) hasty; hotheaded; imprudent 149

recuperate (*v.*) convalesce; improve 80

redundancy (*n.*) needless repetition of words; verbosity 64

redundant (*adj.*) using more words than necessary; wordy; verbose 62

refuge (*n.*) shelter; place of safety 28

rejuvenate (*v.*) make young again 32

relevant (*adj.*) applicable 66

renovate (*v.*) make new again; renew; modernize 80

replenish (*v.*) refill; provide a new supply for 64

replete (*adj.*) well-filled; abundantly stocked; full 62

reprehensible (*adj.*) deserving to be **reprehended** (blamed or scolded); blameworthy; censurable 12

repugnance (*n.*) extreme dislike; aversion; loathing 108

repugnant (*adj.*) offensive to one's taste or feelings; objectionable; distasteful; disgusting 106

rescind (*v.*) revoke; dismantle 66

resilience (*n.*) elasticity; flexibility 166

resilient (*adj.*) 1. capable of quickly recovering or adjusting after misfortune or illness; buoyant; flexible 2. capable of springing back to original shape after being stretched, bent, or compressed; elastic 164

resourceful (*adj.*) adroit; able to deal sensibly with new situations 134

restraint (*n.*) moderation 52

resurge (*v.*) sweep back; surge again; rise again 170

resurrect (*v.*) raise from the dead; bring back to life, use, or attention 171

resurrection (*n.*) coming back into use after disuse or decay; revival; restoration 171

revere (*v.*) honor and admire; worship; respect 112

revival (*n.*) rebirth; resurrection 171

revoke (*v.*) annul by taking back or recalling; cancel; rescind 66

ridicule (*v.*) make fun of; deride; mock; taunt 57

ridiculous (*adj.*) deserving to be laughed at; foolish; absurd; preposterous 59

rigor (*n.*) 1. harshness; strictness; severity; inflexibility 2. severe or harsh circumstance; hardship 196

rostrum (*n.*) platform on which a person stands while delivering a speech; stage 202

sagacious (*adj.*) wise; discerning; shrewd 53, 141

sagacity (*n.*) keen perception and sound judgment; intelligent application of knowledge; insight; shrewdness; wisdom 52

sage (*n.*) person respected for wisdom, breadth of knowledge, and sound judgment; savant; scholar 139

salutary (*adj.*) healthful; wholesome 122

sanction (*v.*) approve; authorize 83

sanitarium (*n.*) 1. health resort 2. institution for the care and treatment of invalids and convalescents 191

sanitize (*v.*) make sanitary; free from dirt or germs 193

sarcastic (*adj.*) sneering; cynical 145

sate (*v.*) satisfy 13

satiable (*adj.*) capable of being satisfied or appeased 12

satiate (*v.*) satisfy to excess; weary or disgust with too much; sate; gorge 13, 62

savant (*n.*) scholar; sage 139

scapegoat (*n.*) one who bears or is made to bear the blame for the mistakes or crimes of another or others 26

scathing (*adj.*) very harsh; bitterly severe; caustic; searing 135

scrupulous (*adj.*) conscientious; meticulous 1

searing (*adj.*) burning; scorching; caustic 135

sedentary (*adj.*) 1. requiring much sitting 2. accustomed to sit or rest much of the time or to do little exercise 57

sediment (*n.*) matter that settles or sits at the bottom of a liquid; dregs 59

seemly (*adj.*) becoming; fitting; decorous 203

self-possessed (*adj.*) having or showing control over one's feelings and actions, especially in tense situations; calm; cool; serene 164

self-possession (*n.*) calmness; composure; equanimity 166

sentiment (*n.*) attitude; feeling; opinion 187

sentimental (*adj.*) too emotional; cloying 62

serene (*adj.*) calm; self-possessed 164

shield (*v.*) defend; protect; serve as a **shield** (protective cover) for 112

shifty (*adj.*) evasive 149

shirk (*v.*) get out of doing one's work or duty; evade; avoid 36

shirker (*n.*) one who evades work or duty 37

simulate (*v.*) 1. give a false indication of; pretend; feign 2. assume the appearance of; look or act like; imitate 135

simulated (*adj.*) made to look genuine; fake; artificial 136

sluggish (*adj.*) slow in movement; torpid; lethargic 31, 198

smidgen (*n.*) particle; bit; iota 174

sneer (*v.*) express scorn or contempt; scoff 144

snob (*n.*) person who admires and tries to associate with people of wealth and position, while ignoring others as inferior; one who has an offensive sense of superiority 139

socialize (*v.*) take part in social activities; mingle 95

society (*n.*) all people; humanity; humankind 93

solar (*adj.*) having to do with the sun; produced by or coming from the sun 193

solarium (*n.*) glass-enclosed room for sunbathing; sun-room 191

solstice (*n.*) either of the two times a year when the sun reaches its farthest point from the equator 193

somber (*adj.*)   1. dark and gloomy; dimly lighted   2. depressing; melancholy   106

somberness (*n.*)   gloominess; dreariness   108

soothsayer (*n.*)   person who claims to be able to foretell events; predictor; prophet   116

sordid (*adj.*)   dirty; filthy; squalid   198

sovereign (*adj.*)   1. free; self-governing; independent; autonomous   2. supreme in power or authority   84

sovereignty (*n.*)   supreme and independent political authority; independence   85

specific (*adj.*)   definite; clear-cut   93

splendor (*n.*)   1. great brightness; brilliance   2. richness; splendid surroundings; magnificence; grandeur   196

sponsor (*n.*)   one who supports or assumes responsibility for another person, or for a thing; supporter; backer   27

sponsorship (*n.*)   financial support; backing   28

spouse (*n.*)   one's partner in a marriage; husband or wife   139

spurn (*v.*)   refuse with contempt; scorn; reject; decline   107

squalid (*adj.*)   dirty; filthy; sordid; wretched   198

squalor (*n.*)   filthiness resulting from neglect or poverty; sordidness; wretchedness; misery; degradation   196

stamina (*n.*)   power to endure or withstand fatigue, illness, hardship, etc.; endurance; vigor; strength   84

status (*n.*)   1. position one holds in relation to others; rank; standing   2. high position; distinction; prestige   186

steadfastness (*n.*)   loyalty; persistence; perseverance   113

stimulus (*n.*)   something that incites to activity; goad; impetus   186

stoic (*n.*)   person who is indifferent to joy or grief and endures pain or misfortune calmly, without flinching   144

stoical (*adj.*)   indifferent to pain or pleasure; impassive; imperturbable   146

stratum (*n.*)   any of several layers (as of earth, rock, or other material) lying one upon the other; level; section   202

strife (*n.*)   bitter conflict; fighting; discord; antagonism   7

stupor (*n.*)   lethargy; coma; torpor   196

subjective (*adj.*)   based on one's personal feelings; nonobjective   164

submissive (*adj.*)   lacking in independence; docile   31

subservient (*adj.*)   extremely obedient; submissive   85

substratum (*n.*)   layer lying under another; underlying support; foundation   204

succinct (*adj.*)   concise; brief; compendious   192

succumb (*v.*)   1. yield; give in to overpowering force; submit   2. perish; die   107

suit (*n.*)   1. lawsuit; case   2. petition; courtship   146

suitor (*n.*)   1. person who petitions (sues) for something; plaintiff; petitioner   2. man who courts a woman, seeking to marry her   144

superficial (*adj.*)   shallow; sketchy; cursory   174

supersede (*v.*)   take the place of; replace; force out of use; supplant; succeed   66

supplant (*v.*)   replace; supersede   66

supportable (*adj.*) tolerable; bearable; sustainable 108
surfeit (*n.*) excess; overabundance; glut 62
surrogate (*n.*) person appointed to act for another; deputy; substitute 170
sustain (*v.*) 1. withstand; endure 2. support; keep going; maintain 107
sustainable (*adj.*) bearable; tolerable; supportable 108
sustenance (*n.*) food; nourishment 108
swerve (*v.*) turn away; deviate; veer 122

tactical (*adj.*) having to do with tactics 90
tactician (*n.*) expert in tactics 90
tactics (*n. pl.*) 1. art of arranging and maneuvering military or naval forces to gain the advantage in combat 2. any methods used to gain an end 88
tactile (*adj.*) 1. having to do with the sense of touch 2. perceivable by touch; tangible; palpable 31
tangible (*adj.*) touchable; palpable; tactile 31
taunt (*v.*) ridicule; deride; mock 57
tedious (*adj.*) tiresome because of length; dull and wearisome; boring 193
tedium (*n.*) wearisomeness; boredom; monotony 191
teem (*v.*) be abundantly stocked; abound 62
temperance (*n.*) avoidance of extremes; moderation 52
tempestuous (*adj.*) wild; stormy; turbulent 122
tenable (*adj.*) capable of being held, maintained, or defended; defendable; justifiable 12

tenacious (*adj.*) holding firmly; stubborn 13
tenacity (*n.*) stubbornness; courage 13
tepid (*adj.*) moderately warm; lukewarm 174
terminal (*n.*) either end of a transportation line; terminus 186
terminate (*v.*) 1. bring to an end; put a stop to; end 2. come to an end; close; stop 79, 188
termination (*n.*) end; conclusion; cessation 80
terminus (*n.*) 1. end; finishing point; boundary; extremity 2. either end of a transportation line; terminal 186
testiness (*n.*) irritability 151
testy (*adj.*) easily annoyed; irritably impatient; irascible; edgy 149
textile (*adj.*) capable of being woven; suitable for weaving 31
textile (*n.*) cloth; fabric made by weaving 31
texture (*n.*) surface of something woven 32
theatricality (*n.*) showy display of emotion; histrionics 88
thrive (*v.*) be fortunate; prosper; succeed; flourish 116
thriving (*adj.*) flourishing; prospering; successful 118
thwart (*v.*) frustrate 16
timid (*adj.*) fearful 8
timidity (*n.*) fear 8
torpid (*adj.*) sluggish; inactive; lethargic 198
torpor (*n.*) loss or slowing of the power of motion or sensation; sluggishness; inactivity; stupor; lethargy 196
totalitarian (*adj.*) having to do with a government in which one political party has complete control and excludes all others 93

touchy (*adj.*) easily perturbed 12
tractable (*adj.*) docile; obedient 31
translucent (*adj.*) letting light through, but not able to be seen through clearly 79
tremor (*n.*) 1. trembling; shaking; vibration 2. involuntary shaking of the body; shudder; shiver 196
tremulous (*adj.*) trembling; quivering; timid 198
trepidation (*n.*) fear; fright; trembling; apprehension 79
trivia (*n. pl.*) matters of very little importance or significance; trifles; trivialities 175
trivial (*adj.*) little; petty; insignificant 203
triviality (*n.*) unimportant matter; trifle 176
turbulence (*n.*) commotion; wild disorder 124
turbulent (*adj.*) 1. causing turmoil or unrest; boisterous; unruly 2. full of wild disorder or violent motion; tempestuous 122
tutelage (*n.*) instruction; coaching; mentorship 146
tutor (*n.*) teacher; coach; mentor 144

ubiquitous (*adj.*) present, or seeming to be present, everywhere; omnipresent; universal 95
unambiguous (*adj.*) easily understood; clear; luminous 122
unappeasable (*adj.*) implacable; unforgiving 6
unassailable (*adj.*) not open to attack or doubt 8
unassuming (*adj.*) not bold; not arrogant; unpretentious; humble 68
uncivil (*adj.*) rude; impolite; ill-mannered; boorish 149

uncomplimentary (*adj.*) detracting; disparaging; unfavorable 149
unconscionable (*adj.*) unscrupulous 2
unequivocal (*adj.*) unambiguous; clear 37
unethical (*adj.*) not conforming to the rules of right conduct 89
unfilial (*adj.*) not befitting a son or daughter; undutiful 57
uniform (*adj.*) 1. all alike; not differing from one another 2. always the same; unvarying; identical 93
uniformly (*adv.*) steadily; evenly; smoothly 95
unintelligible (*adj.*) incapable of being understood; difficult to comprehend; incomprehensible 12
universal (*adj.*) present everywhere; omnipresent; ubiquitous 95
universally (*adv.*) in all places; everywhere; in every case 93
unrelenting (*adj.*) implacable 6
unscathed (*adj.*) uninjured; wholly unharmed 136
unscrupulous (*adj.*) having no concern for what is morally right or proper; unconscionable 2
unscrupulously (*adv.*) unconscionably 3
untenable (*adj.*) not able to be defended 12
usurp (*v.*) seize and hold without right; commandeer; arrogate 68
usurper (*n.*) one who wrongfully takes or assumes the office, rights, or powers of another 66

vacillate (*v.*) keep changing one's mind; hesitate 151
vacillating (*adj.*) constantly changing one's mind; indecisive; wavering 149

vain (*adj.*) conceited 53
vainness (*n.*) conceit; vanity 52
valid (*adj.*) having force; well-founded; sound; legally binding 79
validate (*v.*) make valid; give legal force to; confirm; authenticate 80
validity (*n.*) force; effectiveness; legal soundness 80
valor (*n.*) personal bravery; intrepidity 80
vandal (*n.*) one who willfully destroys or damages valuable private or public property; defacer 27
vandalism (*n.*) mischievous defacement or destruction of property 28
vanity (*n.*) excessive pride in oneself or in one's appearance; self-admiration; vainness; conceit 52
vanquish (*v.*) subdue by superior force; conquer; defeat; overcome 7
veer (*v.*) swerve; change direction; deviate 122
venal (*adj.*) easily bribed; open to corruption; purchasable; crooked; mercenary 149
vendor (*n.*) person who sells; seller 151
venture (*v.*) place in danger; risk; gamble; hazard 118
venturesome (*adj.*) inclined to take chances; adventurous; daring; bold 117
veracious (*adj.*) truthful; undistorted 149
verbose (*adj.*) using or containing an unnecessary and wearisome amount of words; wordy 149
verbosity (*n.*) wordiness 151
verify (*v.*) confirm; authenticate 122
versatile (*adj.*) 1. capable of turning easily from one occupation to another; able to do many things well; many-sided 2. having many uses or applications; adaptable 31
versatility (*n.*) adaptability 32
veterinarian (*n.*) one who is professionally trained and authorized to treat the diseases and injuries of animals 160
veterinary (*adj.*) having to do with the medical treatment of animals 161
vibration (*n.*) shaking; trembling; tremor 196
vicinity (*n.*) environs; district; neighborhood 94
vigor (*n.*) power; strength; stamina 16, 84
vigorous (*adj.*) strong; powerful; energetic 18
vigorously (*adv.*) forcefully; energetically 18
viral (*adj.*) of or caused by a virus 188
virus (*n.*) 1. disease-causing substance or organism so tiny that it cannot be seen with an ordinary microscope 2. anything that corrupts a person's character or mind 186
volatile (*adj.*) capable of evaporating rapidly; likely to shift unpredictably; unstable; inconstant 31
volatility (*n.*) instability 32
voracious (*adj.*) excessively greedy in eating 64

wan (*adj.*) pale; ashen; pallid 198
wanness (*n.*) unnatural sickly pallor 196
ward (*n.*) 1. person under the care of a guardian or court 2. division of a hospital 139
wardrobe (*n.*) 1. closet where clothes are kept 2. one's collection of clothes 141

wavering (*adj.*) hesitating; vacillating   149

windshield (*n.*) front window of an automobile, protecting its occupants from the wind and weather   113

wordy (*adj.*) using more words than needed; verbose   149

wretchedness (*n.*) misery; unhappiness   196

zany (*n.*) clown; buffoon   144

zeal (*n.*) enthusiasm; ardor   51

zealous (*adj.*) enthusiastic   40